7/45

Mother

With love from Jay

Xmas 1945

AGAINST OBLIVION

Keats was accompanied to Rome and attended in his last illness by Mr. Severn, a young artist of the highest promise, who, I have been informed, "almost risked his own life, and sacrificed every prospect to unwearied attendance upon his dying friend."

Had I known these circumstances before the completion of my poem, I should have been tempted to add my feeble tribute of applause to the more solid recompense which the virtuous man finds in the recollection of his own motives. Mr. Severn can dispense with a reward from "such stuff as dreams are made of." His conduct is a noble augury of the success of his future career—may the unextinguished Spirit of his illustrious friend animate the creations of his pencil, and plead against oblivion for his name!

PREFACE TO SHELLEY'S "ADONAIS."

Seymour Kirkup A.
Rome 1822

JOSEPH SEVERN

from the pencil drawing by Seymour Kirkup, reproduced in William Sharp's
Life and Letters of Joseph Severn

AGAINST OBLIVION

The Life of Joseph Severn

By

SHEILA BIRKENHEAD

With 8 half-tone illustrations

CASSELL AND COMPANY LTD.

London, Toronto, Melbourne and Sydney

TO

F.

First Edition   .   .   . *May* 1943
Second Edition   .   .   . *June* 1943
Third Edition   .   .   . *April* 1944

PRINTED IN GREAT BRITAIN BY JARROLD AND SONS LIMITED, NORWICH
444

CONTENTS

LIST OF ILLUSTRATIONS

INTRODUCTION

My acquaintance with the Severns began one wet afternoon at Charlton, when I found an album of their sketches. Then I read Mary Severn's diary and some of her letters. It was Mary in whom I was most interested at first. She seemed strangely modern for her times. Who could have imagined a young lady in the middle of the last century supporting, not only herself, but her family, by her painting? From their sketches, their caricatures and their letters I got to know the Severns. I knew what they looked like, what they thought, and how they talked and behaved. I longed to bring the family to life again.

Six months of Joseph Severn's life are well known and have been often described; the fifty-eight years he lived after Keats's death are usually dismissed in a sentence. The one Life of Joseph Severn, published in 1892, entirely ignored the period in London when the family fortunes were low, which to me is one of the most amusing. I am still enchanted by Mrs. Severn's indomitable remark when, after days of staving off writs and bailiffs, she extravagantly hired a hansom cab and sank back on to the seat, "Well, however poor I am, there are certain things I cannot give up— Hansoms, cold cream and violet powder." Then there were Mary's letters from Windsor, when she was painting the Queen's children, with descriptions of Her Majesty—"If she would only sit in warm rooms she really would be better looking. . . . Her hands were blue and shaking so she could hardly point to the pictures."

If Severn's life had ended when he left England in 1861 it would still have been an interesting one. So many people had entered it—Leigh Hunt, Shelley, the eccentric Countess of Westmoreland, Trelawny, Richmond, Ruskin, Gladstone. But, at the age of sixty-seven, he boldly embarked on a new career as representative of Great Britain in Rome, where he remained through the Garibaldi risings and the Fall of the Papal Government.

Had it not been for his devotion to Keats his name would have been forgotten. All that has been written about him is as the friend of Keats. This book is about Joseph Severn. But it is not only about the friend of Keats. That is why I have called it "Against Oblivion."

All the dialogue is as far as possible authentic. Where Severn reported words spoken by Keats I have used them, otherwise anything he says is taken from his own letters written at the time. I have followed the same course with other characters such as Joseph himself, Shelley, Haslam, Wordsworth, Gibson, the young Severns and Charles Newton.

The two periods of Severn's life which were spent in Rome are covered by his long letters home. The middle period, spent in London, was easy to visualize because of the Severn children's habit of employing any idle moment by making a quick sketch of their surroundings and adding a few lines of dialogue or explanation below. Scenes described are taken from these drawings, and the conversation either from the captions or from letters or diaries.

I must express my gratitude to the late Mr. Edgcumbe, Curator of Keats House at Hampstead, who first told me about the collection of unpublished Severn letters at Keats House, and to Mrs. Stanley Unwin for allowing me to reproduce the Severn Family Miniature, and particularly Joseph's little water-colour of Keats on the voyage. All these had been placed somewhere in the country for safety during the war and I am most grateful to the present Curator of Keats House, Mr. Preston, for bringing them to London, so that I might have them photographed. I must also thank Mrs. Stanley Unwin, granddaughter of Thomas Severn, for permission to read the letters in her possession, Miss Claudia Gale, daughter of Claudia Severn, for sending me a copy of her paper about Mary Severn, which included many family reminiscences told her by her own mother, and Lord Ilchester for allowing me to quote from the Journal of Henry Edward Fox.

But above all all other help I must acknowledge that given me by my mother-in-law, Joseph's granddaughter, who has inherited all the Severns' good taste and interest in art and music, combining with them as incomparable gaiety and a wit untinged with malice.

PROLOGUE

(1803)

JOSEPH'S leg was aching. He had sat in the same position on his damask-covered stool for close on an hour now. Dare he risk a movement? He stole a glance at his father's stern profile and determined to endure his discomfort a little longer. His father's expression was forbidding, and Joseph knew that, had it been one of his own children who was mutilating this lovely Air of Purcell's, they would have had short shrift. As it was, his black brows were drawn down in a scowl and one hand drummed impatiently on his knee. His pupil bit her lip as she staggered through a difficult bar and then plunged, with relief and a rapidly increasing tempo, into a phrase that she really knew. Joseph's attention wandered.

For the hundredth time that afternoon he began cautiously to examine the room they sat in. His father had not exaggerated when he had described the house as the most elegant of all that he visited. It had only been completed six or seven years ago. They had pulled down the ancient manor house in the hollow and replaced it with this handsome modern building set on the hill, to accord with the new fashion which made a good prospect essential. Externals are very important to children, and Joseph had really enjoyed sitting in this room, in spite of the discomfort of the cramp in his leg. It seemed to him that no room could be more beautiful—the lofty windows with enormous gilt mirrors poised between them, the double doors of gleaming mahogany, the delicately-coloured carpet, the marble figures holding up the mantel, and the glittering chandelier that cast little icy sparkles of light on to the snowy mouldings of the ceiling.

The plaintive melody staggered drunkenly to an end and the young performer gave a sigh of relief. She turned, smiling, to the dark face of her master. But charming though she looked in her crisp muslin dress, with her ringlets bobbing round her gay little face, she evoked no answering smile from Mr. Severn. Joseph, watching, thought that the inhabitants of this fairyland were as beautiful as their surroundings; but, his critical sense asserting itself, he added a mental note that some, at least, were not as accomplished as they should be. Why, this little girl must

A*

be quite as old as himself, and he could have played that piece better than she two, or even three, years ago when he was only seven years old. Evidently his father's thoughts were running in the same direction, for he was frowning heavily and the smile had faded from his little pupil's face.

Fortunately the storm was averted by a voice from the room next door. The child jumped down from the piano-stool with a cry of, "Coming, Mama," sketched a curtsey to Mr. Severn, and would have run from the room if he had not called her back to say, in a tone of reproof,

"You cannot hope to excel, Miss Anne, if you do not practise a great deal more."

"Oh, I will, indeed I will," she promised, in an agony to be gone, and then turned appealingly to the door which had just opened. Her mother came in—a middle-aged woman, stylishly dressed in lilac silk, with white satin sleeves, and a frill of white muslin round her neck.

"In trouble again, Anne?" she said reproachfully to her daughter. Then she turned to Joseph's father:

"I fear you will never make of her as good a performer as her sister."

Mr. Severn bowed silently. She waited a minute for a polite protest. It was not forthcoming. A moody, unexpected man, she thought, but what a good teacher! Her eye fell on Joseph, who had risen from his footstool.

"And is this boy the author of the drawings you showed me?" James Severn melted slightly. "Yes, Ma'am."

"I had not thought him so young," she said, looking rather surprised, and then, addressing Joseph kindly, "I hear you wish for permission to see the contents of our picture gallery?"

"Oh yes, Ma'am, if you please," said Joseph eagerly, encouraged by her kindliness and condescension. "I should like it above all things."

She smiled at his eagerness, and thought him very appealing with his big dark eyes and his curling brown hair. Graciously she gave Mr. Severn her permission to take Joseph to the picture gallery, and then, with a rustle of silken skirts and a "Come, my love," to her daughter, she left the room.

Mr. Severn, for all his reserve, was almost as excited as Joseph. Music was James Severn's profession (he could play five instruments), but he was passionately interested in painting, though his knowledge of the art fell lamentably short of his enthusiasm. He could not resist a sale of pictures, and when money was not over-plentiful at home he would for ever be bringing in newly-bought treasures and calling to his wife to come and admire them. Joseph's mother never failed to play the expected rôle of appreciative audience. Nevertheless it was an additional pleasure to the father to find his eldest son, at a very early age, showing as much enthusiasm as himself for these oddly-assorted purchases. Joseph never seemed to tire of staring up at the canvases which came and went in their cottage at Hoxton with almost tidal regularity, and would listen, fascinated, for hours while his father explained their subjects and discussed their merits.

What excitement, then, when the little boy began to show signs of a precocious talent himself. When he was no more than five years old he had drawn a portrait of his father in profile. The proud father had been able to report to his wife that, in the opinion of an artist friend, it was "in everything but firmness, excellent." From that moment James Severn had set himself to develop his son's talent. He would take him for long walks through the fields that surrounded the village of Hoxton. He would choose some object—a group of tall elms, or a wayside inn—and set the boy down to paint it. Only last week he had selected an ivy-mantled cottage, and had borrowed a chair, in his high-handed way, from the old lady who lived in it, for Joseph to sit on. This old lady had watched the progress of the picture and had shown her appreciation in the most practical fashion by rewarding the artist with a large slice of cake.

But now that the boy was getting older his father had hit on the happy idea of taking him to the country houses where he taught music, so that Joseph might have the opportunity of studying pictures by famous artists. Together they wandered, entranced, into the picture gallery. Mr. Severn, who always made up his mind very swiftly and had scarcely ever been known to change it, had no use for anything but landscape. His progress down the long room was a series of sharp rushes. At the first landscape he paused, examined it with interest, grunted appreciatively, and then he was off again, striding down the gallery, searching for another shaded pond or wooded valley, passing a smooth-faced Bellini Madonna and a sophisticated Van Dyck lady with no more than a glance between them.

Joseph, on the other hand, pursued a methodical course down the room, drinking in everything. He was fascinated by the portraits of past members of the family, and especially by a picture

which was the most lately hung—a likeness of the lady of the
house by Sir Joshua Reynolds. So engrossed was he that he was
startled when he turned to find the original of the picture—the
lady in the lilac dress—standing at his side. She too was examining
her portrait.

"There is an object worthy of your study," she said, regarding
her likeness complacently. "Not for the subject—though it is
commonly admitted to be a most perfect resemblance—but because
Sir Joshua was acknowledged to be the greatest artist then living,
and as such he was received in the highest circles. If you cultivate
the talent you have been given, you too may hope to better your
position in the world."

As she was speaking she handed a portfolio to Joseph.

"There," she said, "I will lend you these engravings to copy.
Take great care of them, and you may bring them back when your
father comes again."

She left him stammering his thanks, with the warm glow of
one who has given great pleasure without the slightest inconvenience
to herself.

Joseph was in ecstasy. Not only was he thrilled to have these
precious engravings to copy, but the good lady's words had lit a
flame in his heart. Hitherto he had worked at his painting because
he loved it and was happier when he was doing it than at any
other time. From now on he would work with a passionate
determination to excel—and thus to reach a position where he
would be looked up to and respected by the glamorous creatures
who inhabited this world so different from his own. He too would
be received "in the highest circles." As he walked across the park
with his father towards the village, Joseph in imagination was
alighting at the house from a chaise and four—climbing the lovely
shallow-stepped staircase to the picture gallery—strolling down it
with his hostess, who was eagerly soliciting his opinion of every
picture. They would pause at last before the lady's portrait, and
there, beside it, would hang— Joseph had no time to decide
on the subject of his masterpiece, for he was disturbed by a sharp
cuff on his ear.

"Step up," said his father brusquely. "We won't be home
till midnight if you dawdle so."

Clinging tightly to the precious portfolio, Joseph obediently
broke into a trot.

CHAPTER I

THE ENGRAVER'S APPRENTICE

(1810—1815)

THE firelight leaped and danced on the low-beamed ceiling, and the room was filled with the cheerful noise of a large family having its supper. Knives and forks clattered, chairs shuffled, laughter mingled with cries of protest and appeals for aid. The Severn family had hearty appetites and loud voices; the room seemed full of their exuberant youth. Mrs. Severn sat at one end of the table, her white mob-cap on her still brown hair, her blue eyes sharp to perceive any budding quarrel or injustice, her face showing her happiness. These were the moments she liked best in the day, when her children gathered round the table to enjoy the meals which she had prepared for them. She smiled affectionately round on them all. Her eldest daughter Charlotte, with her smooth fair hair and placid comely face, was sitting next to her. Five-year-old Charles sat on her other hand, his round pink cheeks smeared with gravy. Next to him sat Tom. He was only nine, but already he was showing great promise as a musician. He could not only sing beautifully—they could all do that—but he won praise from his father, a severe critic in anything to do with music, for his performance both on the harpsichord and the violin. He had confided to her the other day that his ambition was to play the organ like his grandfather, James Severn's father, who had been organist at the church in Leadenhall Street. At the moment he was dividing his attention between the food and a musical score which he was balancing on his knee. He would take a good mouthful and then bend, munching, over the music.

To all her family music had seemed as essential as food from a very early age. She was glad they had all inherited this trait from herself and James, and she loved to hear them sing together. James was teaching them one of Handel's anthems now in the evenings. He was late getting home to-night. His chair stood empty at the other end of the table, and next to it sat his youngest daughter, Maria. She was three years older than Tom and had a merry vivacious face, dark hair and blue eyes. Full of gaiety and always laughing, she was joking now with Sarah across the table.

13

Sarah was the cleverest of her daughters, thought Mrs. Severn, but more restless than the others. Charlotte had never been anything but contented. As a baby she had scarcely ever cried, and she had been a quiet happy child. Now she was sixteen and, if Mrs. Severn was not mistaken, would soon be married. A neighbour of theirs in Hoxton, a Mr. Giles, had been calling on them frequently and seemed very taken with her. They had known him for some years and he was a respectable hard-working man who made enough money to support a wife and family. He was some years older than Charlotte, but that was all to the good. Yes, Charlotte would be happy, her mother was certain. But of two of her other children she was not so sure. Sarah and Joseph were more restless than the others. Joseph, she knew, sighed in secret after greatness and distinction, and she did not think he was happy in his work. It had seemed such a good arrangement at the time. . . .

Soon after Joseph's fourteenth birthday Mr. Severn had begun to wonder what he was going to do with his eldest child. It was out of the question for a music-master, with a wife and five other children to support, to pay for an artistic education for his son, and in addition to keep him, perhaps for several years. Everyone knew that it took a long time to make an artist, and still longer for him to establish himself—if he ever did. Yet James Severn was loth to stifle his son's talent. At last a solution occurred to him. It came to him quite suddenly when he entered the house one day to find Joseph painstakingly copying the design on some old plate. The very thing! He would apprentice the boy to an engraver. It took some little time to accomplish. Most of the advertisements demanded a premium of anything from one hundred pounds to three. But at length the business was arranged with a Mr. William Bond, who stipulated only that the father should give an undertaking about the board and lodging of his son. This was agreed upon. Mr. Bond was impressed by the drawings which Mr. Severn showed him and was well pleased at gaining such a promising pupil. Joseph was fascinated by the canvases at Mr. Bond's house, which were far superior to any of his father's haphazard purchases, and the idea of drawing from oil-paintings, which he had so far never attempted, thrilled him. He was apprenticed to Mr. Bond for seven years.

At first he had been happy and excited in his new life, telling his mother how much he was learning from the reproduction of paintings by Singleton. But for some little time now he had told her nothing about his work, and seemed unwilling to talk about it when he got home in the evenings after his long tramp from Mr. Bond's house in Newman Street to his home in Hoxton. His natural high spirits were becoming chilled into listlessness and he seemed thinner every day.

As for Sarah, although she was affectionate and devoted to her brothers and sisters, she was not content like Maria to laugh and play with them all day long. She would sit in a corner, reading, for hours on end, until her mother asked her to help her with the cooking or sent her to run some errand in the village. She and Joseph would talk together about books and writers of whom Mrs. Severn had never heard. When *she* was a girl it had been needlework and painting and music that she had studied, and her parents had not encouraged too much book-learning. Then young James Severn had come as apprentice to her father and a new life had begun for her. He had quickly fallen in love with the beautiful girl who shared his love of music and painting. His dark good looks had captured her heart, and when his apprenticeship was ended, Miss Littel became Mrs. Severn.

He had decided then to teach music, and had made quite a good living from his profession. Although, as he grew older, his temper became difficult, Mrs. Severn had never regretted her marriage to him; they were so completely different in character, yet they admired in each other qualities which they themselves lacked. She was stimulated by his restless energy, by his moods of boisterous good spirits, and by the headstrong intensity of his feelings; while he took strength from her quick sympathy and imperturbable good humour—from her serenity which remained unaffected by changes in fortune, by ill or good chance, by rage or despair. Money was often not too plentiful for their family of six, but she always managed somehow. The children were always fed, the house was always spotless, and Mrs. Severn always serene. Sometimes James was rather hard on the children, but then, at other times, when he was in a good mood, he could be a charming father. He would tell the children stories, and sing and act for them. Once he had so kindled Joseph's imagination by his dramatic interpretation of the Ghost in *Hamlet* that the little boy would not go to bed until he had been allowed to make a drawing of the dreadful apparition.

Mrs. Severn thought herself a most fortunate woman. Her reward for her constant sympathy and tact was the love of her husband and the adoration of her children. She had brought up her family in the knowledge and fear of God and they were all good Christians—unlike some of these dreadful radicals one heard so much about.

The door opened suddenly, and Mr. Severn came in.

The noise ceased abruptly as all eyes turned on him to see what mood he was in. Then it began again almost at once when they observed that he was carrying with him a picture, which he propped up on a chair against the wall. Mrs. Severn, taking her cue faultlessly as usual, rose from the table in order to admire the picture. It was a portrait of a man in armour, but the face with its dark glowing eyes, its heavily marked brows and the square cleft chin, was very like her husband's.

"Is it—you, James?" Mrs. Severn hesitated. Her answer was a roar of delighted laughter.

"I thought you would think so, my dear. No, I found it in ——'s shop." He mentioned a little picture-dealer whose name was only too familiar to them.

"Oh, but it is astonishing, James! I would have sworn it was your portrait!" cried the obliging Mrs. Severn.

"I have not bought it. But the likeness was so singular that I persuaded —— to let me bring it home with me to-night to show it to you. They say it is Lord Strafford, but I have no use for these rubbishy portraits.[1] They want £2 for it. Well, they must want. I shall take it back in the morning."

He walked over to the table, rubbing his hands together in high good humour, and, helping himself liberally to the food, he began to ask Tom questions about the score he was studying. Conversation broke out again round the table, only to cease as Mr. Severn suddenly asked in quite a different voice,

"Is Joseph come?"

"Not yet," was the gentle reply.

"He always comes when dinner is half over," said her husband, frowning.

"Yes, poor lad, and all the nice cabbage cold," Mrs. Severn replied tactfully.

"Ha! Serve him right! Serve him right!" he cried, adding, "Drat the young dog!" in quite an affectionate tone.'[2]

A sigh of relief went round the table. Mr. Severn ate his supper quickly and pushed his chair back.

---

[1] Story of Strafford picture, William Sharp, *Life and Letters of Joseph Severn*, p. 8.
[2] Imaginary conversation in letter from Joseph in Rome to Maria, Jan. 21st, 1821.

"You may clear the table," he announced in his grand manner. This was less of a formality than it might seem, as one of the things most certain to provoke an outburst was for what he termed "housework" to be done in his presence. When Mrs. Severn had sent little Charles off to bed she began to clear the table, her daughters helping her. Mr. Severn took his violin out of its case. Gripping it under his chin he ran the bow over the strings, while with his other hand he twisted the wooden pegs to tune the instrument. With his head thus bent over the violin, he looked quickly up under his thick black brows as Joseph came into the room.

Joseph's handsome face was pale. His young wrists showed thin and bony as he took off his beaver hat and seemed about to throw it on to a chair. He paused when he saw the picture balanced there and went over to look at it. After several minutes' study he straightened up with a sigh, saying, "I should like to copy that picture."

"There is no possibility of *that*," said his father, "for I intend to return it to the shop in the morning. Come, Joseph, you're just in time for us to run over that Mozart quartet."

"Oh, James! Let the poor lad have his supper first," cried Mrs. Severn, hurrying forward with a plate piled high with meat and vegetables.

"The way you cosset your children!" exclaimed Mr. Severn, rolling his dark eyes to the ceiling. "When *I* was a young man—"

"When *you* were a young man I cosseted *you*, my love," Mrs. Severn replied with a smile.

"*Touché!*" cried Mr. Severn and began to sing, waving his bow in time to his song:

> "Blow, blow, thou winter wind,
> Thou art not so unkind
> As man's ingratitude."

He pointed the bow at Tom. "Come, Tom, and serenade your mother, *and* the girls too. Sarah, you can give us an alto— one, *two!*"

> "Heigh-ho! sing heigh-ho! unto the
> green holly:
> Most friendship is feigning, most
> loving mere folly:
> Then, heigh-ho, the holly!
> This life is most jolly."

They were all singing now except Joseph and his mother. Scarcely an evening passed in this house without the family either singing or playing together. They all had good voices and had been used to hearing and discussing music since they were old enough to sing nursery rhymes with their mother. But to-night Joseph did not join in. He finished his supper and then left the room, returning in a short while with what looked like a large box under one arm and in his hand a bundle of paints, brushes, cardboard and paper. He put these on the table and then removed carefully from his pocket a bottle of ink, a quill and a small pot of glue. When the box was emptied it proved to be a miniature theatre—a little stage with curtains drawn up on either side.

Joseph rummaged among the bits of cardboard, found the wings and a back-cloth representing a street of gabled houses, and put them in place. Then he made some careful measurements and began to sketch a small figure on the cardboard. His father had been watching him with a frown. Now he strode over to the table, leaving his other children in mid-song. Their voices trailed off into silence. Mr. Severn scowled down on his eldest son.

"Fiddling about with that child's toy again!" he barked. "You would do better to join your family in a song instead of wasting your time with that rubbish!" He made a scornful gesture with his violin towards the little theatre.

"It's not rubbish, Father," said Joseph. "By changing the scenes I can practise painting architecture and landscape, and now I'm making some studies for the figures." He pointed eagerly to the figure he was sketching. "This is to be Queen Katherine, and I'm trying to reproduce one of Mrs. Siddons's most characteristic attitudes." He hesitated a minute. His father said nothing. His enthusiasm quenched, he went on, his eyes pleading with his father, "Later I thought of making larger drawings from the studies I made of her when I got home from the theatre. I thought I might be able to sell them."

"Sell them!" Mr. Severn gave a snort. "Why can't you stick to the trade to which you're apprenticed? You'll make enough money in that."

"Because I want to be an artist."

"Listen to him." Mr. Severn threw his bow on to the table in a gesture of despair. It slithered across the polished surface and hit the little theatre so that it tottered and would have fallen on its side if Joseph had not clutched it. "A master engraver *is* an artist. There is scope for the ablest draughtsman in so worthy a profession."

"That may be so." Joseph sprang to his feet, his eyes shining, his fatigue forgotten. "It may be the finest calling on earth, but it is not to my liking! Do you hear?" His hands were on the table as he leaned across it towards his father. "It—is—not—to—my—liking! Because I want to *create*. The finest engravings the world has known are only interpretations of what someone else has created. I want to create—myself."

"You are too inexperienced to realize the insuperable obstacles that stand between a man of no fortune and his success as an artist." Mr. Severn spoke coldly. "They can only be overcome by genius. You have to earn your living. As an artist you have not sufficient talent. You would starve."

"How can you know whether I have sufficient talent?" cried Joseph, his voice trembling. "How can I show anyone what I can do—what I *know* I can do? I *must* have training. I must study anatomy. I must—I must attend the Academy Schools."

Mr. Severn heaved a theatrical sigh.

"Hark to the boy. You should be grateful to your father for apprenticing you to an honourable trade and one in which you can use your talents. When you began your apprenticeship Mr. Bond gave me favourable reports of you. Now it is nothing but complaints. Your indifference to the engraver's trade is as foolish as it is reprehensible."

"It isn't my fault!" burst out Joseph hotly. "You apprenticed me to Mr. Bond when I was but fourteen years old. When I saw that I was to draw from real oil-paintings I was delighted. I thought that with Mr. Bond's guidance I should soon become an artist. Had I but known—" he said bitterly. "*You* knew, and you never saw fit to explain to me. When I had copied those Bartolozzi prints he set me to stab the copper. I soon mastered that, and then I thought I should be able to draw again. But no! Mr. Bond said 'he was employing me as an assistant in his trade and not as a tame artist'." His voice broke. "I have been popped unwittingly into slavery and doomed to stab copper for seven long years."

He sat down suddenly and hid his face in the crook of his arm which rested on the table. The wave of his father's wrath broke over him, but he was too tired and miserable to listen.

"Ingratitude—insolence—conceit!" His father's voice roared round him, filling the room. He thumped the table to emphasize his points. He shook both fists in the air. He leaned forward and wagged his finger threateningly under Joseph's nose. And yet, while his furious voice was ringing over his son's bowed head, he knew, and Joseph knew, that whatever happened Joseph would always be his favourite child.

Mrs. Severn entered on this scene. She had been upstairs to see that little Charles was asleep. As she heard her husband's raised voice and saw his flushed face her first thought was, "It cannot be good for him to be so angry."

Then she saw poor Joseph's white miserable face and decided that it was time for her to calm the storm. She went over to her husband.

"There, there, James," she said in her gentle voice. "The poor lad's tired out and must go to bed. And all of you too," she added, turning to the other children, who were still on the further side of the room, where they had stayed, silent and embarrassed, since the singing was interrupted. "Off with you—and quietly. Remember Charles is asleep."

They all went out with subdued "Good nights." Joseph picked up his miniature theatre. As though dazed, he carefully bestowed the pot of glue and the quill and the indian ink in various pockets, and went to the door.

"Good night, Mother. God bless you," he said, using the same words he had spoken every night since he was two years old. He spoke holding the door open with his free hand, his eyes on his feet. He half went out, and then reopened the door to mutter rapidly in a low voice, "Good—night—Father—God—bless—you," before he shut it again. His father was putting his violin back in its case. He snapped the lid to with a vicious click but did not answer.

For nearly an hour after he had said his prayers and snuffed out his candle Joseph lay awake, listening to his mother and father talking in the room below. At last their steps creaked up the narrow stairs. They were still talking quietly.

"Very well, my love, I will go to Newman Street to-morrow. We will see what accommodation can be made. I can't have the boy ill."

That was his father's voice. Not for the first time Joseph gave thanks to God for his "angel-mother." [1]

Mr. William Bond gave in. It was pointed out to him—Mrs. Severn thought he could hardly have failed to notice it for himself—that Joseph was a delicate boy and was becoming ill from

[1] Sharp, *op. cit.*, pp. 9-10.

too long hours of work in a stuffy little room, not enough fresh air, and constant worry and frustration. Mr. Bond agreed that he should have certain holidays, on condition that he would be more assiduous in his work at other times. Joseph kept the agreement, and Mr. Bond no longer found him staring moodily out of the window when he should have been working.

On the other hand, Joseph had more time away from his work. This he divided between reading and painting. True to his determination to be worthy of a higher position in the world, he tried to enlarge his store of knowledge. He read every book on history that he could find. He read poetry, letters, essays—everything he could lay hands on. His enthusiasm covered every form of learning. He even wrestled with some books on mathematics, but soon gave them up for more congenial studies. His enthusiasm was infinite. But his efforts to educate himself were so wild and unplanned that his memory became stocked with a curious literary hotch-potch. Soon he was to have guidance.

He began to paint small portraits in water-colours, for which he charged half a guinea. As time went on he found he could raise his price a little. But he felt more and more strongly that he would never make any considerable progress in his art until he had proper training. As Joseph neared the end of his seven years' apprenticeship it became clear to Mr. Bond that, if he were not allowed to attend the Royal Academy classes, he would feel nothing but hatred and bitterness for his master. He had done good work for the engraver, who was anxious to be able to make use of him when he was no longer bound to him. So, almost a year before he had completed his seven years, Mr. Bond capitulated, and the determined young man, now in his twentieth year, had his way. His delight knew no bounds.

Even the discovery that wealth and influence counted for more than talent in these classes failed to quench his enthusiasm. The Royal Academy Student Classes were held at that time in Somerset House, where the ceilings had been decorated by Angelica Kauffmann, Cipriani and Sir Joshua Reynolds, first President of the Academy. There of an evening the students would assemble— laughing, fooling and pushing each other aside in a rush to secure a pile of the boxes on which they perched while they were drawing. They were a motley crowd. Some, like Joseph, were poorly but neatly dressed, some in threadbare coats and neckties that were none too clean. And here and there you would see a lordly fellow in Hessian boots who would thrust the others aside, taking as his right the largest pyramid of boxes and the best place to sit. These illustrious few, who gave the impression of conferring a favour on students and master alike by their presence, were the sons of Royal Academicians.

Then a sudden hush would fall as a little man entered, "small but with the presence of Jove," as one of his pupils described him.[1] He wore a black chip hat on his white hair. His quick temper showed in the lines round his mouth, and his darting eyes missed nothing. This was the famous Fuseli, Keeper and Professor of Painting at the Academy Schools for nearly twenty-five years. Even the Hessian boots seemed to feel the force of his personality. He was himself a successful artist, and had written a book of aphorisms on painting; that he was not more popular with the majority of his pupils was his own fault. He made no attempt to disguise his contempt for the English. He despised them as a race of barbarians who thought of art only as a luxury, not as life itself.

"You English!" he would cry, throwing his arms above his head in despair. "Vy, you are good for nothing but to use bad language and drink beer!"

One day Joseph hurried from his work at Newman Street to attend a lecture which the great Turner was to give at the Schools, on the subject of perspective. When he arrived, in good time, he was in despair to find that every seat was already occupied. He immediately rushed off to Fuseli to ask him if there was any way of getting a place. The little Keeper's expression became even more sardonic.

"Offer any of the audience a pot of beer in exchange," he said, "and you will get a seat anywhere—and at once!"

Sometimes he was not so restrained. There were occasions when the Schools would echo to his voice of thunder.

"Sir, you are a damnation fool!" he would roar, and once, beside himself with rage, "You are a set of wild beasts, and I am your cursèd Keeper."[2]

Nevertheless this formidable old man could usually tell surprisingly quickly which of his students deserved encouragement. He soon saw that Joseph grudged neither time nor labour in his determination to become a good draughtsman. When he was studying in the "Antique Class" he would walk back to Hoxton after the class was ended, eat a hasty supper and settle down to another two hours of work on Laocoön or the Dying Gladiator.

---

[1] George Richmond, *Richmond Papers*, p. 10.
[2] *Ibid.*, pp. 8-9.

Life became easier for Joseph, when Sarah married. She let him have a room in her house in Goswell Street, and he would sleep there several nights a week. Sarah would always have a good hot dinner ready for him. He could work there in the evenings undisturbed, or sometimes they would sit together by her fire while he confided in her all his dreams and aspirations. Sarah would listen and admire and prophesy that all his dreams would come true.

CHAPTER II

ACADEMY STUDENT

(1818—1819)

WHILE Joseph was still an apprentice to Mr. Bond his life had been divided almost entirely between his home, Newman Street and the Academy Classes. Now that he had completed his seven years with the engraver he began to work up a little connection as a miniature-painter; the world was opening to him and he had time to make new friends.

At twenty-three, although small and still rather thin, Joseph was a strikingly handsome young man. His dark hair was naturally curly. Strongly-marked eyebrows arched over large brown eyes. His mouth was full under a straight nose. His manner, too, was attractive. His open face, his ready enthusiasm and good spirits, the laughter which bubbled up so easily from the optimism and serenity which were his heritage from his mother—all these drew people to him. His manner had a charming diffidence and his modesty was disarming.

Some of his new friends were fellow-students at the Academy Art Schools. There was pale, boyish George Richmond, a few years younger than Joseph, who shared his love of music. Walking home after the classes they would argue about Handel and Purcell and Mozart, and why there were no great English composers living. There was young Edwin Landseer, with whom he was set, on his first day in the Life Class, to draw the Feet of Hercules from a model. There was William Haslam, so friendly and reliable, who at twenty-one was working in his father's firm of solicitors. He had been Joseph's companion on that always-to-be-remembered evening when Mrs. Siddons had emerged from her retirement to play Queen Katherine in *Henry VIII*.

Then there were three brothers whom he met with Haslam—George, John and Tom Keats. He met George, the second brother and the business man of the family, first. Their father and mother were dead, Joseph learned, and he worked in the office of his guardian—a Mr. Abbey, wholesale tea-dealer in St. Pancras Lane. Joseph soon realized, from the way his new friend spoke, what an intensely strong affection bound the three

24

brothers together. The youngest, Tom, was very tall and thin and delicate, and John, the eldest brother, was a medical student at Guy's. Soon Joseph was friendly with all three. Or rather, he was friendly with the two younger brothers; for the eldest his feelings were too complicated to be expressed by so simple a word.

John Keats already radiated the powerful attraction of genius. He was shorter than George—in fact, he was not much over five feet tall. But he was so well made, being strong, broad-shouldered, muscular and compactly built, and moreover his bearing was so erect and manly, that one scarcely noticed his lack of inches. It was only when he was reading, or rapt in some deep reverie, that one realized that he was a small man. Then his chest would fall in, his head would bend forward "as though weightily over-burdened," Joseph described it later, and his eyes "seemed almost to throw a light before his face." [1] It was these brilliant eyes which immediately attracted one's attention at a first meeting. They glowed as though with an inward light, wonderfully bright and of a curious hazel colour. It was almost as an afterthought that people who met him noted the other details of this remarkable face, the wide sensitive mouth, the forehead broad and powerful, the high cheek-bones and boldly-modelled nose. "The character and expression of Keats's features would arrest even the casual passenger in the street," wrote one of their mutual friends [2] after his death.

John Keats made no secret of the fact that when he had passed his examinations he had no intention of practising as a doctor. He could live for a year or two on his share of the money which their grandmother had left the brothers. He intended to leave Guy's when he came of age next year, and to devote himself to writing poetry as his profession. Poetry was the only thing worth the attention of superior minds, he said, and compared to it all other pursuits were mean and tame. The greatest men in the world were the poets, and to rank among them was the chief object of his ambition. His brothers did not try to dissuade him, although they knew that his decision would anger their guardian. Their admiration for their brother amounted almost to worship, and they had perfect confidence that he was born to be exalted and to exalt their name. [3]

George was the practical man of affairs of the trio. He managed their finances and neither John nor Tom questioned what he did.

[1] Sharp, *op. cit.*, p. 20.   [2] Colvin, *John Keats*, p. 31.
[3] Henry Stephens, quoted by Colvin, *op. cit.*, p. 31.

"George always stood between me and any dealings with the world," [1] John Keats was to say sadly, later on, when troubles were gathering round him, and George was far away, and Tom dead. George's common sense certainly relieved his elder brother of responsibilities and left his imagination unburdened by everyday cares. But it was tall, narrow-chested Tom who shared his life of the spirit most completely. George said that there was no man living who understood John as well as Tom did. [2] He could understand his abnormally sensitive reactions. He understood how anything beautiful or uncommon—a sight, a sound, a scent— which would evoke the passing thought in others, "How beautiful that is," would pierce John Keats with a pleasure that was almost pain. It was this hypersensitiveness, this extra-intensity of feeling, which made him a poet and which, at the same time, left him so vulnerable to the emotional blows which were to fall on him as one by one those he loved were to be torn away from him.

Although he was a healthy, normal young man, with good spirits and fond of company, John Keats was already conscious that he had greatness within him, even though it might never be recognized as such by the world.

To Joseph his new friend's knowledge seemed infinite. Dazzled, he followed Keats, and learned to love with him his heroes— Chaucer, Spenser and Shakespeare. His untrained love of poetry grew, he loved to hear Keats linger over some phrase when he was reading aloud, savouring its beauty and betraying his pleasure with "one of his delightful stares."

John Keats, for his part, must have been touched by Joseph's enthusiasm and his genuine appreciation of beauty. His charm of manner made him a pleasant companion, and he showed his pleasure and interest so naïvely in every new discovery, that Keats once burst out laughing and assured him that he was "the most astonishingly suggestive innocent!" [3] He was able to show Keats new beauties, too, in a world where his own judgment was less untrained. Early in their friendship he took Keats to see Titian's "Bacchus" at the National Gallery, which was mirrored later in the description of "Bacchus and his crew" in Keats's poem, "Endymion." After this they would often go to picture exhibitions, and the sculpture galleries together. But their favourite expedition was to the British Museum to see the Elgin Marbles, and soon

---

[1] *Letters of John Keats*, p. 345.   [2] *Ibid.*, p. xxxiv.
[3] Sharp, *op. cit.*, p. 31.

Joseph was introduced by Keats to Mr. Haydon, the painter, whose efforts had led to the Marbles being bought for the nation.

What an extraordinary creature that artist was! Joseph was both fascinated and repelled by him. At their first meeting he felt battered by the strength and exuberance of his personality. Keats was strongly impressed by him. He wrote a sonnet on their first meeting which Haydon replied to with a promise to send it on to the young poet's hero—Wordsworth. The friendship between them grew, and so Joseph, too, came to know him better and was able to form some sort of estimate of him as a man. And yet in a way it seemed to Joseph that he was *not* a man. He was larger than life. He was cast in heroic mould. His emotions seemed more tempestuous and elemental than those of a mere man. As he told how he had quelled this enemy with a letter to the Press and shattered another in argument over a dinner-table, his eyes would flash beneath his great domed forehead, his belligerent chin would jut uncompromisingly and he would seem to swell with self-confidence and pride. It was his own honest conviction that he was the chosen of the Almighty, the greatest painter of all time, martyred and frustrated by malevolent enemies.

He was as fervent in his loves as in his hates, and he soon conceived a passionate admiration for Keats. Joseph was often a third in the long discussions in Haydon's studio in Great Marlborough Street. There they would talk, while the candle-light flickered on the Grecian casts and threw dancing shadows on to the half-finished canvases that crowded around them. Keats was dazzled by Haydon's enthusiasm and energy, and, like so many others among this strange man's contemporaries, for some time he was bludgeoned into seeing his pictures through the artist's own eyes as what he *intended* them to be, and believed that he had already achieved the heights he described so eloquently. Every sort of subject would be discussed during these evenings. Not only sculpture and painting—with, always, an interval for Haydon to take a short gallop on his hobby-horse, the decline of historical painting and his intention of resuscitating it—but literature, the classics, politics and religion. "I have enjoyed Shakespeare with John Keats more than with any other human being," [1] Haydon said afterwards.

Joseph enjoyed and learned much from these evenings. The only jarring note was struck when Haydon got on to the subject of religion. He was a fanatically religious man but adopted a

---

[1] Colvin, *op. cit.*, p. 66.

curious, almost proprietorial attitude towards God. He believed implicitly that God *must* be on his side in any dispute, however trivial, and that those who thwarted him must automatically be the agents of Satan.

"I always rise up from my knees," he said to Keats, "with a refreshed fury, an iron-clenched firmness, a crystal piety of feeling that sends me streaming on with a repulsive power against the troubles of life." [1]

To Joseph, whose mother had taught him a truer Christianity, such presumption was horrifying, but he too was fascinated by Haydon's grandiose schemes, his gigantic canvases, his exuberance, his arrogance and his restless vitality.

On his twenty-first birthday Keats fulfilled his intention of giving up his medical career so that he might concentrate entirely on poetry. His first book of poems was published in the following spring. All his friends waited, breathless, for the anticipated applause of the world to burst on their ears. Haydon, in his grandiose manner, wrote to Keats of one poem in the volume: "It is a flash of lightning that will rouse men from their occupations and keep them trembling for the crash of thunder that *will* follow!" [2] But, apart from lukewarm reviews in two of the leading periodicals, the book was scarcely noticed by the outside world. Joseph did not see Keats for several months after this, for he had gone away to the country alone, to start work on a new poem called "Endymion."

When Keats returned to London in June, Joseph would often walk across the fields to Hampstead, where the three brothers were now in lodgings in the house of a postman called Bentley. He would take one or two of his miniatures with him, so that he might have the excuse of finding backgrounds for them, for he was still so shy and modest that he lacked the confidence to arrive without some reason to explain his presence.

Through the Keats brothers he made many new friends. They were the centre of a group of gay young men, and attracted to them, too, the friendship of men slightly older than themselves, such as Haydon, Leigh Hunt, Charles Wentworth Dilke, who was by profession a Civil Servant and in his leisure hours a student of English literature, Charles Brown, and Charles Cowden Clarke, son of the headmaster of the school at which the Keats brothers had been educated.

[1] Letter from Haydon to Keats, *Letters of John Keats*, p. 27.
[2] *Ibid.*, March 1817, p. 14.

Joseph would visit all of these and was popular with their female relatives by reason of his good looks and his gentle manner. Of the very young men there was John Hamilton Reynolds, who was considered by Leigh Hunt to complete, with Keats and Shelley, the trio of rising young poets. He was soon to renounce his literary ambitions when he wanted to marry, and to settle down as a respectable lawyer. There was James Rice, too, another young lawyer, who, although always delicate, and often ill, was a great talker and was regarded as the wit of their circle. Charles Wells was the youngest of their friends—he was only seventeen years old at this time, and had been a contemporary of Tom's at school.

These young men formed a group of friends. They were not always in London at the same time, but some of them would see each other several times a week, dining together or going to the theatre or to dances or to Haydon's studio or the British Museum, or meeting for an evening at Reynolds's home, where his lively sisters were an attraction. Besides the easy comradeship of youth there was another emotion which was common to them all—to the shrewd Dilke and the outspoken Brown no less than to seventeen-year-old Wells—and that was admiration for and confidence in John Keats's genius.

Keats left London again in the autumn, and Joseph's visits to Hampstead were fewer for a time. Somehow the walk was not so alluring after his day's work when the pleasure of John Keats's company lay no longer at the end of his journey. Then news came that Keats had finished "Endymion," and was back in Well Walk with the Bentleys. As soon as he could get a free day Joseph went up to Hampstead to see him, and found him alone. Tom, who had always been delicate, had produced some alarming symptoms. His cough had got worse and he had several times spat blood. George had taken him to Teignmouth, hoping that the milder climate would do him good. Keats told Joseph that he would be coming to stay in London for a little while, as he was going to act as dramatic critic for the *Champion* while Reynolds was away for a Christmas holiday. He was already busy revising and copying out his new poem for publication.

During the next few weeks Joseph dined several times with Keats—Wells often making a third, as Keats was staying with him while he was in London. Keats would insist on drinking claret, which he loved, and afterwards, when the glasses were empty, they would each choose a musical instrument to imitate,

and with a great deal of laughter they would play what they called
"a concert." [1]

On other evenings they would enjoy a different type of music,
when they went together to the house of Vincent Novello, the
organist at the Portuguese Embassy Chapel in South Street. This
was an easy-going, cosmopolitan household, where life was ruled
by music. Vincent Novello was half Italian, and had been educated
in France, while his wife was of German extraction. Keats was
fond of music and enjoyed himself when Charles Cowden Clarke
first took him to the house in Oxford Road. Charles was a constant
visitor there and was later to marry Novello's daughter, Mary,
who at this time was still a child. Joseph and Keats went several
times together, and Joseph was enchanted by the exquisite render-
ings of Mozart and Haydn that he heard there. The drawing-room
was a pleasant room whose walls were papered a delicate pink and
decorated with water-colours. In the centre stood a sofa table
which was littered with books and prints, and at one end of the
room was a small but fine-toned organ. Here Novello would sit
and play, in the way that caused queues of fashionable carriages
to block the traffic in South Street outside the Embassy Chapel.

There would be a pause for talk and then he would play again,
or Leigh Hunt or one of the Robertson brothers would sing.
Years afterwards Novello's little daughter, who was sitting so
quietly in the corner, was to record her memory of John Keats,
"leaning against the side of the organ, listening with rapt attention
to my father's music." She also mentioned his "favourite position
one foot raised on his other knee." It was in this position that
Joseph made a sketch of him one evening at the Novellos' as he sat
listening to the music. Unlike Mrs. Hunt, Mrs. Novello was a
practical, economical woman, and the "feast of music" was followed
by refreshments in the form of bread and cheese and what Charles
Lamb called "true Lutheran beer." [2]

One afternoon, at the turn of the year, Joseph dressed himself
with particular care. His sister, Sarah, had lately married, and he
was lodging with her in her house in Goswell Street. This made
his life much easier by eliminating the long walk from his father's
house at Hoxton to his work in Newman Street, off Oxford Street.
Although her house was small, Sarah had contrived to keep a room
in it for Joseph. It was his first studio. On this particular evening
she was fussing round him, bringing him a freshly-laundered necktie,

<hr />

[1] *Letters of John Keats*, p. 74.   [2] Mary Cowden Clarke, *My Long Life*.

brushing his coat and showing other evidence of her determination that her brother's appearance should do her credit. At last she was satisfied and let him go, waving goodbye as he set off on his walk to Haydon's new studio in Lisson Grove.

The artist greeted him boisterously as he led him into his studio and told him to observe the progress that he was making on his huge picture of "Christ's Entry into Jerusalem." Then his host went to admit the other guests. Keats and Reynolds, now back from the country, arrived together. They all stood round the fire, chatting and gazing at the gigantic canvas opposite them. Haydon had followed the example of many Renaissance artists by introducing the faces of his own friends and famous men of his own day in the crowd surrounding Christ. Wordsworth was already there, and Keats too was to have a place. Severn asked Keats how his poem went on. Haydon turned to Keats and said in a low voice,

"Keats, don't show your lines to Hunt on any account, or he will have done half for you."

Keats laughed, but Reynolds burst out,

"Yes, it's true. I told him in the theatre the other night that you were getting on to the completion of four thousand lines. 'Ah!' says Hunt, 'had it not been for me they would have been seven thousand!'" [1]

He was about to say more when the door opened and Leigh Hunt walked in. In appearance he was the romantic's ideal of a poet—a slender figure with jet-black hair and dark soft eyes. He entered talking. Joseph had met him many times before, and was used to his flow of conversation and his love of holding the centre of the stage in any gathering, though he was not so bad when there were no ladies present. When greetings had been exchanged, Hunt began at once to pace up and down the room in front of Haydon's huge canvas, inspecting each head in turn and keeping up a continuous flow of comment, not all of it complimentary, for since he and Haydon had been living as neighbours in Lisson Grove they were frequently squabbling. Haydon never accepted criticism of any sort, and a quarrel might have developed if the door bell had not pealed at that moment.

A few minutes later Joseph felt his heart beating as a tall, man followed Haydon into the room. Introductions were made. It appeared that the distinguished new-comer already knew both Hunt and Keats. As he turned to warm his back at the fire

[1] *Letters of John Keats*, p. 52.

Joseph studied him eagerly. His left hand had already stolen into
its favourite position, in the bosom of his waistcoat. His manner
was grave and he answered Hunt's questions deliberately, in a
deep, rough voice. His face was noble, with rather bony features
and burning, deep-set eyes under a jutting brow. Wordsworth
was at this time forty-eight years old and already the doyen of
English letters. Joseph remembered, as he watched him, that
Keats had said only the other day that there were "three things to
rejoice at in this age—'The Excursion,' Haydon's pictures and
Hazlitt's depth of taste." [1]

The conversation at supper was monopolized at first by Leigh
Hunt and Haydon, who were expatiating on the charms and
advantages of a vegetarian diet. Both had recently been converted
to vegetarianism by Shelley. Leigh Hunt was in rhapsodies over
these vegetable banquets.

"The delicious cauliflower swimming in melted butter," he
urged, "the peas—the beans—never profaned by animal gravy——"

The poet of the Lakes bore it for a while in patience. Then,
holding up his hand, he interrupted, begging leave in his deep,
grave voice to ask a question. Leigh Hunt nodded eagerly, and all
leaned forward to hear what he would say. Joseph noticed a little
expression of sly humour at the corner of his austere mouth.

"If," he said deliberately, "by good chance in these banquets
you meet with a caterpillar, do you not thank your stars for the
delicious morsel of animal food?" [2]

There was some laughter, and Hunt, rather confused, turned
the conversation to other matters. Joseph, although feeling that
the remark was not quite of the kind that he had promised Sarah
to store in his memory to repeat to her later, could not help thinking
that there was a good deal of common sense in it. Wordsworth
was later proved more right than he knew. Leigh Hunt and his
friends became daily thinner and paler under their new régime.
But they persevered, encouraged by Haydon's appearance of ruddy-
faced health. One dreadful day they detected him in the act of
emerging from a chop-house. When they taxed him indignantly
with treachery, he admitted with *bonhomie* that for some time past
he had not felt the vegetable fare to be sufficient, so he had formed
the habit of going round the corner each day after he had eaten his
dinner and consuming a good beef-steak. This ended the fashion
for a vegetable diet among his friends. Only Shelley continued,
and that was because he felt a genuine aversion to eating meat.

[1] *Letters of John Keats*, p. 80.   [2] Sharp, *op. cit.*, p. 33.

Leigh Hunt assured Joseph dramatically that his constitution had received a blow from which he would never recover.

When the supper was ended, chairs were pushed back and tongues were loosened. Joseph did not talk much, but a thrill of delight ran through him when he heard Haydon ask Keats to recite his classical "Ode to Pan" from the new poem "Endymion," which he had just completed. Haydon knew Keats's admiration for "The Excursion," and he realized what pleasure praise from its author would give him. Joseph felt almost as excited and nervous as though it were his own work which was to be heard. His faith in John Keats as a poet, like that of all his friends, had been unsubdued by one failure and was to survive another, seemingly even more complete, to burn undimmed through years of oblivion after his death. It was a remarkable testament to Keats's personality, this unforgettable impression that he made on those who knew him.

But his friends were to receive no encouragement that night. John Keats repeated his Ode "with natural eloquence and great pathos," wrote Joseph afterwards. "When he had finished, we all looked to Wordsworth for praise of the young poet. After a moment's pause, he coolly remarked, 'A very pretty piece of Paganism,' and with this cold water thrown upon us we all broke up." [1]

Joseph walked part of the way home with Keats, who had evidently been thinking over what Haydon and Reynolds had said about Hunt, for after walking some minutes in silence he said, "You know how independent my writing has been. I refused to visit Shelley that I might have my own unfettered scope—and after all, I shall have the reputation of Hunt's *élève*. His corrections and amputations will, by the knowing ones, be traced in the poem."

He paused. Joseph said nothing, and then Keats shrugged his shoulders and smiled.

"Now, is not all this a most paltry thing to think about?" he said in a lighter tone. "It is, to be sure, the vexation of a day, nor would I say so many words about it to any but those whom I know to have my welfare and reputation at heart." [2]

Then his thoughts turned again to his poem.

"I have heard Hunt say, and I may be asked—why endeavour after a long poem? To which I should answer, Do not the lovers

---

[1] Severn's "Reminiscences"; quoted by Sharp, *op. cit.*, p. 33.
[2] *Letters of John Keats*, p. 53.

B

of poetry like to have a little region to wander in where they may pick and choose, and in which·the images are so numerous that many are forgotten and found new in a second reading? Do they not like this better than what they can read through before Mrs. Williams comes downstairs?—a morning work at most." [1]

Joseph remembered their conversation a few weeks later, when they were both dining with Leigh Hunt. Hunt had lately had to leave his pretty little white house at Hampstead, with its large windows and country surroundings, and was living as neighbour to Haydon in Lisson Grove. In the intervals of dashing off some melody on his harpsichord he would impartially recite poetry, sing in a charming tenor, or settle down to an animated discussion of Shakespeare or the iniquities of the Prince Regent. There was always company in the parlour and the talk was cultured and gay. But the observant visitor might have noticed a certain artificiality about the whole ménage—that behind the delightful façade and the light-hearted host's emphasis on the delights of the senses, behind the conversation about love and food and poetry and music, poor improvident Mrs. Hunt was struggling desperately to make both ends meet, and, it was to be feared, not succeeding very well.

On this evening the only other guest besides himself and Keats was Percy Bysshe Shelley. This was the first time that Joseph had met him, although Keats and Shelley were already acquainted, and he was surprised at his youthful appearance, with his pinkish girl's skin, his aureole of golden hair and his restless blue eyes. He greeted Joseph in his usual gentle, courteous manner, but, as always, he could not resist the temptation to say something which would shock a stranger. As soon as they had drawn their chairs up to the supper-table he led the talk on to religion. Leigh Hunt, as befitted the liberals' hero, was a self-confessed atheist. Shelley's gentle manner contrasted strangely with his high-pitched voice and flushed face as he warmed to his subject.

"As for that detestable religion, the Christian—" he cried, with an eye on Joseph, who shifted unhappily on his chair but was too shy to express his distaste for this sort of opening. Seeing, no doubt, that he was succeeding in his attempt to shock his new acquaintance, Shelley turned to Hunt and began to outline his plan for a poem which he said he intended to write, in which Christ would be shown as a mountebank, and the miracles as his tricks. [2]

This was too much for Joseph. His indignation was so violent

---

[1] *Letters of John Keats*, p. 52.   [2] Sharp, *op. cit.*, pp. 116-117.

that it overcame his diffidence. The Hunts were astonished to hear him interrupting, in a voice which trembled with anger:

"The fact that since Christ lived all the greatest men have been Christians must alone place the Christian religion beyond the reach of such low ridicule."

Shelley immediately denied that this was so, and each began to count on his fingers the great men who were Christians and those who were not. The argument raged all the evening, with Joseph and Shelley as the two protagonists, and Hunt skating agilely over the surface of the argument, conducting little skirmishes and withdrawals against both sides. Keats listened for the most part in silence, with an occasional smile as Joseph's enthusiasm banished his shyness still further.

When they came to Shakespeare, Shelley attempted to prove that the great poet was no Christian by quoting from *Measure for Measure*. Keats smiled again as Joseph rapidly produced counter-quotations from the speeches of Portia, Hamlet and Isabella. Hunt and Keats declared that Joseph had the best of the argument, whereupon Shelley made a sudden graceful surrender, and assured Severn that he would study the subject and later write an essay on it. Joseph was very well pleased with this ending to their argument.

He was happy, too, when a few evenings later, as he was working late in his room at Goswell Street, John Keats "burst into his lodging." In an excited voice he told Joseph of his astonishment, after the scene with Wordsworth a few nights earlier, when the great man called on him in person and invited him to supper. Keats had accepted and was now on his way home after what he declared had been a memorable evening. From his elation it seemed clear to Joseph that Wordsworth's conduct had been very different from their last meeting.[1] Perhaps he had afterwards been ashamed of his remark.

During the spring and summer of 1818, Joseph was working hard on his enlarging practice as a miniature-painter, and was able now and again to make portraits of some of his friends. Thus he painted all three Keats brothers, and also John Hamilton Reynolds and Haslam. In January and February he walked often across the fields to Hampstead to see John Keats. One of the strongest bonds between them was their love of nature. Joseph noted colours and forms with an artist's eye, but he never ceased to be astonished by Keats's power of observation. "Nothing seemed to escape

[1] Sharp, *op. cit.*, p. 31.

him," he said afterwards. "The song of a bird and the undernote
of response from covert or hedge, the rustle of some animal, the
changing of the green and brown lights and furtive shadows, the
motions of the wind—just how it took certain tall flowers and
plants—and the wayfaring of the clouds: even the features and
gestures of passing tramps, the colour of one woman's hair, the
smile on one child's face, the furtive animalism below the deceptive
humanity in many of the vagrants." [1]

Watching the movements of the wind seems to have been a
constant pleasure to him, especially when it blew across a field of
oats or barley. He would spring on to a stile or the low bough of
a tree to watch every movement of what he called "the inland sea."
"The tide! the tide!" he would cry delightedly, and the sight of
the wind stirring the surface of the field would even awaken him
from the dark, withdrawn moods which sometimes came upon
him quite suddenly during their walks. Joseph was so contented
to be with him that he never questioned or resented these moments
when Keats would scarcely answer a direct question, when his
happy expression stiffened into gloom and his eyes seemed to grow
even larger, troubled and unquiet. These moods would come on
him quite suddenly. One moment he would be full of spirits, his
eyes glowing with pleasure at all the little incidents of life around
them. Then, with no warning, his mood would change and the
gleam in his eyes would deepen into a gloomy abstraction.

Joseph soon learned that it was useless to try to dissipate the
shadow when it had once enveloped him. Only the sudden impact
of beauty could rescue him, and the wild passage of the wind
always seemed to pierce his gloom and call him back from the
shadows where his mind was wandering.

In March, John Keats went off to join Tom at Teignmouth,
where he had spent the winter watched over by George. Perhaps
he was not sorry to leave London, for there had been an outbreak
of quarrelling between his friends. (Haydon was no longer on
speaking terms with Hunt or with Reynolds.) In any case, he felt
that he must go, for Tom's health seemed to have benefited from
the milder climate and John felt that he should be encouraged to
stay at Teignmouth. George must return to London, because it
was not long now before he was to be married to Georgiana Wylie,
and—even more final separation—he and his bride had decided
to emigrate to America, where he hoped to make a fortune.

Joseph knew how John Keats was suffering behind his reserve

[1] Sharp, *op. cit.*, p. 20.

at the thought that the trio of brothers was so soon to be broken up. But he did not try to dissuade George from his purpose, for he knew what high hopes he had of founding a business with what capital he could take with him, and making enough money in a short time to be able to support a family. Joseph guessed that he also hoped in this way to be able to send money home to his brothers.

He did not see John Keats again until he and Tom returned to London, in the last week of May, for the wedding. Tom Keats seemed to be stronger, so that John felt able to accompany George and his bride to Liverpool, where they must embark on their ship. From there he proposed to keep travelling North and to have a holiday. He asked Haslam and Joseph in turn to accompany him on a walking tour, but Haslam could not leave London and Joseph dared not. In the first place, he had no money, scarcely enough for the moderate bills of the country inns where they would have stayed, still less to pay his fare North. In the second place, he had made quite a good connection as a miniature-painter, and to leave it now would mean starting laboriously again from nothing when he returned.

But Keats felt that he must get away. He was exhausted and depressed after his great burst of creation in the Spring. "Endymion" had been published in April, with an introduction by Keats in which he warned the reader to expect "great inexperience, immaturity, and every error denoting a feverish attempt, rather than a deed accomplished." While he was occupied with the corrections of "Endymion," he had found time to write two, at least, of his loveliest Sonnets in Shakespearean form and another long poem, entitled "Isabella or The Pot of Basil."

In the end Keats went with another friend—Charles Brown. Brown was nine years older than Keats, a plump, bald, bespectacled man, with a lively cultivated mind: a man of deep loyalties, obstinate prejudices and a downright frankness of speech. He had a practical mind, cared nothing for convention, and in humour was inclined to be coarse. Joseph had met him, and liked him, at Charles Dilke's house, which was, in a sense, Brown's home too. For the two friends had built together a pleasant white house on the edge of the Heath, in one half of which lived Dilke and his family, and in the other the bachelor Brown, waited on by his Irish maid, Abigail, with whom, Joseph soon learned, her master was on the most intimate terms. The garden was their mutual property, and many were the hours Dilke and Brown spent pacing round their small domain planning daring changes in the beds next year.

Joseph said goodbye to the little party as they climbed into the coach at The Swan and Two Necks, in Lad Lane. George Keats he would not see again for years, perhaps never. But his heart was wrung by his intuition of what John Keats must be feeling about the approaching separation from his brother, and from his sister-in-law too, for whom he felt an affection deeper than for any other girl save his little sister Fanny. How Joseph wished that he had been able to leave London, to accompany Keats on his walking tour after their departure. But it could not be. So he waved goodbye, and walked sadly back to Goswell Street.

Once at work he had soon forgotten everything outside. He could never be unhappy for long, and by the time his sister Sarah had called him down to dinner he had a fine appetite and had recovered his natural good spirits.

Joseph was lucky in getting a number of commissions about this time, and since he was still doing work for Mr. Abbey, as well as studying at the Royal Academy Schools, his days were never long enough for all he had to do in them. At the beginning of August Mrs. Dilke began to be worried about Tom Keats's health, which seemed to have made a sudden change for the worse. Her husband wrote to John, advising him to return home at once.

As it happened, he was already on his way home. The six-hundred-mile tramp through Scotland in all weathers, culminating in the climbing of Ben Nevis in a thick mist, the poor food and sitting about in damp clothing, had resulted in his developing a heavy cold. He presently became feverish. The physician whom he consulted in Inverness strongly advised him to give up his idea of continuing his tramp to Edinburgh and down into Cumberland, and so, reluctantly, he left Charles Brown to walk on alone. He sailed from Cromarty in a sailing-smack, and after a nine-day passage was back at Hampstead on August 18th.

Joseph heard of his return and of Tom's illness from Mrs. Dilke. She described John's appearance at their house on the following day. "He was as brown and as shabby as you can imagine," she said. "Scarcely any shoes left, his jacket all torn at the back, a fur cap, a great plaid, and his knapsack. I cannot tell you what he looked like." [1] When, after the hard life he had

[1] *Letters of John Keats*, p. 212.

been leading, he sank contentedly into the softness of one of Mrs. Dilke's arm-chairs, he relaxed and quoted comically, "Why, Bottom, thou art translated!"

Soon after Keats's return Joseph was struck down by typhus fever and nearly died. The devoted nursing of his "angel-mother" brought him through this dangerous illness. Keats came to see him when he was convalescent, bringing John Hamilton Reynolds with him.[1] But after their visit Joseph saw little of his friend that autumn. Directly he was able, he returned to the classes at the Academy and worked hard in his spare time, feeling that he must double his concentration to make up for the weeks he had lost. Only rarely did he see John Keats, but when he did he was dismayed by his friend's haggard and distraught appearance. Tom was becoming daily weaker, and by October, when Joseph was about again after his illness, John was only able to leave his brother for a few hours at a time.

One day, when they happened to meet, Keats was urged by Joseph to come out for a walk, but he said that he did not feel strong enough to take any unnecessary exercise. His eyes, usually so alert, were strained and anguished. His manner was lethargic. It seemed an effort even to speak. When he was just back from Scotland he had told Joseph that he intended to devote himself to study, as in his stern self-criticism he felt that he must acquire more knowledge to enable him to realize the poetry that was within him.

He may have been made firmer in his resolve by the scathing reviews of "Endymion" that appeared that autumn in two of the most powerful periodicals of the day—*Blackwood's Edinburgh Magazine* and the *Quarterly*. The former, indeed, was more a personal attack than a criticism. *Blackwood's* had already published a libellous attack on Leigh Hunt, and now they turned on Keats, whom they affected to regard as his disciple. The anonymous writer ended his insulting article, "We venture to make one small prophecy, that his bookseller will not a second time venture £50 on anything he can write. It is a better and a wiser thing to be a starved apothecary than a starved poet; so back to the shop, Mr. John, back to 'plasters, pills and ointment boxes. . . .' But, for Heaven's sake, young Sangrado, be a little more sparing of extenuations and soporifics in your practice than you have been in your poetry."

All Keats's friends were furious at the pettiness and unfairness

[1] *Letters of John Keats*, p. 171.

of the reviewers. But after one short outburst that he "would write no more," he quickly determined not to allow them to influence him. "Praise or blame has but a momentary effect," he said, "on the man whose love of beauty in the abstract makes him a severe critic on his own works. My own domestic criticism has given me pain without comparison beyond what *Blackwood* or the *Quarterly* could possibly inflict." [1]

But his plan to isolate himself for a time of intensive study was made impossible by Tom's condition. His brother was so ill now that he could scarcely ever leave him. Joseph became still more alarmed about his friend after a conversation with Haslam, who told him gloomily that it was well known that anyone who spent long hours in the room of a dying consumptive was liable to be attacked, himself, by the same disease. He immediately sought out Keats and urged him to take rooms near his brother instead of sharing his bedroom. John refused point-blank.

"Poor Tom looks upon me as his only comfort," he said. [2]

Then Joseph tried to persuade him to let him take his place by Tom's bedside sometimes, so that he might occasionally have an undisturbed night. [3] It was obvious to Joseph that John had really overstrained himself on the walking tour with Brown, and had never thrown off the effects of the feverish chill which had attacked him. He was still suffering from a sore throat. He told Joseph that he had tried to study but that he could not concentrate. Even in another room the sick brother's phantom rose between him and his work.

"Tom's identity presses on me so all day that I am obliged to go out—and although I intended to have given some time to study alone I am obliged to write and plunge into abstract images to ease myself of his countenance, his voice and feebleness—so that I live now in a perpetual fever." [4]

Soon he could not even write, but still he would not accept Joseph's offer to take his place by Tom's bedside. Poor Tom was now a living skeleton, torn with coughing. He had become exceedingly nervous and was terribly affected by anything which disturbed him emotionally. His brother watched over him night and day. A visit from their young sister, Fanny, upset him so much at the moment of parting that it was never repeated. John did not even dare to tell him when the letter he was writing at his bedside was to far-off George. Slowly his strength ebbed, and

---

[1] *Letters of John Keats*, p. 222.   [2] *Ibid.*, p. 230.
[3] Sharp, *op. cit.*, p. 37.   [4] *Letters of John Keats*, p. 216.

John told Joseph that with it he felt more and more of his own vitality being drained away.[1]

Early on the morning of December 1st, Charles Brown was awakened in bed by a pressure on his hand. It was John Keats, come to tell him that poor Tom was dead.[2] The happy trio of brothers was shattered now indeed.

Directly he heard the news Joseph hurried up to Hampstead to persuade John to go with him to Cornwall for a few weeks, thinking that a change of scene might help him to recover from the blow. Keats did half agree with the idea, but the weather for some weeks after Tom's death was so cold and wet that the half-formed plan fell through. He left the lodgings which held so many poignant memories for him, and went to live with Brown in the house which he divided with Dilke. There he began work on a new poem, "The Fall of Hyperion."

Joseph too was hard at work, with a secret excitement that would allow him no rest.

He had had no premonition that winter's day when he had hurried into Somerset House in time for the Antique Class. He had brought with him a drawing he had made of two fighting gladiators, and when the class was ended, and the students were collecting their things together, he made his way through the crowd to where the old Keeper was standing. Although he was now over seventy years of age, Fuseli was still a formidable old man, and would stand no nonsense from his pupils. Several times lately he had delighted Joseph with one of his rare words of praise. The class that evening had passed off peacefully enough, so Joseph judged it a good moment to show him his drawing, on which he had spent many long evenings.

Fuseli took the drawing and stood for a minute, silently scrutinizing it. Joseph listened anxiously as he made a few gruff criticisms. Then, with an exclamation of annoyance, Fuseli turned towards the crowd of students who were now just moving towards the door, and raised his voice. "Gentlemen!" he shouted; "you vill find an announcement on the vall outside vich may interest you." The movement towards the door became accelerated. Everyone wanted to see for himself what this announcement could be. Fuseli turned back to Joseph, who was still waiting at his side. He nodded his white head with its little black cap not unkindly and hurried off. Joseph followed more slowly, talking to

[1] Sharp, *op. cit.*, p. 37.   [2] Charles A. Brown, *Life of John Keats*, p. 53.

B*

Edwin Landseer, who had also lingered behind the rest. Their fellow-students were jostling each other round the notice. As Joseph and his companion came into the ante-room the excitement communicated itself to them too.

"What is it, Severn? Can you see?" It was little George Richmond, the baby of the class, still in his early teens. His fair hair fell over his cherub-like face as he jumped, trying to see over the heads of those in front of them. The news came back in fragments to them from the fortunate front rank. It was a Grand Prize in Historical Painting. Yes, in oils. What was the subject? Oh, some quotation from Spenser. The interest of most of the crowd of students evaporated when one of them read out from the foot of the notice, "The Prize has not been awarded for twelve years, as no competitor has proved himself sufficiently worthy of it."

"Old Fuzzly's stolen the Medal, depend upon it!" cried a wag, and the crowd melted away into the street. Their shouts and laughter were lost in the busy clatter of the Strand, and a chill breath of air blew in from the open door. Joseph and George Richmond were left alone in the hall. They read the notice carefully. Neither of them thought for a moment of competing. Richmond had only just begun his studies, and Joseph's first effort with oils was a picture he had not yet finished. They read through the particulars. The size of the canvas was to be 4 ft. 2 ins.× 3 ft. 4 ins.—an ordinary half-length. Time—there was more than a year to do it in. Subject—Joseph stiffened:

"Out of his hand she snatcht the cursèd knife . . ."

Rapidly his eyes flew over the lines that followed, but he had no need to read, he knew them by heart already. The subject of the Prize Picture was to be the scene in the Cave of Despair, when Una snatches the dagger from the faint-hearted Knight. How often had he heard John Keats repeating those lines—almost chanting them—in his musical voice. Keats would repeat whole stanzas of *The Faerie Queene*, and Joseph's musician's ear had recognized their beauty so that he had come to love the poem almost as well himself. A battered copy of it was one of his most precious possessions. He felt a sudden bound of self-confidence within him. It seemed like Fate that this should be the subject for the Competition. Surely it was a sign to him. He felt a sudden sense of a power directing him, as though all the reading and re-reading of that precious volume had been an unconscious preparation for this moment. Surely he would do something better than those others to whom the lines were just "a quotation from Spenser."

Joseph found his beaver hat and, turning up his coat-collar, stepped out into the busy Strand. It was raining slightly and a cold wind blew the drizzle in his face. The traffic rattled past him over the cobbles.

Cold and wet, he let himself into No. 6 Goswell Street, the small house which belonged to Sarah and her husband. They would be out this evening, he knew. He went through into the little kitchen, where he found some cheese and a loaf of bread. A further search revealed a small piece of cold meat. He chuckled.

"What a lucky dog I am," he muttered as he carried his booty up the narrow stairs to his room. There was not much furniture in it: a table in the window covered with an untidy pile of books and papers, a chair by the table, and another by the old harpsichord which stood in a corner. This was Joseph's dearest possession. He had brought it here when his parents had moved from Hoxton to Mason's Court, off Shoreditch. His father had an organ in his new home and there was no room for the harpsichord as well. He went over and lit the oil-lamp and rummaged among the books and sketches and letters which lay about on the table. He went through them twice, and then, with an exclamation of annoyance, began to search the drawers. Suddenly his toe struck what he was seeking, a book which had been put—or more likely dropped—with several others on the floor under the table. He pulled it out. It was a shabby volume, bound in calf, but scratched and faded. The gilt letters on the cover had faded too, but were still readable, *The Faerie Queene*. He turned the pages impatiently until he came to the scene in the Cave of Despair. He began to eat and read at the same time.

The light from the window behind him faded, and the room was in darkness except for the pool of light round the lamp. It was a cold night. He got up and stamped his feet to warm himself. The cheese and the meat and half the loaf were gone. He picked a piece of paper from the floor and began to make rough sketches on it. . . .

From that day forward Joseph was passionately determined to win the Prize. First of all he must accustom himself to painting in oils. As luck would have it, he had just finished his first oil-painting—a picture of Hermia and Helena from *Midsummer Night's Dream*. He told no one that he had begun to make studies for the figures in the Cave of Despair.[1] At the same time he continued to

---

[1] Sharp, *op. cit.*, pp. 22-23.

accept gratefully any commissions for miniature portraits in water-colours. He could charge up to three guineas for them, and they were the only source of money with which to pay for the canvas, brushes and paints and all the paraphernalia that he needed for the Prize Picture.

During the turn of the year he spent all his spare time with Keats, whom he saw "almost daily." They would go for long walks together, and often Keats would come to London on purpose to go with him to the National Gallery, or the Sculpture Galleries at the British Museum. One day Joseph arrived at their rendezvous —the room containing the marbles from the Parthenon. He came hurrying in, to find Keats sitting as though transfigured; his glowing eyes were wide open, but seemed as if they saw nothing of what lay in front of them; his expression was so radiant, and yet so withdrawn, that Joseph stole away, afraid to break in on his dreams. Not so a foppish young acquaintance. Joseph had scarcely left when a vapid youth settled himself comfortably on the seat beside Keats and showered him with a rain of fashionable inanities. At length, remembering the purpose of his visit, he unconsciously compensated Keats for the boredom of his con-versation by posturing with an eye-glass in front of the marbles and, after quizzing them for a minute or two from various angles, returning to let fall the gem,

"Yes, Mr. Keats, I believe we may now safely admire these works." [1]

To outward appearance John Keats had recovered from the blow of Tom's death. He was able to write again, he could still laugh and joke and illustrate his stories by inimitable imitations of the people he was describing, reproducing their mannerisms and their voices in so droll a fashion that one could not help but laugh. But, while he had always been a creature of moods, brilliantly talkative at one moment and the next still and aloof, Joseph quickly noticed a difference in the quality of his moods. It was not that his moments of gaiety were unnatural, but that the contrasting quietness was no longer a gentle silent abstraction, but more a sudden collapse of his eager vitality into apathy, which was more like despair than depression. Yet in spite of these changes Keats's creative powers were never more active. During Christmas-time he was working on "Hyperion." As the New Year dawned he wrote "a little poem called 'St. Agnes Eve'." [2]

---

[1] Sharp, *op. cit.*, p. 32.   [2] *Letters of John Keats*, p. 296.

One day early in February he suggested that Joseph should come with him to call on a new friend of his—a Mrs. Brawne—the widow who had taken Brown's house for the summer while he had been in Scotland with Keats. Apparently she was still living in Hampstead with her three children.

Joseph had not been in their house for more than a few minutes when he realized that Keats was in love with Mrs. Brawne's eldest daughter, Fanny. He studied her while he was conducting a grave conversation with her mother. She was eighteen years old, he knew, small, slight in build, and moved with natural grace. Joseph could not hear what she was saying, but she seemed to be teasing Keats. Her face was not beautiful. It was too long and narrow for beauty, but her pale complexion was lovely, and her face was soft-looking, showing no bone through the firm young flesh. She wore her light-brown hair smoothly parted in the centre, and a blue ribbon was threaded through it to match her eyes. Mrs. Brawne turned to speak to Keats, and Joseph had a few minutes' conversation with her daughter. She was lively and amusing, but, for himself, he found the mother more charming than her daughter. Fanny Brawne's was not the type of beauty that appealed to him, and her high spirits were too boisterous for his taste. He thought the clear, straight gaze of her blue eyes was the most attractive thing about her. No, her vitality and good spirits had obviously attracted Keats. She radiated youth and good health. He half turned and caught John's eyes on him with a curious expression in them. Fanny turned too, with a swift graceful movement, and gave Keats a teasing smile.

As they walked together down the road towards Brown's house, Joseph thought it over. Her appearance was elegant, she was lively and amusing, and he could see that Keats was in love with her. But she seemed to him unworthy of love from such a source. He was sure she did not realize how far above other men Keats was. Still, John was only twenty-three, and there were many other girls in the world.[1]

Joseph would have been astonished had his friend told him the truth—that he and Fanny Brawne were already engaged to be married. But since Tom's death John had become increasingly reserved about the things which really mattered to him, and in any case, although he was Fanny's accepted suitor, he had no money for them to marry on, so it seemed more sensible to keep their engagement secret. But alas, the torment it caused him!

[1] Sharp, *op. cit.*, pp. 38-39.

For, being apparently an unattached young female, she continued
to receive flattery and attentions from other men, often in front of
Keats. And being also of a lively disposition, and very young and
fond of admiration, she even flirted a little with them. This was
agony to John. "He doesn't like anyone to look at or speak to
her," [1] said one of the Dilkes. He even suffered secretly as he
listened to some of the gallant compliments paid to her by Brown,
and Joseph himself was the cause of a little jealousy after their
call. Fanny Brawne had to reassure him. "You must be satisfied
in knowing that I admired you much more than your friend,"
she said. [2]

If Joseph had stopped to consider the matter he might have
guessed how far things had gone with Keats. He might have
realized how Tom's death had laid him open to love. When
George was leaving for America John had said, "My love for my
brothers, from the early loss of our parents, has grown into an
affection 'passing the love of women.' I have been ill-tempered
with them, I have vexed them, but the thought of them has always
stifled the impression that any woman might otherwise have made
on me." [3] And now George was three thousand miles away and
Tom was dead. He was doubly defenceless against love's onslaught.

John Keats seemed to be withdrawing further from the world.
As so often happens when people are in love, he could find no
interest in the company and occupations which he used to enjoy.
The Reynolds sisters, for instance, with whom he and his brothers
had always been on the most friendly terms, were staying with
Mrs. Dilke that February. His only comment was, "The Miss
Reynoldses have been stopping next door lately—but all very
dull." [4] In fact, he was not only beginning to go out less into the
world, but Joseph noticed that he was losing touch with many of
his old friends. He stayed indoors a great deal with the object—
or was it an excuse?—of ridding himself of his sore throat. Hunt
got on his nerves with his too-facile ecstasies; Haslam he did not
see, but occasionally wrote to, and knew that he was happily engrossed in a love-affair; Charles Cowden Clarke he admitted he
had not seen "for God knows when." He had not been to the
Novellos' since December, when he and Brown had declared
themselves "devastated and excruciated with bad and repeated
puns." [5] John dismissed it as "a complete set-to of Mozart and
punning," [6] and decided not to go there again. He made efforts

---

[1] *Adonaïs*, Dorothy Hewlett, p. 269.   [2] *Letters of John Keats*, p. 362.
[3] *Ibid.*, p. 69.   [4] *Ibid.*, p. 297.   [5] *Ibid.*, p. 249.   [6] *Ibid.*, p. 297.

to be allowed to see more of his little sister, but their guardian made it very difficult.

The only friends he saw much of now were Brown, with whom he was living, the Dilkes, the Brawnes and Joseph, who came often to the house and sometimes stayed the night in what Keats called "his little crib." Haydon he had not seen since, with much difficulty, he had raised £30 to lend him, which he could ill afford. Nor had he seen Reynolds for some time. Reynolds had now renounced his literary ambitions. The last time they met, John complained, "Reynolds is completely buried in the law: he is not only reconciled to it but hobby-horses upon it." [1]

Joseph was working hard on his studies for the Prize Picture. He sent his first oil-painting, of "Hermia and Helena," to the Academy, accompanied by a miniature of Keats which he had just finished. He wrote a note to John, asking his permission to submit the miniature. John replied: "Of course I should never suffer any petty vanity of mine to hinder you in any wise; and therefore I should say, 'Put the miniature in the exhibition' if only myself was to be hurt. But, will it not hurt you? What good can it do any future picture? Even a large picture is lost in that canting place—what a drop of water in the ocean is a Miniature. Those who might chance to see it for the most part if they had ever heard of either of us—and know what we were and of what years—would laugh at the puff of the one and the vanity of the other. I am however in these matters a very bad judge—and would advise you to act in a way that appears to yourself the best for your interest. As your Hermia and Helena is finished, send that without the prologue of a Miniature. I shall see you soon, if you do not pay me a visit sooner—there's a Bull for you." [2] Both pictures were accepted, but they were badly hung and attracted no attention.

Keats described one of their days together to his brother George, sending a typical page of their London life across the ocean to the settlement in Kentucky.

"On Monday," he wrote, "we had to dinner Severn and Cawthorn, the book-seller and print-virtuoso; in the evening Severn went home to paint, and we other three went to the play, to see Sheil's new tragedy ycleped 'Evadne.' In the morning Severn and I took a turn round the Museum—there is a sphinx there of a giant size, and most voluptuous Egyptian expression, I had not seen it before."

Early in May, that year of 1819, nightingales were nesting on

[1] *Letters of John Keats*, p. 315.   [2] *Ibid.*, p. 289.

the Heath and even in the garden at Wentworth Place. One night Joseph went with a party of friends to the Spaniards Inn. During the evening he missed John Keats and went outside to look for him. He found him, at length, lying beneath the pine trees, and listening entranced to the song of a nightingale overhead.[1] A day or two later Keats took a chair into the garden at Wentworth Place and wrote out, during the morning, the "Ode to a Nightingale," "in and out and back and forth on a couple of loose sheets of paper."[2] Later in the day Charles Brown saw him folding the scraps of paper carelessly away behind some books in his room and rescued them.[3] By the time John Keats left London that summer he had written four other odes which were to become immortal: "To Psyche," "To Melancholy," "On Indolence," and the "Ode on a Grecian Urn."

Joseph was engrossed in his picture for the Prize. He had spared no pains to make it the best of which he was capable. He had accustomed himself to the use of oils, he had made innumerable studies for the figures, and at the same time he had worked at his miniatures in order to pay for all the new materials he needed. His work seemed to eat money. The picture became a passion with him—a secret passion, as he had confided in no one at home for fear of his father's anger. All his work had to be done at Sarah's house in the room she lent him, and he would lock the door carefully when he left it.

As the summer faded he began to have bouts of despair. He had so many difficulties. Not the least of these was lack of money. In the end he was forced to sell all his little treasures to pay for painting materials. Even his watch and his beloved books had to go. August passed, September drew to its close. He had no money for fuel. He sat long hours in his fireless room, painting the limbs of the figure of Despair from his own naked, shivering legs reflected in the chilly depths of the mirror.

At the beginning of October he snatched a respite from his work to visit Keats, who had just returned to London and had taken rooms in Westminster. Apparently he had abandoned the idea of making a living from his poetry and was determined to earn some money from journalism and reviewing. The Dilkes had lately moved to Westminster to be nearer their son, who was going to the school there, and on whom his father doted. When Joseph heard that Mrs. Brawne had taken on the Dilkes half of

---

[1] Sharp, *op. cit.*, p. 40.   [2] Colvin, *op. cit.*, p. 354.
[3] Charles Brown, *Life of John Keats*, p. 54.

the white house at Hampstead he was not surprised that Keats, in his new venture, had thought it better to live away from the unsettling atmosphere of Wentworth Place.

Joseph found him in high spirits when he called at 25 College Street. He showed Joseph several short poems and odes which he had written since they had last met. Joseph was charmed with them, but he was greatly disappointed when, having enquired "how 'Hyperion' went on," he heard that John had decided not to finish it. Joseph had always felt a personal interest in this poem, because it was he who had persuaded Keats to re-read *Paradise Lost*. In vain did he protest against "Hyperion" being discarded. When Keats had read a few passages to him Severn cried indignantly that it might have been written by Milton himself, and that he *must* complete it. John only laughed and said that he did not want to write a poem that might have been written by Milton, but one that was unmistakably written by no other than John Keats. He seemed more interested in a new poem he was finishing, "about a serpent-girl named Lamia." [1]

Then he put his manuscripts aside and told Severn that he had decided not to write any more poetry for the moment, but that he was going to try his hand at journalism, because it was essential for him to make some money. Not only did he owe money to Brown and to his publisher on his own account, but he had also had bad news from George in Kentucky. His "mercantile speculations" had not been successful. His wife had just had a child and he needed money badly. John had to write telling him that they could neither of them get from their guardian, Mr. Abbey, any of Tom's share of their inheritance, which he had left them, because their aunt had just filed a suit in Chancery against them. Mr. Abbey thought that she could be persuaded to withdraw it, but until this was done he could give them nothing.

Next Keats had hoped to raise some money from the tragedy which he and Brown had written together, with a part specially designed to suit Kean. They had sent it to Elliston, the manager of Drury Lane, but now they heard that Kean was probably leaving England for a visit to America, so it seemed that their tragedy would have to wait. He could hope for no money from that source for some little time. Nevertheless he had promised George that he would not spare any exertion to benefit him by some means or other. "If I cannot remit you hundreds, I will tens, and if not that ones," [2] he had written.

---

[1] Sharp, *op. cit.*, pp. 40-41.   [2] *Letters of John Keats*, p. 422.

He told Joseph that his next step had been to ask Haydon to repay the £30 which he had lent him. Haydon had replied that he was unable to repay it. Keats commented that he could well understand that this might be so, but what had hurt him was that "he did not seem to care much about it—and let me go without my money with almost nonchalance." [1]

He stood up and began to pace up and down the little room. "I shall endeavour, for a beginning, to get the theatricals of some paper. When I can afford to compose deliberate poems I will," [2] he said. Severn, sitting listening, was delighted to note his resolute bearing, but, studying his appearance, he was afraid that his holiday had not done him as much good physically as his friends had hoped. "I will settle myself and fag till I can afford to buy pleasure—which if I never can afford I must go without." [3]

Joseph reluctantly admitted that he supposed it was the wisest course to pursue, and left his friend, promising to return in a few days to hear the rest of "Hyperion" and the whole of "Lamia." But it was more than a week before he was able to get to College Street, and then it was only to find that his friend had gone. He had returned to his old home with Brown at Wentworth Place. Poor Keats! His stern resolutions for a régime of hack-writing and self-denial had melted away when he saw his love again. She was kind and he was at her mercy. She dazzled him. There was "nothing in the world so bright and delicate." [4] He tore himself away and returned to Westminster for a few days, but his purpose weakened, his strength had been sucked from him.

Before the end of the month he was back with Brown and living under the same roof as his "dearest girl." Severn followed him there the next Sunday and was distressed to see the change in him. Gone were the resolute confidence, the hopes for the future. His mind seemed in a fever. Apathy and depression alternated with moods of forced, almost violent, gaiety. He told Joseph that he and Brown were working together in the mornings on a comic fairy poem, and in the evenings he was reshaping "Hyperion" into the form of a Vision. That his friend had not entirely finished with "Hyperion" was the only comfort Joseph carried away from that uneasy visit.

The last day of October came. It was the last day, too, for entries for the Prize. It was cold and damp, and a leaden sky

[1] *Letters of John Keats*, p. 419.   [2] *Ibid.*, p. 395.   [3] *Ibid.*, p. 393.
[4] *Ibid.*, p. 435.

threatened to bring darkness before its time. Joseph had slept
but a few hours during the last three nights, and the first pale
light of dawn had found him gazing at his picture, questioning
if he had made the right decision in this part, or if he would have
done better to leave that other corner unchanged. Almost it was
a relief to have it taken from him, to *know* that he could do no
more. Some days before, he had written a note to Keats, asking
him to call and see the finished picture. John replied from
Hampstead:

"I am glad to hear you have finished the picture, and am more
anxious to see it than I have time to spare: for I have been so
very lax, unemployed, unmeridian'd, and objectless these two
months that I even grudge indulging (and that is no great in-
dulgence considering the lecture is not over till nine and the
lecture room seven miles from Wentworth Place) myself by going
to Hazlitt's Lecture. If you have hours to the amount of a brace
of dozens to throw away you may sleep nine of them here in your
little crib and chat the rest. When your picture is up and in a
good light I shall make a point of meeting you at the Academy
if you will let me know when." [1]

But he was not to see the picture until a few days before the
verdict of the judges was published. In the meantime Joseph
had been through alternating fits of hope and depression. During
the first days of November, when his picture had only just gone,
he chided himself for his conceit in thinking that he could learn
to paint in a new medium, during one year, well enough to enter
for a Prize. Almost he regretted his effort, but after a few nights'
sleep his natural buoyancy returned, and although he could scarcely
believe that he, Joseph Severn, had dared such an ambitious
attempt, he no longer regretted the amount of work he had poured
into it, and realized that in the painting of the picture he had
learned a great deal. His mind, he confided to his friends, had now
relaxed to "a certain despairful ease."

He broke the news to his father and to Mr. Bond. The engraver
seemed scarcely interested and his father flew into one of his
passions, rebuked his son for his conceit, reproached him for not
sticking to the safe profession to which he was apprenticed, and
ended by prophesying that nothing but humiliation would be the
reward of such presumption. Joseph's mother, as always, was
sympathetic and understanding, but even she was not very hopeful.
Joseph attended the classes at the Academy every evening, but

[1] *Letters of John Keats*, p. 438.

November passed without any news. Early in December a rumour
spread that the Council had decided to award a Gold Medal for
the first time for twelve years. December the tenth was the date
when the name of the victor was to be published. The name of
every competing student was whispered behind knowing hands in
turn. Joseph had the dubious satisfaction of hearing himself
mentioned as "the dark horse that might win."

He could persuade neither his father nor Mr. Bond to come to
the Academy to see the picture where it hung with all the other
entries. But a few days before the tenth, John Keats called on
him early in the morning and insisted on their proceeding together
to Somerset House. Although Keats admitted that he had always
imagined quite a different setting for the scene, he was delighted
with the picture. He protested that he had no knowledge of the
technique of painting, but, after careful consideration of the other
canvases, he must admit that he liked it the best. He asserted
stoutly that if it didn't gain the Medal it would be the most honourable of the failures.[1] Joseph knew that Keats had no expert
knowledge, but his faith in his artistic intuition was so strong that
he felt greatly encouraged.

At last there dawned the tenth day of December. It dragged
by, hour by hour, each longer than the last, until at 8 o'clock that
evening the President and Council of the Royal Academy filed
solemnly into the Council Room. All the students had been
invited and they were there, in their best clothes. The excitement
and solemnity of the occasion made the atmosphere tense. The
Council lowered themselves with dignity into their chairs on the
daïs, which had been specially prepared for the evening; at a
gracious signal the students subsided, shuffling, into theirs, which
were smaller and harder. The President, Mr. Benjamin West,
rose slowly to his feet. He was eighty-one years old and very
popular with the students because, unlike some successful painters,
he was a generous friend and adviser to young artists. An ex-
pectant stillness enveloped the room in which the old voice was
easily heard.

"Prizes are to be given to three students," it said, "and the
Gold Medal for painting, so long unawarded, is to be bestowed
upon a young candidate whose efforts are all the more praiseworthy
in that he is entirely self-taught." [2]

The old man paused, and perhaps his mind went back to

---

[1] Sharp, *op. cit.*, pp. 26-27.   [2] *Ibid.*, p. 27.

Pennsylvania seventy years ago, and he saw himself again as a young Quaker boy, making colours from leaves and berries, and brushes with the hairs he pulled from his cat's tail.

The silence was agonizing. Joseph's heart was jumping in his chest, as though it could bear its imprisonment no longer. The President brought his wandering thoughts back to the present and to another young man who was just beginning his artist's life. He peered downwards at the paper he held in his hand and announced briefly,

"The name of the Gold Medallist is Joseph Severn."

Joseph's heart gave a convulsive leap and dropped rapidly into his stomach. The room rocked. Everywhere blurred white faces had turned towards him. He felt the blood rise burning to his cheeks and awoke suddenly to a friend nudging him with a sharp elbow.

He concentrated all his strength on rising to his feet, and edged awkwardly past the knees to the main aisle. Once out in the open his courage flooded back, and he stepped boldly up to receive the Gold Medal from the hands of the President himself. In after days he could scarcely remember what happened after that. In memory he could feel the sudden cold weight of the medal pressing on his hand, he could hear the old voice murmuring good wishes for his future as an artist, then a glimpse of Fuseli's face, relaxed for once into an approving smile . . . and his next vivid recollection was of bounding up the narrow creaking staircase at Mason's Court. He ran into his father's room without knocking. His mother followed with a light. James Severn had gone early to bed after an outburst when he had heard where Joseph was spending the evening. He sat up in bed, blinking, his night-cap askew on his black head. "What in heaven's name is the meaning of this intrusion?" he barked.

Joseph was panting and incoherent.

"Father! The Medal! The President! Mr. West! Not for twelve years! They've given it to me!"

His father's expression changed to one of astonishment and then disbelief.

"If this is a pleasantry—" he began.

But Joseph sank down on his knees beside the bed and thrust the great Gold Medal, weighing fully half a pound, into his father's hand. The physical contact seemed to carry final conviction, and James Severn flung his arms round his son's neck and kissed his cheek, turning to cry to Mrs. Severn that he had always told her this would happen. Joseph and his mother exchanged happy, understanding smiles. Then he was made to sit on his father's bed, and with the family round him—even little Charles had been woken by the uproar—he had to tell them the story of that exciting evening from the very beginning.

CHAPTER III

DEPARTURE

(*September* 1820)

It was past midnight when the hired carriage came jolting over the cobbles of Shoreditch. The night was overcast and cold. Joseph gazed gloomily out of the creaking window. He had been up since dawn and now he felt tired and ill. He checked in his mind the preparations he had made for the first great journey of his life.

In the morning he had visited Sir Thomas Lawrence, the new President. After a prolonged tour of Europe, painting scarcely any but crowned and coroneted heads, Sir Thomas had returned to London to find himself elected, on the very day of his arrival, President of the Royal Academy, in place of old Benjamin West who had just died. Joseph told him how he had won the Gold Medal the year before, and that he was leaving London now to accompany a sick friend to Rome and would work there in the hope of winning the travelling studentship. Sir Thomas had listened kindly, and had written two letters of introduction for him: the first to the great sculptor Canova, the other to an old German artist who was living in Rome.

Next Joseph had collected the sum of £25, owing to him for a "miniature of a lady in a white satin bonnet and feathers." He had made a few purchases and called on one or two friends who lived conveniently near, to tell them of his sudden departure. Then he had gathered together what he needed from Sarah's house and had said goodbye to her. She had promised tearfully to keep his room for him just as he left it. She would not move his books or pictures. They would all be ready for him when he came back.

Now he was on his way home and the hardest moment was at hand, when he must say goodbye to his family, from whom he had never before been parted. His spirits drooped even lower as he recalled the long, bitter arguments with his father during the last three days. There had been nothing like them since before he had won the Medal. What great expectations his father had formed then, and how sadly they had lacked fulfilment. As he looked back, Joseph thought there had never been so unlucky a year. His elation had been short-lived. No new commissions had come as a result of his triumph; in fact, it had only served to rouse such envy and jealousy amongst the other students that the Academy Classes had become too unpleasant for him to continue to attend.

George Keats had returned home from America. You would have thought that would have been a happy occasion. But he had stayed a bare three weeks, and then he was gone, back to his wife and child waiting in Louisville, and taking with him every penny he could lay hands on. Joseph's private opinion was that he had taken some which should by rights have been left with John, whose financial position was desperate. Charles Brown agreed with Joseph in thinking that George had behaved shabbily towards his brother. Then what had happened? Scarcely had George left than John Keats had collapsed. Joseph shivered now as he remembered Brown's vivid description.

"At eleven o'clock, he came into the house in a state that looked like fierce intoxication. Such a state in him, I knew, was impossible; it therefore was more fearful. I asked hurriedly, 'What is the matter? You are fevered?' 'Yes, yes,' he answered, 'I was severely chilled,—but now I don't feel it. Fevered!—of course, a little.' He mildly and instantly yielded, a property in his nature towards any friend, to my request that he should go to bed. I entered his chamber as he leapt into bed. On entering the cold sheets, before his head was on the pillow, he slightly coughed, and I heard him say—'That is blood from my mouth.' I went towards him; he was examining a single drop of blood upon the sheet. 'Bring me the candle, Brown, and let me see this blood.' After regarding it steadfastly he looked up in my face, with a calmness of countenance I can never forget, and said,—'I know the colour of that blood; that drop of blood is my death-warrant; I must die.' I ran for a surgeon; my friend was bled; and, at five in the morning, I left him after he had been some time in a quiet sleep." [1]

For two months after that he was an invalid, his only pleasure the visits and the little notes from his love next door. Then, towards the end of March, he was well enough to come to London for the first public exhibition of Haydon's picture, "Christ's Entry into Jerusalem," which was finished at last. There Joseph had seen him. He said he felt better and would think himself quite well were he not reminded every now and then by faintness and a

[1] Charles Brown, *Life of John Keats*, pp. 64-65.

tightness in his chest. He talked of the possibility of his going as surgeon on an Indiaman to improve his health.[1] He told Joseph that when he was ill he had not only been forbidden to write poetry but was advised not even to read it because the doctors said it was "too great an excitement." Now he was getting ready to turn out of Wentworth Place, because Brown had let his house, as usual, for the summer months, and was going on another walking tour. He was wondering, when Joseph saw him at the Private View, if he should accompany Brown to Scotland on the smack for the benefit of the sea voyage. But a week or two later he had given up the idea and taken lodgings near the Leigh Hunts at Kentish Town, a village between Hampstead and London.

Joseph was lucky in getting several favourably-priced commissions for miniatures that summer. At the end of June he had a brief letter from Leigh Hunt, telling him that Keats had had another hæmorrhage and was moving into their house so that they might nurse him. Joseph had gone there to see him whenever he could get away from London. At first he was horrified at Keats's weakness and appearance of exhaustion. But later he seemed to rally and, in spite of his own forebodings, his friends began to hope for his recovery. Joseph wrote to Haslam in the second week of July saying:

"It will give you pleasure to say I trust he will still recover. His appearance is shocking and now reminds me of poor Tom, and I have been inclined to think him in the same way. For himself—he makes sure of it—and seems prepossessed that he cannot recover—now I seem more than ever *not* to think so and I know you will agree with me when you see him." [2]

While Keats lay ill his new volume of poems was published. "Lamia" was in it, "Isabella," "The Eve of St. Agnes," and the great unfinished fragment "Hyperion." Joseph was delighted with it and felt confident that this at last must bring fame to its author. Then he heard that his friend had left the Hunts and had gone to stay with Mrs. Brawne at Wentworth Place. He was so busy with his miniature-painting that it was hard to find time to go on the coach all the way to Hampstead. He imagined that Keats must be quite recovered, if he were paying visits.

It had been a complete shock, therefore, when Haslam had come to him, three days ago, with the news that the doctors thought the only hope of saving Keats's life was for him to winter in Italy. He had been ill ever since the end of June. Far from paying a

---

[1] *Letters of John Keats*, p. 484.   [2] Colvin, *op. cit.*, p. 466.

visit to Mrs. Brawne, she had taken him in out of kindness, after he had flung away from Hunt's house, in a state of painful agitation, because a letter, written by Fanny Brawne, had not been given to him by the servant until two days after its arrival, and then it had already been opened. He had talked wildly of going back to his lodgings with Mrs. Bentley, where he had lived with his brothers, but Mrs. Brawne had insisted on their right to nurse him, and since then he had been tended by her daughter and herself at Wentworth Place.

Haslam told him that Keats had realized by the end of the summer that his only chance of life lay in leaving England for the winter. Joseph could appreciate how much such a decision must have cost him if his feelings towards Miss Brawne were unchanged. Then Haslam sprang the surprise. Not one of Keats's friends could accompany him. He had written to Brown asking if he would go, but there had been no reply. Brown was still on a walking tour in Scotland, moving from place to place, and evidently the letter had missed him. Now the weather was getting colder every day, September fogs were clouding the Heath, and it was obvious to everyone that if Keats were to leave England it must be very soon. His friends, unknown to Joseph, had arranged everything. Taylor, Keats's publisher, had paid him £100 for the copyright of "Endymion" and had raised a further £100 from various friends. It had been settled that Keats should go to Rome, and his passage was booked on a barque called the *Maria Crowther*, which was to sail from London on the 18th of September. Haslam explained the position in a strained, hesitating voice. He would have gone himself if it had not been for his wife. She was expecting a baby. Then he turned to Joseph, his face grave.

"Severn, why should you not go?" he said. "For otherwise he must go alone, and we shall never hear anything of him if—if he dies."

His honest eyes pleaded with Joseph. They faced each other a moment in silence. Then Joseph spoke.

"I'll go."

Haslam's face shone with relief and affection.

"But you'll be long getting ready?" he questioned anxiously. "Keats is actually now preparing. The *Maria Crowther* sails in three days. When would you be ready?"

"In three days' time," said Joseph decisively. "I will set about it this very moment."[1]

[1] Sharp, *op. cit.*, p. 48.

It was only afterwards, in the bustle of preparation for his departure, that he suddenly thought that he might try for the Academy's travelling studentship, which would give him the means to live abroad for three years.

The carriage was moving more slowly. Joseph leaned forward and saw the graceful new spire of St. Leonard's Church and knew that he was home. The carriage drew up at 109 Shoreditch, about twelve doors from the church, where a narrow entrance led into Mason's Court. His heart seemed to turn over as he thought of parting from his mother. Yet she had understood and sympathized with him in his sudden decision. It had been easy for him to explain his feelings to her. How could he leave Keats to go alone—to suffer, or perhaps to die, solitary and uncared for, in a foreign land? No other friend could go. Either Joseph must accompany him or Keats must, in his own phrase, "march up against the Battery" alone.

He climbed slowly out. He looked up and down the silent street. He eased the collar of his heavy travelling-coat. Then, suspecting that the man was watching him, although the night was too dark to see his face, he turned and plunged into the alley-way leading to Mason's Court. He felt his way across the little square of grass round which the old gabled houses clustered. Then he shattered the stillness with a knock on the door of No. 4. Almost immediately it was opened by his mother.

As she put down her candle to help him off with his caped travelling-coat she thought, not for the first time, how handsome her Joe had grown. Though to-night, to be sure, he was very pale. He gave her the miniature that he had finished a few days before and which he had collected from his room in Sarah's house. It was painted on ivory, measuring roughly four inches by five, in which small compass he had contrived a portrait of every member of his family. Tom sat with his hands on the keys of a harpsichord. Charles, Maria and Charlotte were painted full-face, Sarah, his mother and his father in profile. He handed it to her carefully, determined that he should have at least their portraits with him on his journey. Then he gave a swift glance to her face under the crisp white muslin cap, and seemed to see a troubled look which changed the usual gentle sweetness of her expression. He kissed her on the cheek and she answered his unspoken question.

"He's hardly spoken since he came in."

She pressed Joseph's hand and smiled at him.

"It's because he loves you so much," she said. "He has always loved you more than the others. Not only because you're the eldest, but because he's so proud of your being an artist."

Joseph sighed. He held his mother's hand for comfort, as he had so often done as a small boy in the face of his father's bewildering changes of mood.

"Well," he said, in a voice of mock-drama, "I must face the fiery ordeal," and he opened the door of the parlour and went in.

He was prepared for another bitter argument, for passionate reproaches and prophecies of disaster if he insisted on rejecting his father's advice to stay in England. But he was not prepared for what he saw. On the left, by the window, Maria and Tom were putting clothes into a large trunk. Near the fire sat their father. He was sunk down in his armchair, his head bent forward, and on his face an expression of such extreme grief that Joseph checked the words of greeting on his lips. He thought desperately but could find nothing to say. Finally he walked over to the fire, threw himself into the armchair opposite his father and buried his face in his hands.

What a wretched evening. He longed to cut short this gloomy departure and to be already on his way. On his way to Rome. But even that name seemed to have lost its enchantment, and if it had not been for the thought of Keats he would have given in. For he knew that there was a great deal of truth in his father's arguments. It was quite true that by leaving England he was giving up his hard-won connection as a miniaturist. It was equally true that the Academy might not think it suitable to award the travelling scholarship to a student who had already got himself to Rome without its aid. But these considerations were as nothing beside his love and admiration for his friend. Since Keats would need him in Rome, to Rome he would go, and his natural optimism comforted him with the thought that no doubt commissions would be forthcoming when he got there.

He was never one to anticipate adversity. He was to annoy people all his life by never seeming to appreciate the gravity of his position, even when apparently facing ruin. Nevertheless, he thought a little grimly to himself that he would be anticipating the great adventure with more eagerness if his stomach were less queasy. He had been suffering for the last week from a liver complaint. He lifted his head from his hands as Tom touched him on the shoulder.

"I think we should be off. Help me with the trunk."

His mother and sister had finished the packing and fastened the two heavy catches. Tom went to one end of the trunk and Joseph to the other. They strained and heaved, changed their grip and tried again, but they could do no more than shift the massive trunk a few inches along the floor. At length Joseph straightened himself, panting, and called to his father to come and help him. There was no reply from the chair by the fire. He raised his voice.

"Father, will you help us? We cannot lift the trunk."

His father stood up and turned to them a face frozen with anger. His hands were clenched, and his voice when he spoke was husky.

"If that trunk could never be lifted except with my aid, by God I would not touch it!"

He stood there with every limb stiff, as though paralysed by his rage. Only his eyes, beneath the painfully contracted brow, moved from face to face. Joseph was completely taken aback. But there was no time to waste in arguing. He must be off or the boat would sail without him. Tom went quickly out and brought the driver of the carriage in to help. Together the three of them carried the trunk to the carriage. Then the brothers went back into the house. With only a glance at his father, who was still standing, silent, by the fire, Joseph kissed Maria and left a message for Charlotte. Since she had married she lived at Hoxton, and, in his hurried departure, he had not found time to pay her a last visit. Then he turned to go upstairs to say goodbye to his younger brother, Charles, who, in spite of violent protests, had been sent to bed some hours ago, being only fourteen years old.

But, as he moved towards the door, his father suddenly leaped forward and barred the way. He stood in the doorway with his arms flung wide; his face was pale and he panted as though he had been running. Joseph checked a moment and then laid a hand on his father's arm, trying to move it so that he could pass. The touch seemed to let loose the flood of fury that had been dammed up in that rigid figure. With a cry he swung his arm and hit his son a tremendous blow on the side of his head which sent him crashing to the floor. He would have sprung on him and hit him again, as he lay there, if Tom had not leaped forward and caught him round the waist, pinning him against the wall.[1]

Mrs. Severn helped Joseph to his feet, while Tom held his father prisoner. Dazed and shocked, Joseph supported himself by an arm round his mother's shoulders. He could not take his

[1] Sharp, *op. cit.*, p. 51.

horror-struck gaze from his father. He would never, to the end of his life, forget how he looked at that moment of parting—the blazing blue eyes, the lips drawn back showing his clenched teeth, the thick black hair dishevelled, the stock awry. Mr. Severn made a violent effort to free himself. He kicked and struggled with such frenzy that, although Tom was a strong young man, he had to call his sister to his aid. Joseph's mother hurried him fearfully from the room. With tears pouring down her cheeks she helped him to put on his coat, but his legs were trembling so much and he felt so near to being sick, that she had to support him for a minute before he could climb into the carriage.

"God bless you, my dearest Joe," she whispered, reaching up to his hand as she stood beside the carriage. "Keep yourself warm, and be careful of rich food while you are still unwell." She paused, and her voice broke as she added hurriedly, "And pray God for your poor father. He doesn't know what he is doing—" For one moment she stood, a silhouette framed in the doorway of the carriage, then she was gone.

Joseph stretched out his hand as though to reach into the house and draw her back to him. His throat ached and tears rose into his eyes. How could he leave his mother in such a plight? His father had lost his senses. What if he were never to recover? What if by *his* action he had unsettled his father's reason and condemned his mother and family to a life of poverty and sorrow? Surely it was his duty, as the eldest son, to renounce his venture, to stay with his family, to be their comfort and protector.

But there was another duty calling him—his duty to his friend. Keats must sail on the *Maria Crowther*. On that journey hung his one slender chance of life. No, he could never leave Keats to face the terrible future, with no friend to cheer or comfort him. And, of all Keats's friends, he was the only one unmarried and willing to throw up the small position he had made for himself in London, to risk his livelihood for his friend's sake.

He was so sunk in his thoughts that he scarcely noticed Tom jump in beside him, and it was not until the carriage moved forward with a jerk that he realized that he had seen the last of his home.

The gloom of those cold hours before the dawn, as they jolted towards the docks, seemed to symbolize the painful circumstances of his departure, and he could not prevent his mind from turning over and over every detail of the scene. He knew that his father's love for him was unbounded. He was so proud of Joseph's gifts, and how naïvely he had delighted in his son's company. But, when Joseph looked back, this proven affection served only to make the memory of the blow he had received more horrible, and when he thought of his father struggling to get at him, and his twisted face, he felt himself again overcome by nausea.

Gradually, as they rattled through the streets of London, the gloomy night merged into the chill dawn of September morning. Soon they crossed the Thames and drew up by the docks on the south side of the river. A little group was waiting for them on the wharf and, as the two brothers descended from their carriage, chilled and stiff, one of them came forward to greet them. He was small, but broad-shouldered for his height, soberly and rather untidily dressed. His eyes seemed enormous in his face, which Joseph realized with a pang was even thinner than when he had last seen him.

"Severn!"

"Keats!"

No more was said between them, but Joseph understood the message in the voice and the warmth of the handclasp. Joseph presented his brother to the other gentlemen on the wharf. Among them were John Taylor, whose generosity, in advancing Keats £100 for the copyright of "Endymion," had made it possible for him to undertake the journey; William Haslam, who had first introduced Severn to Keats; and Richard Woodhouse, a clever young solicitor, who had met the poet while acting as reader for Taylor's publishing firm.

"This is our vessel," said Keats, pointing to a small brigantine which lay alongside the wharf.

He led the way up the gangway. His friends followed him on to the deck, where they made the acquaintance of the captain, a powerfully-built man with bright-blue eyes in a kindly brown face.

He led them along the deck and down a companion-way. They clambered down after him and found themselves in a small cabin with two bunks on one side and three on the other. The same thought sprang to all their minds. It was *very* small. The *Maria Crowther* was a boat of only a hundred-and-thirty tons, and most of the available space was used for cargo. What would happen if Keats were seriously ill again during the voyage? This was the only cabin. Five people were to live, sleep and eat in it for the next four weeks.

Joseph was the only one of the party who had no thought for the future as he inspected his new quarters. His liver attack seemed to be coming on again and he felt very ill. Keats led the way back to the deck, where they found a plump, middle-aged lady, who dropped them a curtsy as they introduced themselves. The captain interposed to tell her which were to be her two fellow-passengers.

Mrs. Pidgeon—for such she informed them was her name— gave them a comfortable smile and turned to Captain Walsh.

"And now, Captain, the cabin if you please."

"This way, Ma'am."

They passed on, but not before Tom Severn, who was nearest to the companion-way, had overheard the lady asking the captain "which of those two young gentlemen was the dying man?" [1]

This news made Joseph give a wry smile. It cheered him a little to know that he was looking as ill as he felt.

Soon the vessel sheered off from the wharf and swung slowly down the river with the tide. The young men leaned over the side and talked in a desultory way, or paced up and down the deck. Haslam drew Joseph on one side.

"You must promise to send me an account of your voyage and of Keats's health as soon as you reach Naples," he said. "This journey will be very hard for a man so lately confined to his bed— and it will be hard for you too, Severn. Would to God I could come with you, but it is impossible."

Joseph squeezed his arm sympathetically. Haslam had been married less than a year and his wife was expecting her first child. Joseph had painted her portrait before they were married, and knew what a deep devotion Haslam felt for her.

"I'll do all in my power to make him comfortable, you may be sure. And the warmer climate in Rome will do him good— the doctor said so."

It sounded hollow to both of them. Haslam sighed. "I hope so," he said, staring gloomily down into the muddy river water that curled gently away from the bow. Then, turning suddenly, he gripped Severn's shoulders and with an agonized vehemence he cried,

"Keats *must* get himself well again, Severn, if but for us. I, for one, cannot afford to lose him. If I know what it is to love, I truly love John Keats." [2] His voice broke. "It's his own resignation that forces me to despair."

<hr>

[1] Sharp, *op. cit.*, p. 54.   [2] *Ibid.*, p. 73.

JOHN KEATS
from the miniature exhibited by
Joseph Severn in the Royal
Academy of 1819. Now in the
National Portrait Gallery, London.

JOHN KEATS
from a drawing by Joseph Severn,
in the Dyce and Forster Collection, Victoria and Albert Museum,
London.

THE SEVERN FAMILY MINIATURE.
Painted by Joseph Severn in 1820 and taken by him to Rome.   Original now in Keats
House, Hampstead.

KEATS READING ON THE DECK OF THE *MARIA CROWTHER*
from a sketch made by Joseph Severn on the voyage to Naples. Now in Keats House,
Hampstead.

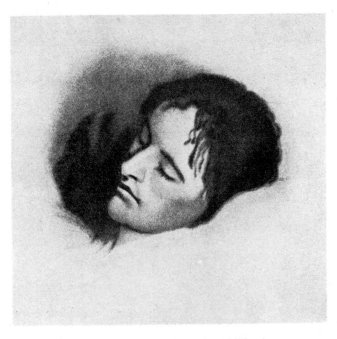

KEATS ON HIS DEATH-BED
Drawing made by Joseph Severn: "3 o'clock M. drawn to keep me awake—a deadly
sweat was on him all this night."

The two friends turned and looked across the deck. Taylor was talking, and as they watched, Keats interrupted him with great animation in his face and manner, and laughed aloud, flinging his head back in a familiar gesture which touched Haslam's heart with memories of happier days. His cheeks were flushed and his eyes shone. Certainly he was not behaving like a man resigned to imminent death. Even Haslam took heart from his appearance. The new surroundings and the voyage down the river seemed to be doing him good. Haslam and Joseph crossed over to the little group and joined in the discussion. Keats was in great spirits. He led the good-humoured attack on Joseph, who suddenly discovered that he had left his passport in his father's house. They all rallied him for his artistic vagueness and lack of method, but Tom and Joseph exchanged uneasy looks, their thoughts drawn unwillingly back to their home and the strange scene enacted there. Tom's face was pale above his blue coat and he was much relieved when Haslam offered to drive straight to Shoreditch and bring the passport to the boat before they sailed.

At four o'clock, after many affectionate farewells, the friends climbed into the little boat which was to take them ashore. Haslam, at Keats's request, was to visit little Fanny Keats at Mr. Abbey's house, and to tell her that he was comfortably settled in his new quarters and that his health seemed already much benefited by the change. Woodhouse took with him a lock of John's hair. Tom was the last to clamber over the side. Joseph embraced him and felt the tears rise to his eyes as the familiar face was gradually blurred by distance until it became unrecognizable.

They went silently down to the cabin, where Mrs. Pidgeon was rummaging in her portmanteau. There the captain joined them and they ate a badly-cooked meal, served by an untidy little cabin-boy. The captain told them that they would wait at Gravesend for another lady who was to come on board next day. Keats cracked jokes all through the meal and soon had the captain chuckling and Mrs. Pidgeon delightedly protesting at his sallies. But, as soon as it was finished, he excused himself on the grounds of sleepiness and climbed into his bunk. Joseph still felt ill, although he had scarcely touched the dinner, and he was tortured by nightmares all night.

Next morning he went ashore with the captain after breakfast to buy some provisions, apples and biscuits. He visited a chemist's, where he had several medicines made up, according to Keats's

C

written directions, and, also at his request, bought a bottle of laudanum. The captain, who was a good-hearted man, tried to find a goat to provide milk for Keats during the voyage, but was unsuccessful. While they were on shore Haslam had been to the ship with Joseph's passport.

Some time after they had eaten their dinner on board they heard the splash of oars approaching. They hurried up on deck. It was already dark, being after six o'clock. Joseph noticed with anxiety that the wind was increasing. A dark cloud thinned for a minute to show the moon, but immediately another rushed to draw a sombre veil over her face. The captain leaned down to help someone up the side. The wind played with the lantern that the mate held above his head, and tossed the shadows into a mad dance. It was a lady who stood on the deck. She was wrapped in a cloak and her face was shadowed by the hood.

She took a step and then faltered and almost fell. Keats and Captain Walsh assisted her down to the cabin. Joseph remained on deck, content to leave the doctoring to Keats. The cold wind made him shiver. Soon he followed the others down to the cabin.

The lady was young and pretty and fair-haired, with a gentle expression and manner.

"A beautiful complexion, but what a frail look," thought Joseph, standing by the companion-way. Keats sat beside her, and, as her manner grew brighter, encouraged her to talk. She was travelling to Naples to stay with her brother, who had been an officer in the Navy and was now a banker. Her name was Miss Cotterell. No, it was not a voyage for pleasure, but for her health. And then it all came out, that she was as far gone in consumption as Keats himself, that the doctors had ordered her to Italy as her only chance of life. Joseph, although deeply pitying her, was distressed to observe her excitement when she heard that Keats had similar reasons for his journey. It was an unfortunate coincidence, and his brow furrowed as he realized that she was in that morbid state when to trace the history of her illness from symptom to symptom was her keenest remaining pleasure.[1] And who would make a better confidant than a fellow-sufferer? As the evening went on Joseph resolved that he would leave Keats alone with her only when it was absolutely unavoidable.

The *Maria Crowther* sailed that night.

[1] Sharp, *op. cit.*, p. 53.

CHAPTER IV

SEA VOYAGE

(*September—October* 1820)

JOSEPH sat on deck. This was their third day at sea. The ship rose and fell rhythmically with the surge of a heavy swell. Until this morning he had had no opportunity to fulfil his promise to Haslam. Now he was writing an account of their voyage for the benefit not only of Haslam but of all Keats's friends and of his own family too. He had decided to write it as a diary, so that he could send all their news at once, whenever the opportunity should offer. He wrote quickly and with scarcely any punctuation save dashes.

"19th Sept. Tuesday, off Dover Castle.

I arose at daybreak to see the glorious eastern gate—Keats slept till seven—Miss C. was rather ill this morning, I prevailed on her to walk the deck with me at halfpast six.—She recovered much—Keats was still better this morning and Mrs. Pidgeon looked and was the picture of health—but poor me! I began to feel a waltzing on my stomach at breakfast and soon I was going it most soundly—Miss Cotterell followed me—then Keats who did it in the most gentlemanly manner—and then the saucy Mrs. Pidgeon who had been laughing at us—four faces bequeathing to the mighty deep their breakfasts—here I must change to a minor key Miss C. fainted—we soon recovered her—I was very ill nothing but lying down would do for me. Keats ascended his bed—from which he dictated surgically like Esculapius of old in basso-relievo— through him Miss C. was recovered—we had a cup of tea each and no more—went to bed and slept until it was time to go to bed—we could not get up again and slept in our clothes all night— Keats the King—not even looking pale.

20th Sept. Wednesday, off Brighton.

Beautiful morning—we all breakfasted on deck—and recovered as we were could enjoy it—about ten Keats said a storm was hatching—he was right—the rain came on and we retired to our cabin—it abated and once more we came on deck—at two storm came on furiously—we retired to our beds. The rolling of

our ship was death to us—towards four it increased and our situation was alarming—the trunks rolled across the cabin—the water
poured in from the skylight and we were tumbled from one side
to the other of our beds—my curiosity was raised to see the storm
—and my anxiety to see Keats for I could only speak to him when
in bed—I got up and fell down on the floor from my weakness and
the rolling of the ship. Keats was very calm—the ladies were
much frightened and would scarce speak—when I got up to the
deck I was astounded—the waves were in mountains and washed
the ship—the watery horizon was like a mountainous country—
but the ship's motion was beautifully to the sea, falling from one
wave to the other in a very lovely manner—the sea each time cross-
ing the deck, and one side of the ship being level with the water—this
when I understood gave me perfect ease—I communicated below
and it did the same—but when the dusk came the sea began to rush
in from the side of our cabin from an opening in the planks—this
made us rather long-faced—for it came by pail-fulls—again I go
out and said to Keats 'Here's pretty music for you'—with the
greatest calmness he answered me only by 'Water parted from
the Sea.'[1] I staggered up again and the storm was awful—the
Captain and the Mate soon came down—for our things were
squashing about in the dark—they struck a light and I succeeded
in getting my desk off the ground—with clothes and books, etc
The captain finding the hole could not be stopped tacked about
from our direction and the sea ceased to dash against the cabin—
for before we were sailing against wind and tide—but the horrible
agitation continued in the ship lengthways—there were the pump
working—the sails squalling—the confused voices of the poo
sailors—the things rattling about in every direction and us poo
devils pinn'd up in our beds like ghosts by daylight—except Keat
he was himself all the time—the ladies suffered most—but I wa
out of bed a dozen times to wait on them and tell them there was n
danger—my sickness made me get into bed very soon each time—
but Keats this morning brags of my sailorship—he says could
have kept on my legs in the watery cabin I should have been
standing miracle!

                          21st Sept.

    I caught a sight of the moon about 3 o'clock this morning—
and ran down to tell the glad tidings—but the surly rolling of th
sea was worse than the storm—the ship trembled to it—and th
sea was scarcely calmed by daylight—so that we were kept fro

---

[1] The title of a popular song of the moment.

2 o'clock yesterday until six this morning without anything—well it has done us good—we are like a quartette of fighting cocks this morning. The morning is serene we are now back again some twenty miles—waiting for a wind—but full of spirits—Keats is without even complaining and Miss Cotterell has a colour in her face—the sea has done his worst upon us.—I am better than I have been for years. Farewell my dear fellow.

J. SEVERN.—show this to my family with my love to them.

When you read this you will excuse the manner—I am quite beside myself—and have written the whole this morning Thursday on the deck after a sleepless night and with a head full of care—you shall have a better the next time."

He had scarcely finished this letter when the captain came over to him and suggested that he and Keats might like to go ashore and stretch their legs. There was scarcely any wind, and what there was was dead against them. The ladies were afraid to face the jump into the little rowing-boat that, at one moment, was level with the deck, and the next had dropped a good five feet below it. But the two young men enjoyed their scramble over the gravel of desolate Dungeness, and Joseph found an opportunity to post his letter to Haslam. They came back hungry and in high spirits, and Joseph made his companions laugh with his description of himself staring, fascinated, at the enormous waves rushing in upon the shore, until a "miserable exciseman" appeared and demanded what he was doing. His stammered explanation that he was admiring the sea only confirmed the exciseman's worst suspicions, and Joseph moved on hurriedly.

But captain and passengers alike became less good-humoured when, after ten days at sea, they were no further than the Solent, and still waiting for a wind. Miss Cotterell had been very ill as they were tacking painfully down the Channel against the head-wind. She was constantly fainting, and sometimes remained unconscious for as long as five or six hours. Keats and Severn at first shared the task of nursing her, but soon Joseph was left alone to care for her, following his friend's directions, for Keats also had a relapse. Miss Cotterell craved for air. Whenever the port-holes were opened Keats would have a terrible fit of coughing which would sometimes end in his spitting blood. But if Joseph were to shut out the cold air which caused his friend so much pain, Miss Cotterell would become very distressed and eventually faint away.

The fourth passenger, whom the two young men had thought

so good-hearted, proved to be very unsympathetic and kept herself as aloof as was possible in such crowded quarters. Once when Joseph, running from one invalid to the other, called her to help, she broke into a tirade which showed him that he need never look for aid from that quarter.

While they lay in the Solent Keats became much better, and even went ashore with Joseph to visit some friends who lived at Bedhampton. There they were welcomed with joy and Keats was resolutely cheerful. Everyone said that he seemed much better than they had expected. It was late when they got back to the ship.

Next morning Keats wrote to his friend, Charles Brown. He had waited, hoping that when he wrote he might be able to describe some definite improvement in his health. But now he felt increasingly certain of his fate and feared that, if he did not write now, he might later lack strength. So he shed the brittle gaiety which had sheltered his inward agony. He must unburden himself. He must write of his love; his love which was deep and full and burningly passionate—and unfulfilled. The pale ghost of Tom warned him of the danger of agitating thoughts like these.

"I wish to write on subjects that will not agitate me much—there is one I must mention and have done with it. Even if my body would recover of itself, this would prevent it. The very thing which I want to live most for will be a great occasion of my death. I cannot help it. Who can help it? Were I in health it would make me ill, and how can I bear it in my state? I daresay you will be able to guess on what subject I am harping—you know what was my greatest pain during the first part of my illness at your house. I wish for death every day and then I wish death away, for death would destroy even those pains which are better than nothing. Land and sea, weakness and decline are great separators, but death is the great divorcer for ever. When the pang of this thought has passed through my mind I may say the bitterness of death is passed. I often wish for you that you might flatter me with the best. I think without my mentioning it for my sake you would be a friend to Miss Brawne when I am dead. You think she has many faults—but, for my sake, think she has not one. . . . If there is anything you can do for her by word or deed I know you will do it. I am in a state at present in which woman merely as woman can have no more power over me than stocks and stones, and yet the difference of my sensations with respect to Miss Brawne and my sister is amazing.

The one seems to absorb the other to a degree incredible. I seldom think of my brother and sister in America. The thought of leaving Miss Brawne is beyond everything horrible—the sense of darkness coming over me—I eternally see her figure eternally vanishing. Some of the phrases she was in the habit of using during my last nursing at Wentworth Place ring in my ears. Is there another life? Shall I awake and find all this a dream? There must be—we cannot be created for this sort of suffering. The receiving this letter is to be one of yours. . . ." [1]

He quickly finished the letter, folded it and put it in his pocket. He did not know if he would ever send it. His spirit had failed him at last, and for the rest of the day he shunned them all and sat alone, his eyes shadowed with despair.

The captain had hoped to put into Portland Roads that evening, but the wind dropped again off the Dorset coast. The next day they were still becalmed, and Severn and Keats went ashore at Lulworth Cove. Here Keats seemed to have a flash of his old delight in nature's beauty, and the two young men spent the morning exploring the tunnels and caverns in the rocky chalk coast. Joseph, watching his companion anxiously, was reassured by the pleasure with which he showed him ledges and fissures in the cliffs that he had climbed as a boy.

It was reluctantly that they returned to the ship, to sit, silent, in the cabin, while Mrs. Pidgeon sulked in a corner and Miss Cotterell lay resting in her bunk. The captain was on deck, anxiously searching the sky for promise of a wind. Keats was writing. After a while he stood up and beckoned to Joseph to follow him on deck. They stood together gazing at the star-scattered sky. Joseph, with a painter's interest, watched the shifting lights and colours on the polished surface of the sea. The chalk cliffs glimmered pale across the water.

At last Keats turned to Joseph, and said that he had a present for him. Joseph looked at him, surprised. Those curious gleaming eyes were fixed on his handsome face. Then they dropped and John Keats began to recite in a low, tremulous undertone, which was almost a chant:

> "Bright star, would I were steadfast as thou art—
> Not in lone splendour hung aloft the night,
> And watching, with eternal lids apart,
> Like Nature's patient, sleepless Eremite,

---

[1] *Letters of John Keats*, p. 520.

> The moving waters at their priest-like task
> Of pure ablution round earth's human shores,
> Or gazing on the new soft fallen mask
> Of snow upon the mountains and the moors—
> No—yet still steadfast, still unchangeable,
> Pillow'd upon my fair love's ripening breast,
> To feel for ever its soft fall and swell,
> Awake for ever in a sweet unrest,
> Still, still to hear her tender-taken breath,
> And so live ever or else swoon to death."

His voice dropped even lower, so that Severn could only just hear the last phrase whispered. He waited, unwilling to shatter the beauty of the silver silence.

Then Keats drew from his pocket a well-thumbed book. It was his volume of Shakespeare's poems. He opened it and showed Severn that on a blank page, opposite the heading "A Lover's Lament," he had written out the sonnet that he had just recited. He closed the book and pressed it gently into Joseph's hand.[1] Then he turned quickly and went below to the cabin.

When Joseph came down he was lying in his bunk and apparently asleep.

Joseph was awakened by the cabin-boy, who shouted down the hatchway that the captain desired him to tell the passengers that a favourable wind had risen at last and, if it held, they would soon be seeing the last of the English coast. Joseph and Keats dressed quickly and went on deck. The wind was becoming stronger, and already the ship was rising and dipping with a lively motion. It was not long before they were both feeling qualms of sickness. There was no dinner eaten that day in the cabin. The captain stayed on deck, with an anxious eye on the rising wind, and the passengers lay, wretched, in their bunks.

It was the beginning of a storm that was to last for three days. By nightfall enormous seas were sweeping over the deck, and the motion of the ship was so violent that Joseph was several times almost thrown out of his bunk. Water rushed up and down the cabin in the darkness. Trunks bumped about the floor. Whenever the ship gave a particularly frightening lurch Mrs. Pidgeon would scream, and once or twice he heard a moan from Miss Cotterell. But although he shouted several times to Keats he could hear no reply. The terrifying noises of the storm drowned his voice and seemed to batter his mind into insensibility.

[1] This book is now at Keats House, Hampstead.

By the hour when a grey light began to penetrate into the cabin his only thought was to cling to the edge of the bunk with cold cramped fingers, and not to be hurled down into the water that dashed their belongings up and down the cabin. Several hours after daybreak he raised himself with a great effort and shouted again to Keats. But there was no reply. He felt so weak and dizzy that he did not even try to get down from his bunk. He knew that such an attempt could only end in disaster.

So the seemingly interminable day passed and night came again. He was desperately afraid that John might die, confined to his berth as he was, without food or assistance of any kind. The storm was as violent as ever, and the cold was intense. It seemed to Joseph that the ship must surely founder. But the dawn of another day found him still lying cold and miserable in his berth. The ship was lurching less violently. She seemed to be lifted irresistibly—then there was a pause—followed by a sickening drop. It was very uncomfortable, but at least it was a regular motion and, as such, reassuring.

After a little while he was able to climb down from his bunk. He held fast to the side of it and worked his way along to where Keats was lying. The water washed six inches deep round his legs. He reached up and shook Keats's shoulder and was delighted to see him turn slowly towards him and even give him a faint smile. He shouted that he was going to try to get up on deck, and Keats nodded. They had had no time to undress, so Joseph had only to put on his greatcoat, which was hanging on the other side of the cabin, swinging violently from side to side. He waited until the ship rolled and then ran downhill to the other side, grabbing something just in time to avoid being thrown over as she lurched back again. After a pause to get his breath he lifted the coat off the peg. It was more difficult to get on, but he managed it at last. Then he groped his way across the cabin.

Just as he got to the foot of the companion-way a face appeared above him. It was one of the sailors, sent by the captain to see if they needed any assistance. His appearance was welcome, as without him he could not have got out on to the deck, because everything had been battened down. He clambered up the companion-way and peered cautiously out. At first he was terrified at the enormous height of the waves that bore down on the little *Maria Crowther*. But soon he gained courage as he saw how gallantly she rode over the green mountains, and then he became fascinated by the grandeur of the scene. He spent the rest of the

*C

day watching the long foam-topped waves and the driving clouds.
Now and then he had to duck to avoid a shower of spray which
lashed the deck but, undismayed, he stayed at his vantage point
until dusk. It was still too rough for anyone to get along the
deck to them with food, but Joseph was alone in feeling the
lack of it.

Next day, although there was still a heavy swell, the sky was
brighter. Joseph and the captain breakfasted in the cabin, with
the boy set to hold the table still. They gave some tea, laced with
rum, to Keats and the two ladies. Again Joseph spent most of
the day on deck in his greatcoat, fascinated by the Atlantic rollers—
"each one as long as Shoreditch." What were his family doing
now? he wondered. Had his father recovered, and were Tom and
Maria missing him?

The storm continued to abate that night, and by the morning
John Keats and Mrs. Pidgeon had recovered sufficiently to join
the other two at breakfast. There was even some laughter when
a sudden lurch sent the cabin-boy sprawling on top of the table
which he was supposed to steady, and threw the coffee-pot,
fortunately nearly empty, into Mrs. Pidgeon's lap and the ham
on to Joseph's knees. They were all impressed, and secretly
rather pleased, when the captain told them that at certain moments
during the storm he had felt grave fears for the safety of the ship.

Miss Cotterell was the slowest to recover. But soon, off Cape
St. Vincent, they were becalmed, and she could sit on deck in the
warm sun. Even so, she would faint as often as four times a day,
although in the intervals she would seem quite well. She was
touchingly grateful to the two young men for their care. Mrs.
Pidgeon was heartily disliked by them all. She was determined
to run as little risk of infection as possible, and would see Miss
Cotterell stiffened like a corpse without offering to assist in any
way.[1]

During the calm weather Keats and Severn sat apart from the
others and read Lord Byron's "Don Juan" aloud to each other.
But when they came to the shipwreck canto Keats flung the
book down, disgusted by its cynicism.[2] The sea was oily-smooth,
and the two friends, leaning over the side of the ship, could see
many strange fish. Once, to their delight, a whale came up to blow.
At the first opportunity Severn brought out his paints and made
several water-colour sketches of the sea, and two of Keats.

[1] Letter to Maria, Jan. 21st, 1821.   [2] Sharp, *op. cit.*, p. 57.

The calm soon gave way to a steady favourable wind, and the voyage continued uneventfully until one day when several Portuguese men-of-war approached them. A shot was fired across their bows. Captain Walsh, who had been shaving in the cabin, rushed up on deck. The *Maria Crowther* was hove to. A great four-decker drifted close to them and her captain shouted across the water with his speaking-trumpet. He asked in English if the little brig had seen any vessels which looked like privateers. When they replied that they had seen no vessels of any kind he signalled them to sail on. The passengers were horrified by the horde of savage, dirty sailors, who crowded the decks and clambered in the rigging which towered above the little *Maria Crowther*, and Captain Walsh was not happy until the whole fleet had disappeared below the horizon.

Later that day they reported the incident to a spick-and-span English sloop-of-war which went about smartly in pursuit of the Portuguese fleet.[1] After this excitement, the rest of their voyage passed quickly. Keats told Joseph that he was planning a poem on the story of Sabrina, and Joseph sat spellbound while he recited long passages from Milton's "Comus" in his beautiful moving voice.

This fresh burgeoning of poetic ambition encouraged Joseph to think that his friend was better and would win his way back to health. But terrible fits of coughing still tore him, and the cramped quarters and poor food were taking their toll. His hair, which had once been a bright chestnut, was now quite dark, and the curl had left it. It hung lank and straight round his thin face. Often Joseph, watching him when he thought he was unobserved, would be pained at the distraught, haunting expression of grief on his friend's face.

Gibraltar was passed, the coast of Barbary slipped over the horizon in a golden haze, and at last, after six weeks at sea, the day dawned when they were to enter the Bay of Naples.

[1] Sharp, *op. cit.*, pp. 57-58.

CHAPTER V

QUARANTINE

THEY were all up at sunrise to catch the first glimpse of the Bay, and the beauty of it exceeded anything Joseph Severn had dreamed of. The white houses, cushioned in green vineyards and just touched by the rising sun, shone tier above tier on the steeply-sloping hills. Vesuvius towered over them, his crest hidden in sun-gilded smoke. The little ship glided gently through the brilliant-blue water, wafted into port by the light dawn breeze. She picked her way daintily between the small craft that studded the bay. Then, turning into the wind, with sails flapping, she dropped anchor near the Castell' d'Uovo.

Almost at once they were surrounded by a jostling crowd of little boats. From all corners of the harbour they came darting out, weighed down with their wares. Some were manned by a single youth, but most were propelled by an oarsman while another figure crouched in the bows, encouraging his companion to greater efforts with shrill cries, howling derision at slower rivals, and shouting abuse at any boat that seemed likely to reach their common prey before him. Some of the boats were piled high with gorgeous heaps of fruit. Joseph's mouth watered as he saw grapes, peaches, figs, melons and many other fruits which were quite new to him.

The group on the *Maria Crowther* leaned over the side of the ship. Wherever they looked, dark faces were upturned to them, brown hands gesticulated and delicious sun-golden fruit was held out to tempt them, while the harsh cries of brightly-coloured parrots added to the uproar. After the monotonous, bad food of the voyage, they were eager to buy fresh fruit. Joseph felt an exquisite sense of pleasure as his teeth sank into a juicy peach.

Just at that moment the discordant shouts increased in volume and bitterness as a man in some sort of uniform approached, seated in the stern of a rowing-boat. With a series of violent gestures to the little skiffs that swarmed round the *Maria Crowther*, he persuaded them to draw apart and to leave a narrow lane, down which he directed his ragged oarsman to approach the ship. Captain Walsh stepped forward to receive him, but the official, though he stood up in his swaying boat, made no effort to come on board. He asked the name of the ship and port of departure.

When he heard that they had come from London he became very excited. He threw his hands above his head and cried that they would have to keep quarantine. They had heard there was typhus in London. Nobody must leave the ship for ten days. He repeated this with great emphasis, then, with a wave of his hand, motioned his man to row him away.

It was a cruel blow, after all the discomforts of their five weeks' voyage—the crowded quarters, the bad food, the storms—to arrive at last at their destination and to be penned up on board for another ten days. Joseph was the least depressed. The deep blue of the sea and sky, the paler blue of the mountains, the vivid shifting colours of the clustering skiffs, all filled him with delight. He felt full of vitality and power. He longed to capture this strange scene with his brush and to give permanence to a moment which otherwise would pass and be gone for ever. He had never before left England, and had but seldom been away from London. His work had left him little time for holidays since he was fifteen years old. Now he was nearly twenty-seven. The alien beauty of Naples and the strange sights and sounds about him filled him with an almost unbearable excitement. He would not mind staying on the ship for months in this bay of enchantment.

Then he felt suddenly ashamed of his selfishness and, contrite, turned anxiously to look for John Keats. He was reassured to find him at his side, gazing entranced at the scene before them. He was relieved to see him so taken out of himself, for of late he had often such a starved expression on his thin face, and so sad a look in his eyes, that Joseph had felt bewildered and helpless in the presence of such misery. But to-day his worn face was serene as he gazed about him. Joseph, encouraged, was about to fetch his paints from the cabin when a naval pinnace came alongside. A young lieutenant sprang on board. The English fleet was in the Bay, and the Admiral, seeing the British flag at the masthead of the *Maria Crowther*, had sent an officer to make enquiries.

He introduced himself as Lieutenant Sullivan. Captain Walsh's offer of refreshment was cordially accepted; a request from the mate that some of the sailors might come on board was authorized by the captain on the one side and granted by the lieutenant on the other—with the proviso that four must remain to man the pinnace. So six sailors clambered on board and were soon exchanging nautical and racy reminiscences with the crew. The passengers, too, were quickly in conversation with the first person outside their little circle to set foot on their ship since they left England. They described eagerly the terrible storm they had been through in the Bay of Biscay. Then Keats opened a new subject by questioning the naval officer about the Neapolitans' revolt against the Austrians. Sullivan seemed to doubt whether the rebels would be successful. He began to tell them his reasons for this opinion. They were all so deeply interested that the little Italian official had to hail them twice before anybody heard him.

Then, speaking in an agitated voice which made him very difficult to understand, he told them that since the English officer and his men had broken the quarantine regulations by going on board, there they must remain until the ten days were over. When he understood this the lieutenant frowned and in a brisk voice ordered the four remaining men to take the pinnace back to his ship for instructions.

The pinnace soon returned with a message that Lieutenant Sullivan and his six men were to stay on board the *Maria Crowther*. It was delivered by a fellow-officer, who rallied Sullivan on his predicament. However, Sullivan took the opportunity to ask that some extra food might be sent, as the *Maria Crowther* had only just got into port after a long voyage. Away went the pinnace again, and was soon back with a store of meat, fruit, bread and, best of all, a plentiful supply of red wine.

After this, as far as food went, they were in luxury. A few hours after the pinnace had brought its precious load, Miss Cotterell's banker-brother appeared. Living in Naples as he did, he was well aware of the strict quarantine regulations, so that he did not attempt to come on board. But he handed them baskets containing every sort of delicacy—fish, chickens, grapes, vegetables and armfuls of flowers. These last gave Keats the greatest pleasure. Indeed, with the stimulation of a new and gay personality in their company, he became, to Severn's joy, almost his old self again.

In a few days' time Charles Cotterell could no longer content himself with shouted conversations from a little boat. His sister looked so wasted and ill that he felt he could not leave her care to the two young men, whom he had thanked again and again for their kindness to her. So he gave instructions to his servants that fresh supplies of food were to be sent daily to the ship, and voluntarily joined their captivity.

For the first day or two this led to an increased gaiety on board. While the sun shone the sea round the *Maria Crowther* was thick with little boats whose occupants had come to make merry at the expense of the sailors from the English man-of-war. Sullivan could speak Italian, but Cotterell, still better, could speak the Neapolitan lazzaroni-patois, and he was quick to reply to the good-natured jokes at the lieutenant's expense, so that the laughter was often turned back on the joker. He translated these exchanges for the benefit of those on board, and they all helped to suggest replies. Keats was by far the quickest, and seemed to enjoy the interchange as much as any of them.

But alas! the weather changed. Rain began to fall heavily. No longer did the gaily-coloured boats throng round the *Maria Crowther*, filling the air with laughter and chatter; no longer did misty shapes glide slowly past in the dusk while a tenor voice echoed across the water and a guitar twanged a sweet accompaniment. The rain hissed on the empty water round them, dripped from the rigging and drummed maddeningly on the deck above their heads. For now they were all huddled in the one little cabin. It had been crowded before, but now there were two extra occupants. However, uncomfortable as they were, there was no other arrangement possible. The forecastle, with six extra sailors to shelter, was absolutely full, and on that little ship there was nowhere else to go.

So there they all lived together, two of them sleeping on the floor at night. This made seven people in what Joseph called, with much truth, "the black hole of a cabin." Miss Cotterell wilted quickly under these conditions and became very seriously ill, and soon, to Joseph's consternation, he saw that her relapse was preying on Keats's nerves. He lost his good spirits and would sit for long periods with his eyes on Miss Cotterell's face, marking every symptom of her decline. Joseph would try to distract him by conversation, but he would answer only with a cold, harsh brevity or not at all. In the foul air of the crowded cabin he could scarcely eat and he became daily more emaciated.[1]

Joseph was himself in better health than he had been for some time. The sea voyage seemed to have dissipated his liverishness, but even he felt at times as though he would stifle in the foetid air of the cabin. Whenever the weather seemed clearer they would emerge eagerly on to the deck, to look longingly at the city they had come so far to see. But they would soon be driven back to the cabin by another downpour, and as there was no way of drying their clothes, they were none of them anxious to be soaked.

[1] Sharp, *op. cit.*, pp. 59-61.

With the exception of a few momentary respites of this sort, they spent the rest of their quarantine in squalid discomfort, which to Miss Cotterell and Keats rapidly became desperate suffering. Joseph could hardly believe that his friend would survive this incarceration. Terrible spasms of coughing convulsed him and he grew daily weaker. It was while he was thus imprisoned that Keats wrote to Mrs. Brawne:

". . . The sea air has been beneficial to me about to as great an extent as squally weather and bad accomodation and provisions has done harm—so I am about as I was—give my love to Fanny and tell her, if I were well there is enough in this port of Naples to fill a quire of paper—but it looks like a dream—every man who can row his boat and walk and talk seems a different being from myself. I do not feel in the world. It has been unfortunate for me that one of the passengers is a young lady in consumption—her imprudence has vexed me very much—the knowledge of her complaint—the flushings in her face, all her bad symptoms have preyed upon me. . . . I shall feel a load off me when the lady vanishes out of my sight. . . . I dare not fix my mind upon Fanny, I have not dared to think of her. The only comfort I have had that way has been in thinking for hours together of having the knife she gave me put in a silver case—the hair in a locket—and the pocket book in a gold net— Show her this. I dare say no more. . . . Oh what an account I could give you of the Bay of Naples if I could once more feel myself a citizen of this world—I feel a spirit in my brain would lay it forth pleasantly—O what a misery it is to have an intellect in splints! My love again to Fanny—"

He sent a message to Fanny's younger sister and to her brother, a word to the Dilkes, another to Brown, and inscribed himself:

"my dear Mrs. Brawne
　　　　Yours sincerely and affectionate
　　　　　JOHN KEATS—"

Then his pen scribbled an anguished postscript:
"Good bye Fanny! God bless you!" [1]

---

[1] *Letters of John Keats*, Oct. 24th, 1820, pp. 522-523.

CHAPTER VI

NAPLES TO ROME

(*October—November* 1820)

THE ten days were over. The morning was cold and a damp fog hung over the harbour, but no weather could have depressed Joseph. In half an hour his foot would, for the first time, touch foreign soil. They were all on deck, muffled up against the weather—Mrs. Pidgeon, with her false air of motherliness; Lieutenant Sullivan pacing the deck, anxious to be back in his ship; Charles Cotterell, hovering anxiously around his ill sister, who sat limply with her eyes fixed unwaveringly on the deck. Joseph felt that she was trying to summon up all her fortitude for the journey to her brother's house. A surge of sympathy stirred in him. She was so young to face so stern a battle.

But where was Keats? He looked about to see if he was talking with the captain, with whom he had struck up a great friendship, and whose kindness to the two friends had been unceasing. But Walsh was busy with one of the seamen coiling some ropes. Joseph hurried aft. He must still be in the cabin. Perhaps he had lain down to rest and had fallen asleep. He stopped quietly at the top of the companion-way and, bending, peered down into the cabin.

At what he saw he turned quite white and a cold horror seemed to run through his body. For a moment he stayed with a sick, empty feeling in his stomach, then he stumbled aft, and in the stern of the ship, with no one near, he sank down on the deck and covered his eyes with his hand. The sight of so much suffering was unbearable. He heard again that ghastly cough; he saw again the poor white face, the terrible pool of blood. Unnerved, bewildered, and cursing his helplessness, he sat there with hot tears pouring down his cheeks, until the sudden fear that Keats would find him thus forced him to compose himself.

He dried his eyes mechanically and, rising to his feet, began to pace across the deck and back. In his mind a cold voice was repeating,

"What he passed must almost have killed a man as strong as myself. How can his poor shattered frame survive?" [1]

[1] Severn's letter to Haslam, Nov. 1st, 1820; quoted by Colvin, *op. cit.*, p. 498.

Thus he paced the deck until Keats emerged from the cabin
amidst the bustle that surrounded the shore-going boat. Mr.
Cotterell insisted on taking them in his carriage to the hotel which
he had recommended—the Villa di Londra.

In spite of all he had heard, Joseph was taken aback by the dirt,
the noise and the smell of the city which had looked so beautiful
from the sea. The streets were filthy. The wheels of their carriage
passed through heaps of slush and rotting vegetables, which lay
steaming on the cobbles. The stench was overpowering, but the
natives did not appear to notice it. The whole population seemed
to live in the streets, and the noise they made was deafening. Red-
capped mariners were hawking fish. Swarthy bare-legged men
devoured macaroni at the street corners, while mothers nursed
their babies in the gutters. Filthy beggars dragged themselves
with uncanny speed along the roadway, calling attention to their
deformities. A troop of ragged children ran beside their carriage
clamouring for "*un piccolo soldo, signore.*" At a narrow corner they
were held up while a herd of cows wandered past them, and Mr.
Cotterell explained that in Naples they were driven to your door
to be milked. A masked religious took advantage of the delay to
thrust a collecting-box into the carriage. Joseph stole a look at
his friend's white, listless face, and could have cried again as he
thought how Keats, in good health, would have revelled in all the
strange sights and sounds around them.

He thought of their long walks together over wild Hampstead
and of Keats's extraordinary faculty of observation that had always
astonished him; of his enjoyment of everything he saw, the
pleasure he felt in a colour, or a flower, or the swaying of the trees.
His eyes had gleamed delightedly as he marked them all; now
they passed dully over everything. Alas, thought Joseph, his
suffering blinds his eyes to everything.[1]

Keats rested when they arrived at the hotel. But in the afternoon they ventured out to see a review of Neapolitan troops.
Joseph was most enthusiastic about their fine martial appearance,
but Keats would not allow that they had any backbone in them.
Neither of them guessed how soon he would be proved right.

In their large airy room at the hotel, with a view of Vesuvius
from its windows, both sat down to write home. Joseph continued
his journal-letter to Haslam, bringing it up to date with a description
of their voyage, of Keats's misery in quarantine, and of the kindness they had received both from Captain Walsh and Mr. Cotterell.

---

[1] Letter from Severn to Haslam, Nov. 1st, 1820.

He was too engrossed in his letter to notice Keats's expression of suffering as he wrote to Brown, the only friend who already knew so much of his love that there was no need for explanation.

"My dear Brown," he wrote. "Yesterday we were let out of Quarantine, during which my health suffered more from bad air and the stifled cabin than it had done the whole voyage. The fresh air revived me a little, and I hope I am well enough this morning to write you a short calm letter;—if that can be called one, in which I am afraid to speak of what I would fainest dwell upon. As I have gone thus far into it, I must go on a little; perhaps it may relieve the load of WRETCHEDNESS which presses upon me. The persuasion that I shall see her no more will kill me. My dear Brown, I should have had her when I was in health and I should have remained well. I can bear to die—I cannot bear to leave her. O God! God! God! Everything I have in my trunks that reminds me of her goes through me like a spear. The silk lining she put in my travelling cap scalds my head. My imagination is horribly vivid about her—I see her—I hear her. There is nothing in the world of sufficient interest to divert me from her a moment. . . ."

The pen rushed on.

". . . I am afraid to write to her—to receive a letter from her—to see her handwriting would break my heart—even to hear of her anyhow, to see her name written, would be more than I can bear. My dear Brown, what am I to do? Where can I look for consolation or ease? If I had any chance of recovery, this passion would kill me. Indeed, through the whole of my illness, both at your house and at Kentish Town, this fever has never ceased wearing me out. When you write to me, which you will do immediately, write to Rome (poste restante)—if she is well and happy, put a mark thus †; if —"

He added some other messages but could not prevent himself from returning to the one subject which filled his mind.

". . . Is there any news of George? O, that something fortunate had ever happened to me or my brothers!—then I might hope,— but despair is forced upon me as a habit. My dear Brown, for my sake, be her advocate for ever. I cannot say a word about Naples; I do not feel at all concerned in the thousand novelties around me. I am afraid to write to her—I should like her to know that I do

not forget her. O, Brown, I have coals of fire in my breast. It
surprises me that the human heart is capable of containing and
bearing such misery. Was I born for this end? . . ." [1]

He finished his letter. Joseph saw him take up a volume of
Clarissa Harlowe, but he seemed unable to concentrate on it. After
frequent changes of position, he put the book down and went over
to the window, where the raindrops had begun to chase each other
down the panes and blurred the lights twinkling in the misty night
outside. At length he turned away from his gloomy vigil over the
city and began to move restlessly about the room, every now and
then glancing at Severn, as though he were about to speak.

Joseph interrupted the sentence he was writing and scribbled
rapidly: "for the present I will talk to him—he is disposed to it.
I will talk him to sleep for he has suffered much fatigue." [2]

Then he laid down his pen and tried to lead John on to talk.
It was not easy. The truth was that Keats was aching to talk to
someone about Fanny and his frustrated love. But by nature he
was very reserved where his deepest feelings were concerned and,
with his illness, secrecy had become an obsession. Even in good
health he had constantly urged Fanny to tell no one of their love.
He had told her, with the prospect of a long engagement before
them,

"I would rather die than share my secret with anybody's
confidence." [3]

As his illness became more acute, he had striven even more to
hide what should have been his dearest happiness. Of what use
to expose a love which could not be consummated? He had no
money. He could not marry. The doctors forbade him even to
think about the poetry which he must write if he was to pay his
debts. [4]

He had kept his secret well. Of all his friends, only Charles
Brown realized the intensity of his passion. There had been no
possibility of concealing from Brown the constant visits of their
attractive neighbour or the intimate terms that he was on with her.
Many were the days when Brown, in order to leave them together,
had descended to the kitchen, to while away the time with his fiery
Irish "Abby." But Joseph had no inkling of the depth of his
friend's feelings for Miss Brawne. Although he had met her
several times he, like Reynolds, had not thought her worthy of the

---

[1] *Letters of John Keats*, pp. 523-524.
[2] Letter to Haslam ; quoted by Colvin, *op. cit.*, p. 498.
[3] *Letters of John Keats*, p. 500.   [4] *Ibid.*, p. 463.

friend whom he adored. He realized that Keats was strongly attracted to her, but she had always responded in such a lively way to his own laughter and good spirits that the atmosphere, when he had been with them, had never been such as might have shown him the truth.

Indeed, when poor Fanny saw the letter that Joseph had just put aside to finish later, she wrote to Keats's sister—"From your brother I never expect a very good account, but you may imagine how lowering to the spirits it must have been when Mr. Severn, who I never imagined it was possible for anything to make unhappy, who I never saw for ten minutes serious, says he was so overcome that he was obliged to relieve himself by shedding tears." [1]

In any case, he had seen little of Keats during the months immediately before their departure, because he had been painting every minute of the long summer days. So he did not realize the agony John was suffering in being parted from her—perhaps for ever.

Gradually Keats was able to bring himself to tell Severn something of his unhappiness. The first halting words made a crack in the wall that reserve had built round his most intimate feelings. Slowly the crack widened under the urgent pressure, the words came more easily, and then the wall crumbled and a flood of frustrated longing surged round Joseph and swept him into an alien, tragic world.

John Keats cried out against the perverse fate which had allowed him to meet, love and be loved by Fanny, only to snatch the prospect of a happy union from him. But his misery and weakness made him incoherent. His frustrated love became mixed with the horror he felt at being unable to write, or even to *see* with the poetic sight that had been his. So that Joseph, even then, did not realize quite how this passion alone was consuming him, apart from the drying up of his poetic inspiration.

Keats was not able to purge himself of all his misery. He did not tell Joseph of his conviction that this passion for Fanny would kill him, that with the certain knowledge, which he felt himself in spite of the doctors, that he was going to die, every thought of her was a sword-thrust in his vitals, and thus a further impediment to any chance of recovery.

Nevertheless the confidence, incomplete though it was, relieved him. Joseph's passionate sympathy and deep emotion did much to soothe him, and he was comparatively calm when they went to bed.

[1] Betty Askwith, *Keats*, p. 264.

"Keats went to bed much recovered," wrote Joseph to Haslam next day. "I took every means to remove from him a heavy grief that may tend more than anything to be fatal. He told me much —very much—and I don't know whether it was more painful for me or himself—but it had the effect of much relieving him—he went very calm to bed. This morning he is still very much better. We are in good spirits and I may say hopeful fellows—at least I may say as much for Keats—he made an Italian pun to-day. The rain is coming down in torrents."

Next morning Keats received a letter from Shelley, urging him to go and stay at Pisa. He showed it to Joseph. It was a charming letter. Shelley's generous soul had been revolted by the critics' attack, and when, in July, he heard of Keats's illness, he had at once written to invite him to Italy as his guest. Keats, although touched by his kindness, had preferred to retain his independence. Almost every literary friend of Shelley's relied on him for financial assist-ance, and Keats was always embarrassed lest he might think that he, too, desired to profit from his generosity. This fear had always, in his relations with Shelley, made him a little abrupt and even ungracious. So it was on this occasion. Although grateful to him for his kindness, he declined the invitation, explaining that their arrangements were already made to spend the winter in Rome.[1]

After four days in Naples they set out on the last stage of their journey, in a small carriage, called a *vettura*. Joseph was sorry to leave Naples, where Charles Cotterell had given a farewell dinner in their honour. But Keats, with his liberal convictions, was upset by the King's betrayal of the new constitution and the apathy with which the Neapolitans themselves seemed to be facing the loss of their freedom and a resumption of the Austrian yoke. The King had fled to his Austrian friends only the day before, and Keats declared that he could no longer bear to stay in a city where men cared so little for their liberty.

"I should die in anguish," he cried, "if I thought I was to be buried amid a people of such miserable political debasement."[2]

The weather was delightful. The *vettura* moved very slowly, so that Joseph was able to walk long stretches of the journey beside it. He was exhilarated by the pure air and the strange surroundings. They passed through mile after mile of vineyards. The vines were festooned like lovely natural garlands from tree to tree, and their

---

[1] Sharp, *op. cit.*, p. 63. [2] *Ibid.*, p. 63.

green chains ran from the hill-tops down to the road in the valley and stretched away up the slope on the other side. He strode along beside the carriage, sniffing the lovely scents blown down from the hills and the briny tang of the never far-distant sea.

Keats, seated in the *vettura*, was listless and unhappy. He could not eat the coarse unpalatable food which was all they could get at the wayside inns. His only pleasure was in the wild flowers that grew everywhere about their path and whose smell became almost overpowering when they came to cross the Pontine Marshes. Joseph would fill the little carriage with flowers. Keats never tired of them, and their scent and colour seemed to kindle in him a strange joy.

At last they saw before them the vast menacing wastes of the Campagna. Keats's interest quickened.

"It's like an inland sea," he said.[1]

Not a tree nor a house could they see in the wide monotony before them. The grass grew yellow from the cracked ground. On a hillock not far from the road a buffalo stood tense for a moment watching them, then plunged away. The dust lay thick beneath the wheels and swirled behind them in a cloud. Ahead of them, near the ruins of a solitary square tower, they saw a moving patch of crimson. As they drew nearer they found it was a cardinal in a bright red cloak. An owl, which was fastened by one leg to a stick beside him, fluttered about indignantly. Attached to the owl was a small looking-glass reflecting the sun, which attracted numerous small birds. When they came near enough the cardinal would shoot them. Two liveried footmen stood at his side and deferentially loaded the fowling-pieces. Already quite a large pile of tiny victims lay at his feet.

They passed this eccentric sportsman, and at the summit of the next hill the carriage came to a standstill. The *vetturino* pointed with his whip.

"*Ecco Roma!*"

The miles of desolate plain, the occasional massive tower, the bare rocks and, in the distance, the historic hills shrouded in mist, all combined to create an atmosphere of solitude and fallen splendour. As they gazed over the barren wastes of the Campagna, Rome seemed like an enchanted city of the dead. But as they drew nearer they met long lines of carts and great wagons drawn by white oxen. Peasants were returning from the city having sold their cheese or olives. Some walked, some rode on

---

[1] Sharp, *op. cit.*, p. 64.

little shaggy ponies, their legs hanging almost to the ground.
Joseph gazed curiously at a group of girls who were striding along
in brightly-striped skirts, their coarse black hair tangled by the
wind. The air was shrill with their laughter and snatches of song.

They entered the city by the Lateran Gate, and almost at once
they were staggered by their first view of the Colosseum. Its size
and the broken grandeur of its outline impressed them deeply.
They passed through the ruins of the Imperial City and turned into
a long, narrow street which the driver told them was the Corso.
Joseph thought it very narrow and the side-walks very poor for
the principal street of a great city. Shops, churches, palaces and
private houses stood side by side, and over the faces of all alike
were scattered verandahs and balconies.

Once the street broadened into a piazza, then it narrowed again,
and soon they turned into the Via Condotti, which seemed to be
lined with jewellers' shops. Their eyes were dazzled as they
emerged from the darkness of the narrow streets into the open
space of the Piazza di Spagna. Directly opposite them a magnificent
flight of steps led upwards to a church with twin towers. "*Santa
Trinità de' Monti*," said the coachman, pointing with his whip.
Water was playing in a fountain, shaped like a stone ship, at the
foot of the steps. All around stood stalls of flowers, piled high
with daffodils and mimosa.

Dr. Clark received them warmly in his house in the Piazza di
Spagna. Keats had written to him from Naples, and the doctor
had already taken rooms for them in a house just opposite his own.
After presenting them to Mrs. Clark, he led them across the
square and showed them their rooms. They were in the house on
the right-hand side of the Spanish Steps, which led from the Piazza
to the church above. On these steps, as they passed, Joseph
noticed groups of strangely-dressed men, women and children,
all lounging about, with nothing more to do, it seemed, than to
bask in the beams of the wintry sun. The steps were thick with
the yellow husks of the boiled beans they were chewing.

"Ah, those?" chuckled Dr. Clark, when Joseph drew his
attention to them. "I prophesy that you will mark a great change
in their demeanour when they discover that you are an artist.
Yes, this is the meeting-place for all the models in Rome. Here
you will find beggars or Madonnas, patriarchs or assassins—all
conveniently assembled at your doorstep."

Keats's room was at the side of the house overlooking the
steps, and Joseph's faced on to the Piazza. The rooms were on

the first floor. Soon after their arrival their landlady sent out to a restaurant, or *trattoria*, for a large dish of macaroni. Keats was exhausted by the long journey and could eat nothing, but the excitement of being at last in Rome made him comparatively cheerful.

"You would never believe this could taste so good," said Joseph with his mouth full. Then, thinking of the good English food at Mason's ·Court—roast beef, cabbage and pudding—he made a face and added, laughing, "though it *looks* like a dish of large white earth-worms." [1]

---

[1] Letter to Maria, Feb. 19th, 1821.

CHAPTER VII

NO. 26 PIAZZA DI SPAGNA

(*November—December* 1820)

DR. CLARK did not confine his kindness to his patient. When he heard that Joseph knew no one in Rome he spoke to John Gibson and returned with an invitation from the sculptor for Severn to visit him. Joseph was delighted but apprehensive. He longed to take advantage of the introduction. Yet, from his experience in London of the lack of interest shown by successful artists in their poorer brothers' struggles, he feared a snub or a cold reception, which would show clearly that Gibson had been more or less forced into extending a vague invitation to Dr. Clark's friend, and thought it poor taste on his part to have taken advantage of it.

But Keats would allow no hesitation. He was gradually gaining strength after the journey, although the doctor would not yet allow him to see any of the great sights of Rome, for fear that they would excite his brain too much. He divided his time between reading, learning Italian, and taking gentle walks on the Piazza. Joseph would accompany him on these strolls, but Keats was much troubled by the thought that his friend's journey to Rome might prove disastrous to him in his career.[1] He had already urged Joseph to present his letter of introduction to Canova at the earliest opportunity, and now, hearing what Dr. Clark had done, he insisted that Joseph should present himself at John Gibson's apartment that very afternoon.

Joseph dressed himself carefully in his best blue coat and put on a fresh white shirt and necktie. Then, having combed his thick brown hair, which at once sprang up again into the same untidy curls, he took his beaver hat from the bed, waved farewell to Keats, and set out on foot for Gibson's studio.

It was a short walk from the Piazza di Spagna to the Via della Fontanella where the English sculptor lived. Although only two years older than Joseph, he had already achieved considerable fame. For the last three years he had been living in Rome, and many of the best-known English collectors had returned to their

---

[1] Sharp, *op. cit.*, pp. 55, 67, and 69.

own country only after they had placed orders for copies of his sculptures to be executed in marble and sent after them. It was well known that the Marquis Canova had expressed the highest opinion of his work.

Joseph turned thoughtfully in at the door of the house he sought. Like most of the dwelling-houses in Rome, it was a large building divided into flats, which were approached by a common staircase. He climbed to the first floor and paused, hesitating, on the landing. There was no bell outside the door, so, after a moment's hesitation, he gave a quiet knock, and was just wondering whether to repeat it when the door was opened by Gibson himself. He was wrapped in a bulky white overall bunched in at the waist with a belt. His black hair was rather long, and Joseph noticed at once his sensitive firm mouth and fine eyes. He introduced himself and Gibson drew him inside with a warm smile. Joseph was beginning to thank him for his kindness in inviting him when there was another, louder knock, and Gibson turned again to the door. An elderly gentleman stood on the threshold, rather short but, to Joseph's eyes at least, most elegantly dressed.

"Please come in, my lord," said Gibson gravely, holding the door wide open for him to enter.

My lord! Joseph's heart missed a beat. He stared at the new-comer with reverence. This was Lord Colchester, who had been Speaker of the House of Commons, and whom Dr. Clark had described as a connoisseur and a patron of artists. Then his excitement turned suddenly to depression. What wretched luck to have arrived at the same time as this great gentleman! He had experience enough of fellow-artists in London to know that when a wealthy patron appeared other considerations would be ignored. Lord Colchester was expressing a wish to see a group ordered by the Duke of Devonshire. Joseph made a wry face and turned towards the door, which still stood open. This was the moment when an unknown young artist withdrew quietly, relieving his host of an embarrassingly alien presence.

He turned rather self-consciously at the door, meaning to bid them a courteous farewell before leaving with as much dignity as he could. But at that moment Gibson looked up and saw that he was about to go. Joseph's words of farewell were checked as he came quickly across and caught him by the arm, apologizing in the most charming manner for not having introduced his two visitors before. He presented Joseph to Lord Colchester and pressed them both to come into his studio.

Lord Colchester looked at everything, even the casts from
nature—hands, legs and arms. Joseph soon lost his unaccustomed
shyness when he found that Gibson showed him exactly the same
attention as he did Lord Colchester. His lordship admired the
clay model of a sleeping shepherd boy, and Gibson admitted that
it was the first really important work he had done in Rome from
his own design.

"I copied Nature pretty close," he said with a grave smile.
Then he quoted Canova's advice to him. "'At the same time as
working from the life go constantly to look at the antique.'[1] How
I wish that I had been born in the days of Praxiteles! I am a
Welshman, but with a soul panting after the perfection of the
immortal sculptors of Hellas."

Then they all came to a halt before the "Mars and Cupid,"
which stood seven feet high. This was the group that the young
Duke of Devonshire had ordered in marble for Chatsworth.
Joseph thought it very fine. After admiring it from every angle
Lord Colchester took his leave, arranging to come again, with a
friend, the following day. Joseph did not like to leave at the
same time as his lordship, so remained standing awkwardly in the
studio. Gibson came back, smiling, and began to question Joseph
about his plans.

"You will find Rome very different from London," he told
him. "Rome above all other cities has a peculiar influence on
the real student. It is *the* University of Art, where art is the
principal subject both of thought and of conversation."[2] He
went on to say how different were the relations of artists with
each other in Rome as compared to England. "Every young
sculptor in England bungles his way as he can. They do not
visit each other's studios, which in Rome is the universal practice.[3]
I always ask for criticism from artists who visit my studio, and when
I go to them, they expect me to point out any faults in their works.
I believe the painters do the same with their cartoons."[4]

They talked a little longer and then Joseph left. Gibson
begged him not to scruple to let him know if there was any way
in which he could help him.

So anxious was Joseph to tell Keats about Gibson's behaviour
that he almost ran back to the Piazza di Spagna. He found his
friend puzzling out an Italian book.

[1] *Biography of John Gibson, R.A.*, p. 50.   [2] *Ibid.*, p. 55.
[3] *Ibid.*, p. 105.   [4] *Ibid.*, p. 221.

"It was a revelation to me, Keats!" he cried, when he had described the scene at the studio. "Making money is all that artists in London think about. But if Gibson, who is a great artist, can afford to treat a poor and unknown painter in this way, then Rome is the place for me!"

Keats was delighted. "A first treat to humanity," he said with his sad smile.[1] Then his expression became more serious and he said that it was time they discussed together Severn's plans for the future. He must start at once upon a picture. He must make at least one sketch that very day. No time must be lost, especially if he treasured some hope of winning the Academy's three-year pension for a travelling student. Knowing Joseph's optimistic nature, he went on to warn him against over-confidence. In the first place, the Academy Council, who were well known to be a lot of touchy old gentlemen, might consider it unsuitable to award the travelling pension to an artist who had already managed to get to Rome without their help. In the second place, he had reason to believe that Severn's winning the Gold Medal had made him many enemies among his fellow-artists in London.

Joseph agreed ruefully, and after a moment's hesitation Keats told him what he had heard at a gathering of artists in London. He had been taken by Hilton to dine with some other artists at de Wint's house. The conversation turned to the recent award of the Academy's Gold Medal after so many years. One of the company scornfully explained that the picture was very inferior, but that as the artist was an old fellow and had made frequent attempts for the prize, the Council had given the medal out of pity, and not for any merit. Keats awaited a flat contradiction from one of the three artists present, besides Hilton, who knew the truth. It was not forthcoming. He had then expressed his disgust at so mean a lie. He declared that he would no longer sit at the table with traducers and snobs; that he knew the winner intimately, had seen the picture and recognized its merits; that, as they well knew, Severn was a young man and the picture his first attempt for a prize of any kind. He had then risen from the table and abruptly left the party.[2] As he described the scene to Joseph, he seemed to live it again. The generous resentment that injustice never failed to rouse in him made his eyes flash, and he seemed to increase in stature.

It was a shock to Joseph to realize the malice his triumph had aroused, but he was deeply touched by Keats's loyal championship and he made a fresh resolve to be worthy of it.

[1] Sharp, *op. cit.*, p. 65.　　　　[2] *Ibid.*, p. 66.

Things went on well enough for the first month after their arrival. Keats seemed to be getting a little stronger, and although Dr. Clark would not yet allow him to visit any of the great monuments of Rome, he was able to stroll on the Piazza in the mild autumn weather, and even to ride about on a little pony. Joseph hired a piano for seven *scudi* a month and would play to him. Kind Dr. Clark lent them some books of music. Among them was a collection of Haydn's symphonies, which proved a delight to Keats. As Joseph sat playing he exclaimed, "This Haydn is like a child, for there is no knowing what he will do next!" [1]

He was strong enough to take a very definite interest in their food. Like everyone living in lodgings in Rome, they had their dinner sent in to them from a *trattoria*. The dishes were brought in a large basket, lined with tin, and the food was kept hot by a little charcoal stove inside. In spite of frequent complaints, the food sent them was so badly cooked as to be almost uneatable, although it was by no means cheap. One day Keats told Joseph that he would tolerate it no longer. He refused to say what he was going to do, but when the porter came as usual with the basket, and was beginning to set the food out on the table, Keats opened the window, which was over the Spanish Steps, and taking each dish, one after the other, emptied the contents deliberately out of the window. He then quietly, but very decidedly, pointed to the basket, which the porter took away without a word.

"Now," said he, "you'll see, Severn, that we'll have a decent dinner." [2]

He was right. In less than half an hour an excellent dinner appeared. The food continued to be equally good on subsequent days, and no mention was made of the rejected dinner on their account.

About this time they made the acquaintance of a young English officer, Lieutenant Elton, who, though tall and handsome, was, like Keats, consumptive. He joined them in their strolls. The fashionable promenade on the Pincio was their favourite place for exercise, as it was sheltered from the north wind, and at first they were always a trio, because, until Keats seemed really better, Joseph could not bring himself to leave him, even to work. The sunny air seemed to give him a certain ease, and as the weather continued warm he was able to walk out every day, although he could only go a very short distance. Sometimes, in the soft

[1] Sharp, *op. cit.*, p. 67.   [2] *Ibid.*, p. 67.

Roman sunshine, Keats would seem almost like his old self, but he was always liable to sudden moods of deep dejection when he could no longer drive away the nightmare shadows that surrounded him.

"I have an habitual feeling of my real life having passed," he wrote to Charles Brown, "and that I am leading a posthumous existence." Any reminder of the happiness he had known was agony to him. "I am so weak (in mind) that I cannot bear the sight of any handwriting of a friend I love so much as I do you. Yet I ride the little horse, and, at my worst, even in quarantine, summoned up more puns, in a sort of desperation, in one week than in any year of my life. There is one thought enough to kill me; I have been well, healthy, alert, etc., walking with her, and now the knowledge of contrast, feeling for light and shade, all that information (primitive sense) necessary for a poem, are great enemies to the recovery of the stomach. Dr. Clark is very attentive to me, he says there is very little the matter with my lungs, but my stomach, he says, is, very bad. . . . Severn is very well, though he leads so dull a life with me. . . . I can scarcely bid you goodbye, even in a letter. I always make an awkward bow."[1]

Soon something made them change the direction of their walks. On their way round the Pincio they had several times noticed a lady in a magnificent carriage. She was handsome, richly dressed, and carried herself with a haughty air. The three young men were much intrigued when they found that this was Napoleon's sister, Pauline Bonaparte, now Princess Borghese. She was a famous beauty, though no longer young, and lived in a splendid establishment apart from her husband. They had heard many stories of her private life, which was notorious, and, like everyone else, they had been to see the statue Canova had made of her, nude to the waist, which was publicly on show in Rome. Keats had dismissed it as "beautiful bad taste."[2]

When next the carriage passed them they all turned to gaze, and were disconcerted to find their interest more than returned. Her quick eye had lighted on the tall figure of Lieutenant Elton and her manner changed abruptly as her haughtiness vanished and she threw him a shamelessly coquettish glance. Every day she was on the watch for them, and her languishing glances, even though he thankfully acknowledged that they were not intended for him, so wrought upon Keats's nerves that he could not bear to stay.

[1] *Letters of John Keats*, pp. 525-527.   [2] Sharp, *op. cit.*, p. 82.

Poor Keats! Something in her behaviour had pierced his indifference and brought him intolerable thoughts of beauty and desire. He had always been intensely jealous. Fanny was so coquettish and fond of admiration. Even in the happy past he had reproached her for smiling on other men. What was she doing, now that he was separated from her? His nerves were so affected that they decided not to go again to the Pincio.

After this Keats and Elton would go for easy rides together—never very far, nor at a pace faster than a walk. Sometimes they would leave the city, by the Porta del Popolo, and ride slowly along the banks of the Tiber. These expeditions left Joseph free to go to the Vatican to study at the feet of Michelangelo and Raphael. He could make sketches of buildings and of ruins, and once he risked his neck climbing to a ledge of the Colosseum to pick a wallflower, that he might show Keats how it had scented all the air.[1]

When they sat indoors Joseph would work on a picture to submit for the Academy pension. He knew that it gave Keats pleasure to see him thus employed, for one of his constant anxieties was the thought of the sacrifice Severn had made to accompany him to Rome, and he feared lest his own misfortunes should involve his friend. For Joseph's sake he would force a gaiety and humour which he did not feel, and would try to interest himself in learning Italian, and even in ideas for a poem which he should write when he felt stronger. But then some random word or thought would strike his defences from him and deliver him, powerless, to the dark enemies he was fighting.

Thus when he brought home a volume of poems by Alfieri, the first words that he read were too much his own, and he threw the book away and would read it no more.

> *Misera me ! sollievo a me non resta*
> *Altro che'l pianto, ed il pianto è delitto.*
>
> Unhappy me! there is no comfort left for me
> Except weeping, and weeping is a crime.[2]

Another evening Joseph was extolling his favourite Tasso. Keats, translated for a moment from the present, said that he "anticipated he should become a greater poet if he were allowed to live." [3] But immediately he shook his head and said how cruel it was to die before he had completed anything great.

"If I had had time I would have made myself remembered." [4]

[1] Sharp, *op. cit.*, pp. 82-83.   [2] *Ibid.*, p. 68.
[3] *Ibid.*, p. 83.   [4] *Letters of John Keats*, p. 468.

When his sufferings were great, Joseph found that music soothed him, and he would sit at the hired piano and play until the fretted nerves were eased.

But in spite of these words of despair, on the whole he seemed calmer and even a little more hopeful, until with tragic suddenness his malady roused and sunk its claws into him again.

CHAPTER VIII

JOSEPH TELLS HIS OWN STORY

December 14th, 1820.

I fear poor Keats is at his worst. A most unlooked for relapse has confined him to his bed, with every chance against him. It has been so sudden on what I thought convalescence, and without any seeming cause, that I cannot calculate on the next change. I dread it, for his suffering is so great, so continued, and his fortitude so completely gone, that any further change must make him delirious. This is the fifth day, and I see him get worse.

December 17th, 4 A.M.

Not a moment can I be from him. I sit by his bed and read all day, and at night I humour him in all his wanderings. He has just fallen asleep, the first sleep for eight nights, and now from mere exhaustion. I hope he will not wake till I have written, for I am anxious that you should know the truth; yet I dare not let him see I think his state dangerous. On the morning of this attack he was going on in good spirits quite merrily, when, in an instant, a cough seized him, and he vomited two cupfuls of blood. In a moment I got Doctor Clark, who took eight ounces of blood from his arm—it was black and thick. Keats was much alarmed and dejected. What a sorrowful day I had with him! he rushed out of bed and said, "this day shall be my last"; and but for me most certainly it would. The blood broke forth in similar quantity the next morning, and he was bled again. I was afterwards so fortunate as to talk him into a little calmness and he soon became quite patient. Now the blood has come up in coughing five times. Not a single thing will he digest, yet he keeps on craving for food. Every day he raves he will die from hunger and I feel obliged to give him more than he was allowed. His imagination and memory present every thought to him in horror; the recollection of "his good friend Brown," of "his four happy weeks spent under *her* care," of his sister and brother. Oh! he will mourn over all to me whilst I cool his burning forehead, till I tremble for his intellect. How can he be "Keats" again after all this? Yet I may see it too gloomily since each coming night I sit up adds its dismal contents to my mind.

Dr. Clark will not say much; although there are no bounds to his attention, yet he can with little success "administer to a mind diseased." All that can be done he does most kindly, while his lady, like himself in refined feeling, prepares all that poor Keats takes, for in this wilderness of a place, for an invalid, there was no alternative. Yesterday Dr. Clark went all over Rome for a certain kind of fish, and just as I received it, carefully dressed, Keats was taken with spitting of blood.

We have the best opinion of Dr. Clark's skill: he comes over four or five times a day, and he has left word for us to call him up, at any moment, in case of danger. My spirits have been quite pulled down. Those wretched Romans have no idea of comfort. I am obliged to do everything for him.[1]

December 24th.

Keats has changed somewhat for the worse—at least his mind has much, very much—and this leaves his state much the same and quite as hopeless. Yet the blood has ceased to come; his digestion is better, and but for a cough he must be improving, that is, as respects his body. But the fatal prospect of consumption hangs before his mind's eye, and turns everything to despair and wretchedness. He will not hear a word about living—nay, I seem to lose his confidence by trying to give him this hope, for his knowledge in internal anatomy enables him to judge of every change accurately, and adds largely to his torture. He will not think his future prospects favourable. He says the continued stretch of his imagination has already killed him. He will not hear of his good friends in England, except for what they have done—and this is another load; but of their high hopes of him, his certain success, his experience, he will not hear a word. Then the want of some kind hope to feed his voracious imagination. . . .[2]

Letter from Haslam received by Joseph about Dec. 24th.

. . . Why have you not kept your diary? I ask you solemnly, for no one thing on earth can give such satisfaction at home as such minute detail as you set out with. If you have discontinued it, in God's name resume it, and send it regularly to me. *Do this,* Severn, tho' at some sacrifice of your inherent dislike of order and of obligation to do a thing—do it, if but because I ask it. . . . Tom

[1] Letter to Mrs. Brawne ; quoted Sharp, p. 69.
[2] Letter to Taylor, Dec. 24th, 1820 ; quoted Sharp, *op. cit.*, p. 80.

has several times called on me, and I understand your father has at last become tolerably reconciled.[1]

January 11th, 1821.   1 o'clock morning (finished 3 A.M.).

. . . Little did I think what a task of affliction and danger I had undertaken, for I thought only of the beautiful mind of Keats, my attachment to him, and his convalescence. In the first fortnight of this attack his memory presented to him everything that was dear and delightful, even to the minutiae, and with it all the persecution, and I may say villainy, practised upon him—his exquisite sensibility for everyone save his poor self—all his own means and comfort expended on others almost in vain. These he would contrast with his present suffering, and say that all was brought on by them, and he was right. Now he has changed to calmness and quietude, as singular as productive of good, for his mind was most certainly killing him. He has now given up all thoughts, hopes, or even wish for recovery. His mind is in a state of peace from the final leave he has taken of this world and all his future hopes; this has been an immense weight for him to rise from. He remains quiet and submissive under his heavy fate. Now, if anything will recover him, it is this absence of himself. I have perceived for the last three days symptoms of recovery. Doctor Clark even thinks so. Nature again revives in him—I mean where art was used before; yesterday he permitted me to carry him from his bedroom to our sitting room—to put clean things on him and to talk about my painting to him.

For three weeks I have never left him—I have sat up all night— I have read to him nearly all day and even in the night—I light the fire—make his breakfast, and sometimes am obliged to cook— make his bed, and even sweep the room. I can have these things done, but never at the time when they must and ought to be done—so that you will see my alternative; what enrages me most is making the fire—I blow—blow for an hour—smoke comes fuming out—my kettle falls over the burning sticks—no stove—Keats calling me to be with him—the fire catching my hands and the door bell ringing; all these to one quite unused and not at all capable—with the want of even proper material— come not a little galling. But to my surprise I am not ill—or even restless—nor have I been all the time; there is nothing but what I will do for him—there is no alternative but what I think

[1] Quoted Sharp, *op. cit.*, p. 72.

and provide myself against—except his death—not the loss of him—I am prepared to bear that—but the inhumanity, the barbarism, of these Italians. So far I have kept everything from poor Keats; but if he did know but part of what I suffer from them and their cursed laws, it would kill him. Just to instance one thing among many. News was brought to me the other day that our gentle landlady had reported to the police that my friend was dying of consumption. Now their law is—that every individual thing, even to the paper on the walls, in each room the patient has been in, shall without reserve be destroyed by fire, the loss to be made better than good by his friends. This startled me not a little, for in our sitting room where I wanted to bring him, there is property worth about £150, besides all our own books, etc.—invaluable. Now my difficulty was to shift him to this room and let no one know. This was a heavy task from the unfortunate manner of the place; Our landlady's apartments are on the same floor with ours—her servant waits on me when it pleases her, and enters from an adjoining room.

I was determined on moving Keats, but what would be the consequence? The change was most essential to his health and spirits, and the following morning I set about accomplishing it. In the first place I blocked up their door so as they could not enter, then made up a bed on the sofa, and removed my friend to it. The greatest difficulty was in keeping all from him; I succeeded in this, too, by making his bed, and sweeping the room where it is and going dinnerless with all the pretensions of dining, persuading him that their servant had made his bed and I had been dining. He half suspected this, but as he could not tell the why and the wherefore, there it ended. I got him back in the afternoon and no one save Doctor Clark knew about it. Doctor Clark still attends him with his usual kindness, and shows his good heart in everything he does; the like of his lady—I cannot tell which shows us the most kindness. *I* even am a mark of their care—mince pies and numberless nice things come over to keep me alive. But for their kindness I am afraid we should go on very gloomily. My eyes are beginning to be unruly and I must write a most important letter to our President, Sir Thomas Lawrence, before I suffer myself to go to sleep. Poor Keats cannot see any letters, at least he will not—they affect him so much and increase his danger. The two last I repented giving, he made me put them into his box—un-read.

3 *o'clock morning.* I have just looked at him—he is in a beautiful

sleep; in look he is very much more like himself—I have the greatest hope of him.[1]

Jan. 15*th*, 1821.

Poor Keats has just fallen asleep—I have watched him and read to him to his very last wink—he has been saying to me "Severn I can see under your quiet look immense twisting and contending—you don't know what you are reading—you are enduring for me more than I'd have you—O that my last hour was come—what is it puzzles you now—what is it happens?" I tell him that "nothing happens—nothing worries me—beyond his seeing—that it has been the dull day." Getting from myself to his recovery—and then my painting—and then England—and then—but they are all lies—my heart almost leaps to deny them—for I have the veriest load of care that ever came upon these shoulders of mine. For Keats is sinking daily—perhaps another three weeks may lose me him for ever.—This alone would break down the most gallant spirit—I had made sure of his recovery when I set out. I was selfish and thought of his value to me—and made a point of my future success depend on his candour to me—this is not all—I have prepared myself to bear this now—now that I must and should have seen it before—but Torlonia's the bankers have refused any more money—the bill is returned unaccepted—"No effects" and I to-morrow must—aye must—pay the last solitary crown for this cursed lodging place—yet more should our unfortunate friend die—all the furniture will be burnt—bed sheets—curtains—and even the walls must be scraped—and these devils will come upon me for £100 or £150—the making good—but above all this noble fellow lying on the bed is dying in horror—no kind hope smoothing down his suffering—no philosophy—no religion to support him—yet with all the most gnawing desire for it—yet without the possibility of receiving it. . . .

I know not what may come with to-morrow—I am hedg'd in every way that you look at me—if I could leave Keats for a while every day I could soon raise money by my face painting—but he will not let me out of his sight—he cannot bear the face of a stranger—he has made me go out twice and leave him solus. I'd rather cut my tongue out than tell him that money I must get—that would kill him at a word—I will not do anything that may add to his misery. For I have tried on every point to leave him for a few hours in the day but he won't unless he is left alone—this

[1] Letter to Mrs. Brawne; quoted Sharp, p. 77.

won't do—nor shall not for another minute whilst he is John Keats.

Yet will I not bend down under these—I will not give myself a jot of credit unless I stand firm—and will too—you'd be rejoiced to see how I am kept up—not a flinch yet—I read, cook, make the beds, and do all the menial offices—for no soul comes near Keats except the Doctor and myself—yet I do all this with a cheerful heart—for I thank God my little but honest religion stays me up all through these trials. I'll pray to God to-night that He may look down with mercy on my poor friend and myself. I feel no dread of what more I am to bear but look to it with confidence.[1]

My hopes of being kept by the Royal Academy will be cut off unless I send a picture by the spring. I have written to Sir T. Lawrence. I have got a volume of Jeremy Taylor's works, which Keats has heard me read to-night. . . . Dr. Clark is still the same though he knows about the bill; he is afraid the next change will be to diarrhoea. Keats sees all this—and his knowledge of anatomy makes every change tenfold worse. He cannot read any letters, he has made me put them by him unopened. They tear him to pieces—he dare not look on the outside of any more.[2]

Now I saw that the doctor no longer had any hope, for he ordered the scanty food of a single anchovy a day, with a morsel of bread. He had no hope for himself save a speedy death, and this now seemed denied to him, for he believed that he might be doomed to linger on all through the spring. His despair was more on my account, for, as he explained, his death might be a long lingering one, attended with a slow delirious death-stage. This was in apprehension his greatest pain, and having been foreseen had been prepared for. One day, tormented by the pangs of hunger, he broke down suddenly and demanded that this "foreseen resource" should be given him. The demand was for the phial of laudanum I had bought at his request at Gravesend. When I demurred, he said to me that he claimed it as his own and as his right, for, he added with great emotion, "As my death is certain I only wish to save you from the long miseries of attending and beholding it. It may yet be deferred, and I can see that you will thereby be stranded through your lack of resources, and

---

[1] Letter to Haslam ; quoted Colvin, *op. cit.*, p. 508.
[2] Sharp, *op. cit.*, p. 91.

that you will ruin all your prospects. I am keeping you from your painting, and as I am sure to die, why not let me die now? I have now determined to take this laudanum, and anticipate a lingering death, while emancipating you." Of course I was horrified, and tried in every way to explain the madness of the act, and to urge the cruelty it would evince to all his friends and indifference to their efforts for him. Again and again I urged this, affirming my right as the principal of these friends, and assuring him that I should never be tired of him or of my ministrations, and that even on the score of my immediate prospects I was in no fear of perdition, for I expected the student's pension from the Royal Academy. This somewhat calmed him, but as I still refused to let him have the laudanum he became furious. He even supplicated me with touching pathos, and with equally touching eloquence described the manner of his death by continued diarrhoea; but on my persistent refusal he grew more and more violent against me, and I was afraid he might die in the midst of his despairing rage. And yet in all this there was no fear of death, no want of fortitude or manliness, but only the strong feeling on my account to which he regarded himself and his dying as secondary.

So for long we contended—he for his death, and I for his life. I told Dr. Clark about the bottle of laudanum and he took it away with him. This was on the second day of our sore contention, and when he learned what I had done Keats became silent and resigned, and sank into solemn seriousness. 'Twas evident that the physician was powerless to mislead the great intelligence the invalid had of his own case. Dr. Clark came to see him many times a day, and it was an awful sound and sight to see Keats look round upon the Doctor when he entered, with his large increasing hazel eyes (for as his face decreased his eyes seemed to enlarge and shine with unearthly brightness), and ask in a deep pathetic tone, "How long is this *posthumous* life of mine to last?" Ever after the loss of the laudanum he talked of his life as posthumous.

Now that his face was so sunk and pale, those hazel eyes became more prominent and less human; indeed at times, owing to the intelligence of Keats when he was questioning Dr. Clark, his eyes had the abstract expression of a supernatural being, and he evidently knew well all that was passing in the Doctor's mind, although the latter was unable to venture a word. After a week of those tragic scenes (and daily Keats asked Doctor Clark the same question as to how long his posthumous life was to last) he became somewhat more calm, and harrowed me by recounting the minutest details of his approaching death.[1]

On finding me inflexible in my purpose of remaining with him, he tranquilly said that he was sure why I held up so patiently was owing to my Christian faith, and that he was disgusted with himself for ever appearing before me in such a savage guise; that he now felt convinced how much every human being required the support of religion that he might die decently. "Here am I," said he, "with desperation in death that would disgrace the commonest fellow. Now, my dear Severn, I am sure, if you could get me some of the works of Jeremy Taylor to read to me, I might become *really* a Christian, and leave this world in peace."[2]

Dr. Clark succeeded in obtaining a copy of Jeremy Taylor's *Holy Living and Dying*, and thereafter I read daily to poor Keats, both morning and evening, from this pious work, and he received great comfort. When he became restless, and when he was willing, I prayed by him, and so a great change and calmness grew upon him, and my task was much lightened. If I had no longer any hope in the prolongation of his life, yet the gentle Christian spirit beginning to soften the rigour of his dying, relieved me more than I can well account for.

He kept continually in his hand a polished, oval, white cornelian, the gift of his widowing love, and at times it seemed his only consolation, the only thing left to him in this world clearly tangible. Many letters which he was unable to read came for him. Some he allowed me to read to him, others were too worldly—for, as he said, he had "already journeyed far beyond them." There were two letters for which he had no words, but he made me understand that I was to place them on his heart within his winding-sheet.[3]

Jan. 28th. 3 o'clock M.

Drawn to keep me awake—a deadly sweat was on him all this night.

(Picture.)[4]

Feb. 11th.

He has been confined to his bed two months, during which time I have scarce ever left him, except just for a run out for a

---

[1] Sharp, p. 84.
[2] Joseph Severn, "On the Vicissitudes of Keats's Fame": an article published in the *Atlantic Monthly*, 1863.   [3] Sharp, *op. cit.*, p. 91.
[4] See drawing facing page 65.

mouthful of fresh air. But no more of this letter on a subject so sad. I am writing to keep up my spirits, therefore I must not write of this. I am trying to paint a picture for the Royal Academy. This picture will be the same size as the last. I have a daily visit from the Architectural Student who is now here from the Royal Academy. His time expires in July next and he seems certain I shall succeed him. He says it depends entirely on myself. Very well does it. Then I shall continue as I did with my last picture, and do my best to be away from you three years. Three years! O how can I bear it![1]

12th February, 1821.

I have kept him alive by these means week after week, He had refused all food, but I tried him every way—I left him no excuse. Many times I have prepared his meals six times over, and kept from him the trouble I had in doing it. I have not been able to leave him, that is, I have not dared to do it but when he slept. Had he come here alone he would have plunged into the grave in secret— we should never have known one syllable about him. This re-flection alone repays me for all I have done. It is impossible to conceive what the sufferings of this poor fellow have been. Now he is still alive and calm. If I say more I shall say too much. Yet at times I have hoped he would recover, but the Doctor shook his head, and Keats would not hear that he was better,—the thought of recovery is beyond everything dreadful to him. We now dare not perceive any improvement, for the hope of death seems his only comfort. He talks of the quiet grave as the first rest he can ever have. I can believe and feel this most truly. In the last week a great desire for books came across his mind. I got him all the books at hand and for three days this charm lasted on him, but now it is gone. Yet he is very calm—he is more and more reconciled to his fortunes.

Feb. 14th.

Little or no change has taken place in Keats since the commence-ment of this, except this beautiful one, that his mind is growing to great quietness and peace—I find this change has its rise from the increasing weakness of his body, but it seems like a delightful sleep to me. I have been beating about in the tempest of his mind so long. To-night he has talked very much to me, but so easily that he at last fell into a pleasant sleep—he seems to have comfortable dreams without nightmare. This will bring on some change—it cannot be worse, it may be better. Among the many things he has

[1] Letter to his sister Maria. (Keats House.)

requested of me to-night, this is the principal, that on his grave shall be this—

"Here lies one whose name was writ in water." . . .

Since, a letter has come. I gave it to Keats, supposing it to be one of yours, but it proved sadly otherwise. The glance of that letter tore him to pieces. The effects were on him for many days—he did not read it—he could not, but requested me to place it in his coffin together with a purse and a letter (unopened) of his sister, since which time he has requested me not to place *that letter* in his coffin, but only his sister's purse and letter with some hair. Then he found many causes of his illness in the exciting and thwarting of his passions, but I persuaded him to feel otherwise on this delicate point. In his most irritable state he sees a friendless world with everything that his life presents, particularly the kindness of his friends, tending to his untimely death. I have got an English nurse to come two hours every other day; so that I have quite recovered my health, but my nurse after coming three times has been taken ill to-day—this is a little unfortunate as Keats seems to like her. You see I cannot do anything until poor Keats is asleep: this morning he has waked very calm—I think he seems somewhat better. He has taken half a pint of fresh milk; the milk here is beautiful to all the senses—it is delicious—for three weeks he has lived on it, sometimes taking a pint and a half a day.

The Doctor has been—he thinks Keats worse.—He says the expectoration is the most dreadful he ever saw—never met an instance when a patient was so quickly pulled down. Keats's inward grief must have been beyond any limit—his lungs are in a dreadful state. His stomach has lost all its power—Keats says he has fretted to death—from the first drops of blood he knew he must die.[1]

Four days before Keats died the change was so great that I passed dark moments of dread. He was aware of it himself. He made me lift him up in the bed many times. The apprehension of death was strong upon him, but its effect was only that of giving him comfort. He seemed only affected when the morning came and still found him alive, and he grieved inwardly until some further change made him hope that the night would bring death. The extreme brightness of his eyes with his poor pallid face were dreadful beyond description.[2]

[1] Letter to Mrs. Brawne; quoted Sharp, *op. cit.*, pp. 89-90.
[2] Letter, March 3rd, 1821; quoted Sharp, *op. cit.*, p. 95.

[During these terrible last days Joseph turned, whenever he
could, to his letter home. Whenever he felt his spirits beginning to
fail he would add a few lines and feel for a moment that he was back
with his family. "I am writing to keep up my spirits," he had
explained in the second instalment of his diary letter. "I cannot be
merry unless I be with you," he had written wistfully, "yet this
train of thought always helps me to be happy." The miniature of
the family stood on the table where he wrote, and he could raise
his eyes from the paper to gain comfort from those well-loved
faces.]

Feb. 19th.

I have just got your letter. O! I have shed tears and tears
of joy to find my dear home the same, all happy and all well. I
thank God for this greatest blessing. O! you cannot know the
delight it is to me. These are the particulars on which I can feed
my comfort. Tell father that the Marquis Canova and I had a
"pipe and pot together" at our first meeting, that he was exceedingly kind to me. The letter of recommendation gave me a most
friendly welcome. I mean our President's letter. He has promised
me his service at any time, and has already written to His Holiness
the Pope to permit me to study in any of his palaces. He seems to
think highly of my views, particularly from my receiving the Gold
Medal amid so much contest. This sets me very high here. There
is great expectation from my works. . . . Tell him that I continue
to think of painting from the English History when I return. I
hope to glean all the knowledge and beauties of foreign art, and
apply them to the Annals of my own Country. This has never
struck any painter. Is it not a lucky thought? I am now thinking
of my future on the plan of Raphael's pictures in the Vatican
Palace. One picture I have in mind is the Golden Age of England,
the Court of Queen Elizabeth, with portraits of all the distinguished
folk of her time, Sir W. Raleigh, Shakespeare, etc. etc. To do this
I hope to take a tour all over England, to collect the antiquities
and records for my purpose. Tell Father something tells me that
he will go with me on the tour. I know his love for all these old
ruins.

My object will be to propose my plan to some English Noble-
man. Father must not doubt my success in this, for there are
several painters here sent out by persons of fortune.

Tell my Mother that poor Keats has lived on bread and milk
for a month past. It is the only thing he can take. I get very

good dinners for twopence, with my half pint of wine (for three-pence) afterwards. I am looking very well and can assure her I am so. . . . I have every personal comfort possible, even to cabbage, altho' not my dear Mother's. Then I have pudding every day. "Ah! still *my* Joe," says my Mother. The puddings are beautiful, rice particularly; plum pudding delicious, they even call it by its English name. The fact is there are so many English here (about 200) that it is almost like London. . . .

[At dawn next day he again took refuge from the tragedy that was his constant companion. To escape from it for a few moments was his only hope of renewing his strength. His family—his prayers—and Keats's poor white face and enormous, glowing eyes. These were his life.]

Feb. 20th.

My good-natured fire says good-morning Maria, so while my kettle is boiling I will give you a little more gossip. Now sit down and make yourself comfortable. How do you do this morning? How are they all at home? How is Mother? Come now sit down and hear what I have got to say. Pull off your bonnet. You know you don't often see me. . . . At some future time I have no doubt my dear Maria but here I shall be able to realize a great deal of money by my Miniatures. You see all the English here are rich, and come to buy pictures. They think of nothing but pictures. I should have liked Father to hear me blow up a fellow just now in Italian. I gave it him in style.[1]

Feb. 22nd.

I have nothing to break this dreadful solitude but letters. Day after day, night after night, here I am by our poor dying friend. My spirits, my intellect, and my health are breaking down. I can get no one to change with me—no one to relieve me. All run away, and even if they did not Keats would not do without me. Last night I thought he was going. I could hear the phlegm in his throat; he bade me lift him up on the bed or he would die with pain. I watched him all night, expecting him to be suffocated at every cough. This morning, by the pale daylight, the change in him frightened me; he has sunk in the last three days to a most ghastly look. Though Dr. Clark has prepared me for the worst, I shall be ill able to bear to be set free even from this, my horrible

---

[1] Letter begun on Jan. 21st, 1821. (Keats House.)

situation, by the loss of him. I am still quite precluded from painting, which may be of consequence to me. Poor Keats has me ever
by him, and shadows out the form of one solitary friend; he opens
his eyes in great doubt and horror, but when they fall upon me they
close gently, open quietly and close again, till he sinks to sleep.
This thought alone would keep me by him till he dies; and why did
I say I was losing my time? The advantages I have gained by
knowing John Keats are double and treble any I could have won by
any other occupation.[1]

He turned to me suddenly on one occasion, and, looking fixedly
at me a long while with a fiery life in his eyes, painfully large and
glowing out of his hollow woe-wrought face, said, "Severn, I
bequeath to you all the joy and prosperity I have never had." I
thought he was wandering again; and soothed him gently. "This
is the last Christmas I shall ever see—that I ever want to see," he
said vehemently, an hour later, and as though no interval had
elapsed; "but you will see many, and be happy. It would be a
second death for me if I knew that your goodness now was your
loss hereafter." [2]

He made me go to see the place where he was to be buried,
and he expressed pleasure at my description of the locality of the
Pyramid of Caius Cestius, about the grass and the many flowers,
particularly the innumerable violets, also about a flock of goats
and sheep and a young shepherd—all these intensely interested him.
Violets were his favourite flowers, and he joyed to hear how they
overspread the graves. He assured me "that he already seemed to
feel the flowers growing over him." [3]

Again and again, while warning me that his death was fast
approaching, he besought me to take all care of myself, telling me
that "I must not look at him in his dying gasp nor breathe his
passing breath, not even breathe upon him." From time to time he
gave me all his directions as to what he wanted done after his death.
He told me with greater agitation than he had shown on any other
subject to put the letter which had just come from Miss Brawne
(which he was unable to bring himself to read, or even to open,)
with any other that should arrive too late to reach him in life,
inside his winding-sheet on his heart.[4]

[1] Letter to Haslam ; quoted Sharp, *op. cit.*, p. 92.   [2] *Ibid.*, p. 202.
[3] Severn's MS. " Recollections " ; quoted *ibid.*, p. 93.   [4] *Ibid.*, p. 93.

He is gone. He died with the most perfect ease. He seemed to go to sleep. On the 23rd, Friday, at half-past four, the approach of death came on.

"Severn—I—lift me up for I am dying. I shall die easy. Don't be frightened! Thank God it has come."

I lifted him up in my arms, and the phlegm seemed boiling in his throat. This increased until eleven at night, when he gradually sank into death, so quiet, that I still thought he slept— but I cannot say more now. I am broken down beyond my strength. I cannot be left alone. I have not slept for nine days, I will say the days since —— On Saturday a gentleman came to cast the face, hand and foot. On Sunday his body was opened; the lungs were completely gone, the doctors could not conceive how he had lived in the last two months. . . .[1]

[On Feb. 26th, while the sky was still dark, two carriages left the Piazza di Spagna. Day was breaking as they drew up at the foot of the Pyramid of Caius Cestius, and the mortal remains of John Keats were carried to the grave without delay. Because of the hostility towards Protestants in Rome the burial had to be over by daylight.

The English chaplain read the prayers; but Joseph Severn scarcely heard his voice. His health had suffered from the pro- longed strain and since Keats's death he had been prostrated. Only by a great effort of will had he been able to rise and dress himself to accompany his friend on his last journey. William Ewing, an English sculptor who had shown him great kindness during the last days of Keats's illness, had helped him to put on his clothes and had driven with him in the carriage. Now he supported him as he stood, swaying, at the graveside. Joseph was greatly affected by the thought that he was the only one present of Keats's devoted band of English friends. In the half- light he saw that Dr. Clark was there and four other gentlemen also, who by their clothes and bearing were his countrymen. Of those present at his interment only Joseph, Dr. Clark, and Ewing had known Keats at all, and, of these, only Joseph had known the real Keats in the full splendour of his fine intellect and ardent imagination.

Above them towered the grey pyramid—proud tomb of a Roman, dead for eighteen hundred years. Lichen had crept over

---

[1] Unfinished letter, never posted, to Charles Brown; quoted Sharp, *op. cit.*, p. 94.

the marble and wild green plants hung from the crevices. Behind it the dark battlements of the city walls stood sentinel over the silent burial-ground, where the daisies and violets clustered in the grass and ran unchecked over the foreign graves.

The earth fell upon the coffin-lid. Beneath it Fanny Brawne's letter lay, unopened, against her lover's heart.]

CHAPTER IX

LADY WESTMORELAND

(1821)

EVERY winter Rome was filled with a gay colony of distinguished English visitors. In their cumbrous travelling-coaches they came rumbling over the Alps, spending a few weeks in France or Switzerland *en route*. Rich and leisured, they came to wander round the ruins, to admire the statues and pictures, to enjoy the social life which they created, and to patronize the arts. With them they brought a retinue of servants, their own cooks and cooking utensils, their own bed-linen, sometimes even their own furniture. They would rent a palace, or part of one, from some impecunious Roman noble, and there they would settle down to entertain and divert themselves.

Their mornings would be passed in visits to the picture galleries, churches or ruins, or sometimes in expeditions to Tivoli or picnics in the Campagna. Or they would visit the studio of an artist or sculptor. Every afternoon there was the fashionable rendezvous on the Pincian Hill, where they rode or drove in their coaches round the promenade, stopping every now and again, when they met a friend, to take a stroll and enjoy the lovely views over Rome.

To the west, beyond the Tiber, they could see the archangel poised on the Castle of St. Angelo, and still further away the great dome of St. Peter's rose against the background of the purple hills. Then the sky would flush into a lovely Roman sunset, while from a hundred churches bells rang out the Ave Maria, signal for the crowds to melt away. There would be three or four assemblies to choose between in the evening. Every lady of fashion had at least one evening a week when she was at home to the *monde*.

The life they led was so many-sided that everyone, whether learned or frivolous, could find enjoyment. It was not surprising that so many English visitors of rank and fashion came to spend the winter in Rome.

Among these people Joseph suddenly found himself well known. The story of his devotion to an unknown young poet and the tragic death of his friend, so far from home, had spread rapidly among the English colony. And when the ladies discovered that the hero of this romantic story was a handsome young man, with easy, pleasant manners, their interest in him became even more marked.

He soon found himself with an invitation to dine out every day, but he would allow himself only an occasional acceptance, because he kept resolutely before him the necessity of winning the travelling pension from the Academy. To complete his picture soon was imperative, not only for his future as an artist, but for his very existence. The necessity of continuous work saved him from complete collapse after Keats had died. As spring matured into summer he rose at four or five o'clock and worked sometimes for as many as twelve hours a day on his picture. But, even so, he found that his countrymen did not ignore him. Seymour Kirkup, a fellow-artist with a small private income which made him independent of his work, had been introduced to him by Ewing at Keats's graveside, and he brought many distinguished visitors to Joseph's studio—Lord and Lady Ruthven, the Duke of Hamilton, and Lord William Russell amongst them.

Joseph was quite dazzled by the position in which he found himself. He wrote naïvely to his father:

"The attention I receive from the English Nobility is most encouraging. We are hand in hand, walking in the same places, living in the same houses." [1]

The Duchess of Devonshire, who was busily directing her private excavations in the Forum, told him that when his picture for the Academy was finished he was to come immediately to her house and they would at once return together in her carriage to view the completed masterpiece. [2]

Another evening he dined with Lord and Lady Ruthven. They were a party of fourteen, and when dinner was over, her ladyship proposed that they should all go to Mr. Severn's studio to see his "Alcibiades"—for Joseph had taken as his subject the moment when Alcibiades emerged from his villa, to be assassinated by the crowd which surged around it. The carriages were ordered, and the whole party drove off to No. 43 Via di San Isidoro and climbed the stone stairs to the second floor, where Joseph had his studio. The picture was finished by then, but it had to wait three weeks for the paint to dry before it could be rolled up and

[1] Letter, April 10th, 1821. (Keats House.)
[2] Letter to Sarah Severn, June 6th, 1821.

sent to England. The ladies were in transports and vowed that he must certainly succeed. Lady Rivers said it was astonishing how he could paint such a wonderful effect of fire and torches.

"Vastly pretty indeed, Mr. Severn."

"The colouring is excessively fine."

"It is altogether charming."

Although the adjectives were not very well suited to the tragic subject, Joseph's heart was warmed by the praise and by the pretty lips that uttered it.

But of all his new acquaintances, there was one who, by force of character, made the others seem no more than charming shadows. The Countess of Westmoreland was remarkable alike for her queenly beauty and her dazzling wit. "Her ladyship is a most superior woman," wrote Joseph to his sister, "having all the really English nobility in her and with much learning—she is about thirty-eight and is a very noble looking lady—the charm in her manner from the many accomplishments blended down in this lady of fashion is very astonishing. She is a beautiful musician and a poetess and seems to be quite acquainted with all the great persons of the time." [1]

He found this great lady infinitely charming and helpful. She proclaimed for him a great future. Sir Thomas Lawrence was an old acquaintance; she flattered herself that he had some little respect for her judgment in artistic matters; she would write to him about Joseph and his picture.

Often, when he was busily painting, Lady Westmoreland's carriage would draw up at the door, and a liveried footman would assist her ladyship to alight and escort her to the door of Joseph's studio. Sometimes she would spend as long as two hours talking with him. She brought a strange air of sophistication and distinction into his poorly-furnished room, with her extravagant bonnets, her fur cloaks and costly shawls. To her Joseph confided his ambition to become a historical painter, and she encouraged him by promising her aid. More experienced men than Joseph had been fascinated by her "wonderful talents and brilliant conversation." [2] To Joseph she seemed a goddess, and he was lost in admiration of her extraordinary vitality, her wit and arrogance.

In July his "Alcibiades" was sent off, but by an accident it missed the messenger at Ancona, and he was in despair lest it

[1] Letter to Sarah Severn, June 6th, 1821. (Keats House.)
[2] *Journal of Hon. Henry Edward Fox*, p. 229.

should not reach London in time for the meeting of the Academy Council. Lady Westmoreland arrived at his studio to find him in a state of depression, but she quickly talked him into good spirits. He wrote that night to his father, telling him what had happened to his picture and saying, "Lady Westmoreland writes by this post to Sir Thomas Lawrence, on my behalf, explaining the short notice I have had to send my picture and praying that the Council, should my picture not arrive in time, will consider my case at their next meeting. I cannot speak in terms too high of this lady's kindness and condescension." [1]

But her kindness did not end there. Nor did poor Joseph's anxieties. For, when his picture had reached London, it entirely disappeared. Again Joseph despaired, and again Lady Westmoreland wrote off to Sir Thomas, telling all the story of Keats's death and Joseph's hard work on his picture. At the same time she promised Joseph that, even if he did not win the pension, she would see that he got commissions for as many miniatures as he cared to paint. It must have been greatly due to her efforts that he was in fact awarded the pension, for when the picture was at last discovered, in a battered tin box in the cellars of the Royal Academy, it was found to have been damaged. But, before he had heard of his success, Lady Westmoreland had put another proposition to him.

Egypt was all the fashion in London that year, and in September she suggested to Joseph that he might accompany her there. She was full of preparations for the journey. She would be taking a savant to explain the mysteries of Ancient Egypt to her. It would be an excellent opportunity for Joseph to see the relics of another civilization. She had chosen him from all the artists in Rome for the honour of accompanying her.

Joseph was flattered at being thus singled out. It never occurred to him that there might be anything in his youth and good looks that could have commended him to her. To him she was a being from another world. But he kept his head, and after thinking it over, decided that he would be foolish to leave Rome just when he was beginning to do well there.

He told Lady Westmoreland of his decision when she was paying one of her visits to his studio. Her brow contracted, her dark eyes became stormy. She was not accustomed to being thwarted. She was usually able to impose her will on other people by her strength of purpose and her arrogant disregard of any

[1] Letter, July 21st, 1821. (Keats House.)

objections. When she failed to influence them she would resent
it bitterly, and often imagined that her friends had been prompted
by malicious ill-feeling against herself. Transfer to the enemy
camp could be surprisingly quick, and as she loved to manage
her friends' lives for them, sooner or later, in spite of her ex-
ceptional intelligence and charm, she would fall out with everyone.

She professed herself not satisfied with his refusal. His reasons
appeared insufficient for missing such a favourable opportunity.
Joseph saw that she was displeased, but in anything affecting his
art he would make no compromise. He told her that around
Rome there were many views and landscapes of which he was
anxious to make studies, so that if he returned to England they
would serve as backgrounds for future pictures. Then, as he
noted the impatience in Lady Westmoreland's demeanour, he
hurriedly added yet another reason, which was that a young artist
named Catherwood, whom he had known in England, had just
arrived in Rome, and that they had arranged to take rooms
together.

Lady Westmoreland questioned him about his friend, and
when Joseph had given a very favourable account of his abilities,
she asked graciously if Mr. Catherwood would not perhaps like to
come with Mr. Severn to Egypt. Joseph was taken aback.

"I—I have no doubt that Mr. Catherwood would feel himself
most honoured by your ladyship's suggestion. I am distressed at
not being able to take advantage of your ladyship's kindness
myself, but—Mr. Catherwood might go without me."

Lady Westmoreland rose impulsively from the rather hard
chair on which she had been sitting, and laid her hand, in its lilac-
coloured glove, on Joseph's arm.

"My dear Mr. Severn, I do not know this young man, but I
would take anyone of your commending, because I feel you
understand me."

She paused for a moment, while she gave him a long, earnest
look from her fine eyes, and then she turned and swept from the
studio.[1]

The following evening, at Ave Maria, Joseph and Mr. Catherwood presented themselves at the Villa Negroni. They were kept
waiting for some time before Lady Westmoreland appeared,
explaining that she had been making her toilette for the French
Ambassador's ball that evening. She was wearing a high-waisted

[1] Letter to Maria Severn, Sept. 15th, 1821. (Keats House.)

ball-dress of tulle over some shimmering golden material. On her head was a turban of gauze with a plume of golden osprey feathers standing stiffly up from her forehead. She wore pearl ear-rings and bracelets, and several rows of magnificent pearls were twisted round her neck. Her movements were graceful and deliberate— as they always were, unless she became agitated.

Joseph presented Mr. Catherwood to her. She was most charming. They talked about Egypt, and she seemed so well informed, and imparted her knowledge in such an agreeable manner, with such amusing little asides and references to contemporary personalities, that both young men were fascinated. As always, her conversation flitted unpredictably from one subject to another, and although they had begun by talking about Egypt, in a short time she was animatedly discussing the truth of the legend of the "masque de fer," and a few moments later was telling them how Lady Caroline Lamb and Lord Byron had met for the first time at her house in London.

As they were descending the stairs after they had taken their leave, Catherwood's admiration for this brilliant woman made him incoherent. Joseph's enthusiasm equalled his friend's, though he still held by his decision not to go to Egypt, and advised Catherwood, for the sake of his art, to stay in Rome. But his friend said that it was a wonderful opportunity, and perhaps the only one he would ever have, of going to Egypt. Travelling with a great lady, there would be such preparations made and so many servants accompanying them, that there would be no danger in the journey. Joseph argued that a knowledge of Rome was a necessary part of an artist's education. But he need not have worried about his friend.

Two days later, when they came home from a long walk round Rome, he found that Lady Westmoreland had been to his studio four times that morning, and had sent her servants to the café where she knew he usually dined.[1]

The landlady was just giving them this news when her ladyship returned again.

Her appearance was most striking. Her close-fitting pelisse was black, with embroidered trefoils down the front, and she wore a bonnet of black satin, surmounted by a plume of black ostrich feathers. A high triple ruff of white lace round her throat was the only light touch in her appearance.

[1] Letter to Maria, Sept. 19th, 1821.

Seeing their concern, she explained that she was in mourning for the Queen, and then, with great distress, added that she must postpone her journey to Egypt until another season. She required more servants. She was in despair at not being able to go to Egypt as she had intended. She had anticipated such pleasure and profit from the journey. But she particularly requested Mr. Severn to hold himself bound to accompany her next season—and, with a gracious smile, his friend Mr. Catherwood also.

Joseph at once replied that nothing would give him more pleasure. She appeared satisfied and her manner became calmer. She declared that she wished Mr. Severn to paint her portrait— a miniature. Again Joseph professed himself delighted and honoured.

"I have written to the Duke of Devonshire of your picture now in hand. He comes here next winter and could do much for you."

Joseph thanked her warmly and, when both young men had accepted an invitation to dine with her on Saturday, she left.[1]

All through that nerve-racking autumn she was unfailingly kind. First there was the anxiety about the picture getting to London in time, followed by the shock of its disappearance. Then, when at last it was found—he got the news in October—there was still the question of whether the Council would consider it. Every morning he awoke worrying about his chances. Every night his last thought was of the pension. Without it he must continue to live from day to day, from picture to picture, just making enough to exist, but with no prospect of security. And what would happen to him if he were ill, or if, when his present patrons left Rome, he could find no more to take their place? But it was only when he was tired that he felt like this. In the ordinary way, his confidence and optimism were unchanged. He refused to confine himself to miniatures only, from which he could always make a small, but steady income. He was determined to make his name as a painter of large historical pictures.

In spite of his many preoccupations, he had not forgotten Keats, and in his spare time he was painting a small full-length picture of him reading, as he had so often seen him at Wentworth Place, behind him the window opening on to the garden, where the old mulberry tree threw its shadow on the lawn. While he was working on this picture he received a package from Shelley,

---

[1] Letter to Maria, Sept. 19th, 1821.

who was still living at Pisa. Inside he found the first copy of *Adonais*, and with it a letter:

"DEAR SIR,—I send you the elegy on poor Keats—and I wish it were better worth your acceptance. You will see by the preface that it was written before I could obtain any particular account of his last moments. . . . I have ventured to express, as I felt, the respect and admiration which your conduct towards him demands. In spite of his transcendent genius, Keats never was, nor ever will be, a popular poet; and the total neglect and obscurity in which the astonishing remnants of his mind still lie, was hardly to be dissipated by a writer, who, however he may differ from Keats in more important qualities, at least resembles him in that accidental one, a want of popularity. I have little hope, therefore, that the poem I send you will excite any attention. . . ."

Joseph's eye ran rapidly over the rest of the letter, and the signature—

"Your most sincere and faithful servant,
PERCY B. SHELLEY."[1]

Then he opened the book and turned to the preface.

"He was accompanied to Rome," he read, "and attended in his last illness by Mr. Severn, a young artist of the highest promise, who, I have been informed, 'almost risked his own life, and sacrificed every prospect to unwearied attendance upon his dying friend.'

Had I known these circumstances before the completion of my poem, I should have been tempted to add my feeble tribute of applause to the more solid recompense which the virtuous man finds in the recollection of his own motives. Mr. Severn can dispense with a reward from 'such stuff as dreams are made of.' His conduct is a golden augury of the success of his future career— may the unextinguished Spirit of his illustrious friend animate the creations of his pencil, and plead against oblivion for his name!"

His eyes were wet with tears when at last he laid down the little book. He could not concentrate on his painting that morning. He had meant to finish off a picture he was painting for Sir William Drummond, but phantoms of Keats kept rising between his brush and the canvas. He could see Keats's face when he had first known him—the eager, vital expression—the glowing eyes—the wide, mobile mouth. How he had enjoyed and savoured

[1] Sharp, *op. cit.*, p. 118.

life. Then the face blurred and he saw him again during those last, terrible nights—ghastly white in the flickering candle-light. The hollow look of his eye-sockets where the lids drooped over his enormous eyes, the transparency of his skin, drawn tight over the high cheek-bones and nose. . . .

Joseph felt the tears in his eyes and, striding over to the wall, chalked in large letters, where his eyes would often see them, the last words of Shelley's preface:

"May the unextinguished Spirit of his illustrious friend animate the creations of his pencil, and plead against oblivion for his name."

Then he returned to his easel and set to work with fresh determination, pausing now and again to smile to himself as he read over the words he had chalked on the wall. Already he seemed to draw inspiration and comfort from them.[1]

Shelley was right in not expecting an immediate stir to be made by his poem. The only violent reaction was from Joseph's family, who were horrified to find his name in the writings of "that atheist, republican and free-liver." Letter after letter implored him to "break off all acquaintance with a man of such vile reputation as Shelley," [2] and prophesied nothing but ruin and disgrace if he persisted in such a friendship.

Still no letter came from the Royal Academy. All day he kept hard at his painting. He had commissions for many miniatures among the English nobility. Lady Westmoreland introduced him to everyone likely to serve him, and in such glowing terms that he was treated with great respect. He had also begun a large picture of Alexander—nine feet by six—which he hoped to be able to sell when it was finished.

He was working at this canvas on Christmas Eve. It was the same size as the picture of "Alcibiades" which he had sent home to the Academy. There was still no news of its success or failure. When the light began to fail he put away his brushes and, taking his coat from the chair, went sadly down the stairs, his feet ringing with a hollow clatter on the stone steps. He walked slowly to the Caffè Greco, where every evening he would dine, in company with some ten or eleven other English artists. He made his way slowly through the crowded, low-arched rooms. The place was full of smoke, and resounded with the clatter of plates and a strange medley of languages. It was the rendezvous of artists in Rome. Painters, sculptors and musicians of every race gathered there. Joseph

[1] Sharp, *op. cit.*, p. 121.   [2] *Ibid.*, p. 121.

found his friends and sat down, feeling tired and depressed and
a little home-sick. It was his second Christmas away from home.
He tried to picture what his family would be doing in Mason's
Court, and ate absent-mindedly, not speaking to anyone.

Richard Westmacott, a young sculptor and son of a Royal
Academician, whispered something to Kirkup and then ordered
a large bottle of the sour white wine which they usually drank.
When it came, Westmacott filled his glass and rose to his feet.

"Here's to Severn, the representative of the Royal Academy,"
he said, "and success to him!"

The toast was drunk with enthusiasm. Joseph was too dazed
to reply for a minute to the shouts of congratulation, but gradually
a warm wave of happiness surged through him as he realized that
the travelling pension was his.[1]

The next few days were a dream. Lady Westmoreland's
delight—Seymour Kirkup's Christmas dinner in his honour,
"with a plum pudding and plenty of music"—and finally the official
letter announcing that the pension awarded was £130 a year for
three years and £80 travelling expenses. Enclosed in the letter
was the unexpected gift of a draft to cover the expenses of his
journey to Rome. His first thought was to write to them all at
home, enclosing "£10 for Sarah to help with the rent. To my
father £5 to have a new coat, for my sake, or what he pleases, and
to Maria, £4 for a new pélisse and bonnet, and £1 to Charles for
fiddlesticks and music."

For three years he need have no anxieties.

[1] Letter to Maria, Dec. 26th, 1821.   (Keats House.)

CHAPTER X

MISS MONTGOMERIE

(*January* 1827—*October* 1828)

JOSEPH sat on the window-sill in his studio, one leg crossed over the other, and gazed out over Rome. He was waiting for Lady Westmoreland. He had found himself doing this very frequently during the last two years, for her ladyship had a complete disregard for time—except as a theory to be discussed with philosophers. Sometimes she would sleep all day and expect her friends to sit up with her all night.[1] She would not realize that even her brilliant conversation began to pall about two or three in the morning. However, Joseph had made it clear from the first that he would do anything to please her, except when it would interfere with his painting, and after several scenes she had accepted this.

Staring out over Rome, he thought of the last six years with wonder. His success had been so sudden that at times he could still scarcely believe that he, Joseph Severn, who was invited to every party in Rome, who in the season received invitations to as many as four dinners a day with carriages sent to fetch him, who talked with Dukes and even Princes and, better still, received commissions from them, was the same person as that impoverished young man who had arrived in Rome six years ago with a dying friend and no prospects.

The transition from obscurity to success had been so sudden that perhaps he was to be forgiven for his conviction that he must surely be a genius. Both his pictures and himself were in great demand. When he began to make money he bought himself new clothes, and now he was "quite dandyish." His complexion had darkened in the Italian sun and his figure had filled out. He held himself more erect and had more confidence in himself. He was strikingly handsome and a gay companion. His high spirits scarcely ever deserted him, he could tell a story amusingly, and his infectious enjoyment of everything he did made him much in demand for parties and picnics and expeditions to places outside the city. It was no wonder that many English ladies had lost their hearts to him, and many Italians too. As for Joseph, he was

[1] Sharp, *op. cit.*, p. 150; also *Journal of Henry Fox*, p. 229.

only too susceptible, but always a hard core of common sense
and self-interest, bred in him when he was a poor, struggling
artist with his way to make, prevented him from taking the
irrevocable step into matrimony.

There had been one occasion on which he had been very near
to it. Two charming young English girls, nieces of Lord Elgin,
had spent nearly two years in Rome with their widowed mother.
He had fallen in love with the elder sister, Maria, who was twenty-
three years old, very gentle and pretty. He had painted her
portrait, they had sung words from *Romeo and Juliet* together, to
music of his own composing, he had holidayed with them in
Naples and accompanied them in their visits to the Vatican. He
had felt at home with them, in a way that relieved the ache for
his own home and family. For although he loved his expeditions
into high society, and savoured his exchanges with titled acquaintances, it was a relief to spend a quiet evening with Maria and her
mother and sister. He would take his chalks down to their
lodgings and sit sketching, while Maria played the piano and her
mother did beautiful embroidery.

She reminded him of his own dear sister, Maria, and he was
tempted— Then Lady Westmoreland returned to Rome, and
beside her tempestuous, impulsive brilliance, her exquisite toilettes,
her air of sophisticated lady of fashion, poor Maria's attractions
began to seem rather insipid, and even her uncritical adoration a
little boring. Lady Westmoreland cajoled, provoked, fascinated,
flattered him, and his evenings were no longer spent in the homely
atmosphere of Maria's family.

The matter was finally decided for him by the mother's tragic
death and the sisters' departure for England almost immediately
afterwards. Joseph comforted them, made all the necessary
arrangements for their journey, did all he could to spare them
further anxieties, but he could not suppress a sense of escape and
of relief that he was still free.[1]

As he remarked later to Lady Westmoreland, with a comical
smile,

"I must confess to a gay and elastic temperament which makes
me suppose that marriage is not altogether my forte!" [2]

Her ladyship did not contradict him.

So many things had happened since he had been awarded the
pension. Although he had never been back to England he had

[1] *Letters*, July 5th, 1822; August, 1822; March 2nd, 1824; April 10th, 1824.
(Keats House.)   [2] Sharp *op. cit.*, p. 151.

seen quite a number of his old friends. Charles Brown had come to Florence, bringing his son—the result of his liaison with the fiery Irish maid at Wentworth Place. For a little time he had shared a house with Joseph in Rome, where his robust common sense had been invaluable. They had only disagreed on one subject. Joseph had confided in him his resolve to become a historical painter, and Brown had done his best to dissuade him. He said that the English did not really understand art, and that he would do far better to stick to portraits.

"If you continue to study portraits, both in miniature and in oils, crowds will be led by vanity to your door, and you will be rich and at ease in your mind. Look to facts. Who has succeeded in historical painting since Sir J. Reynolds? None, save West. I repeat, the English understand it not. What was Sir Thomas Lawrence's advice? Truly, it was wise. You are now the best miniature-painter we have. This is no compliment, you know it yourself." [1]

But Joseph only smiled. He did not fully appreciate his gift for miniature painting and, now that his success had convinced him that he was destined to be one of the great artists of his time, he was determined to move on to work more worthy of his talent.

He had made many friends among the artists in Rome; Gibson and he were very friendly and planned to hold a joint exhibition of pictures and sculptures when they returned to London. Eastlake, Kirkup and Ewing were all intimate friends, and Walter Savage Landor had stayed with him for a while. Then Leigh Hunt had turned up in Italy, with his ailing wife and ever-increasing family. Hunt was one of the arguments that Joseph used to himself whenever he felt a weakness for the married state. But he was delighted to be of service when Hunt wrote asking his help in the arrangements for the interment of Shelley's ashes. That had been an odd experience.

Soon after the arrival of Hunt's letter a strange, black-bearded seaman, Edward Trelawny, had appeared in Rome. He it was who had cremated Shelley's body on the seashore at Viareggio, with the white Alps towering above the beach and Elba shimmering across the sea. In the pocket of Shelley's coat was found a copy of Keats's last volume of poems, "doubled back," said Trelawny, "as if the reader, in the act of reading, had hastily thrust it away." [2]

Mrs. Shelley had wished her husband to be buried beside his

[1] Sharp, *op. cit.*, p. 108.   [2] *Life of Trelawny*, p. 236.

infant son, whose grave was in the Protestant cemetery in Rome,
but the Papal Government had forbidden any further interments
in the ground where Keats lay. So many of the heretics' tombs
had been defaced by the Catholic population that the English
residents had appealed for permission to surround them with a
wall. The Papal Government refused, on the pretext that . it
would spoil the view, but they made a new burial-ground quite
near, with a wall around it, and stationed soldiers there to defend
the Protestant graves.

As they could not get permission to bury Shelley's ashes
beside his son's grave in the old cemetery, Severn and Trelawny
decided that they must remove them both to the new. They
found the stone recording the brief life of Shelley's son, and
opened the grave beneath. To their horror there lay revealed a
skeleton fully five and a half feet long. A mistake must have
been made in the placing of the stone, but they dared not search
any further, for, as Joseph wrote to Brown, they were "in the
presence of many *respectful* but wondering Italians." [1]

So, in the end, poor Shelley's ashes lay alone. But Trelawny
bought a plot of ground so that, when his life was over, he might
lie beside his friend.

The bell at the front door clanged. That must be Lady
Westmoreland. As Joseph turned from the window, his eye ran
over the canvases which leaned against the walls all round the
room. To the left was a "Peasant Girl Praying to a Madonna"
which Prince Leopold had bought the other day when Lady
Westmoreland had brought him to the studio. His Royal Highness
had ordered another picture too. Against the opposite wall stood
an enormous picture, "The Vintage," with twenty-two figures of
Roman peasants painted in an Italian landscape. That had been
bought by the Duke of Bedford for £150 and was waiting to be
sent off to England, where it was to be hung in the next Exhibition.
He had nine pictures actually in hand, all ordered by different
patrons. Ironically, the only picture in his studio which had not
found a purchaser was one for which poor Maria had sat as model—
"Ferdinand and Miranda" he called it. Maria's face gazed up at
him from the canvas with a sweet, slightly insipid half-smile.

Yes, he thought, it was as well we did not marry. I have seen
so many melancholy examples of marriage that (when I am not
in love) I almost make up my mind to be an old fogey to the end

[1] Sharp, *op. cit.*, pp. 122-123.

of my days. I am so full of second thoughts that I think I shall be content to be married to my painting all my life.[1]

The bell rang again, more loudly. He gave a last, satisfied look over the evidence of his industry and hurried to open the door.

Lady Westmoreland stood outside, with a footman waiting deferentially a few steps behind her. She dismissed him with a nod and entered Joseph's apartment. It was very different from the studio where she had visited him in the Via di San Isidoro. Now he was living in the large upper storey of a suppressed monastery in the Vicolo dei Maroniti. Here he had six or seven rooms, one of which he used for the English Academy organized by himself as a humble imitation of the grander, State-subsidized French and Austrian Academies in Rome. The British Ambassador in Naples had contributed £100 towards expenses, and Sir Thomas Lawrence had sent £50 from his own pocket and a large portrait of George IV, which hung at one end of the room where as many as twelve or fourteen English artists would come of an evening to study.[2]

Next to this was his Painting Room, then an ante-room hung with original studies he had made. These all faced north. On the sunny side he had his bedroom, a small room with a fireplace for winter nights which he called his library, and, next to that, the room to which he led Lady Westmoreland. Lastly, on the roof, he had an observatory that gave him a panorama of Rome.

Lady Westmoreland subsided on to the chair Joseph brought forward, with a rustle of silken skirt. The room was some thirty feet long and well proportioned, and so sunny that, even in the winter, a fire was never necessary in the daytime. He had hung copies of pictures by Raphael, Titian and Rubens on the walls. The furniture, although not new, was handsome. Two large folding windows opened on to a balcony and gave a wonderful view over Rome.

"I have come to tell you about my musical party next week," said Lady Westmoreland. "I have decided that we two shall play Mozart's overture to 'Figaro' on the pianoforte. I have the music here and I will leave it with you."

She laid a scroll of music, tied with ribbon, on the table beside her.

"But—"

[1] Letters, Nov. 21st, 1825, and May 26th, 1827. (Keats House).
[2] Letter, Dec. 7th, 1822. (Keats House.)

"We shall do famously together," she added reassuringly, as she noticed Joseph's startled expression.

"B—but I do not think—I scarcely know how—in short, I could not do it," stammered Joseph.

He knew Lady Westmoreland's parties, and saw in his imagination the enormous rooms at the Palazzo Rospigliosi ablaze with candles, shimmering with silken dresses and nodding plumes—the largest room crowded with everyone of distinction in Rome, and all waiting for him, Joseph Severn, to play. No, it was too much.

"My nerves are too weak, Ma'am. I could not play with so many people watching me."

"Pretty vanity of you," Lady Westmoreland replied playfully, rising to her feet with a laugh. "For if we play together *I* shall be the person looked at—nobody will look at you." [1]

And, indeed, her appearance would compel attention anywhere —her tall, well-proportioned figure, and her wonderful carriage, the head and neck set proudly on her fine shoulders. Her complexion was still lovely, and her large, expressive eyes lit up a face of great intelligence and vivacity.

She raised her hand to silence any further objections.

"I will come to-morrow morning and we will try it together on your instrument."

She then enquired about the progress of his picture of an Italian fountain, to be the same size as "The Vintage," and the studies he had been making for the figures. Her interest in his work was so flattering and her comments so intelligent, that Joseph found himself handing her to her carriage without having made any further protest about the duet at her musical party.

As she was about to drive away, she leaned forward.

"Better still, come to the Palazzo Rospigliosi at Ave Maria, and we will try the overture then. Your friend Mr. Eastlake is coming, I believe."

Lady Westmoreland was now established in the Palazzo Rospigliosi for the winter.

Joseph gave up any hope of getting out of it, thanked her, and stood watching, divided between gloom and admiration, while the magnificent carriage, with its liveried coachman and footman, rolled off down the street.

Joseph and Eastlake were shown upstairs into one of the suite of small rooms where Lady Westmoreland usually received. When

[1] Letter to Charles Severn, Jan. 1st, 1827. (Keats House.)

she was entertaining large numbers of people the huge rooms below would be thrown open. The servant placed a large silver candelabra on the table, closed the shutters, drew the curtains and left them. Outside the bells were ringing over the city.

They made uneasy conversation, but kept breaking off as footsteps approached the door. Half an hour passed without anyone disturbing them. Then they heard a light step outside, the door opened and there entered a lovely girl. Her eyes, as she raised them modestly to Joseph, after making him a curtsy, were an intensely brilliant blue in her small oval face. They were large and well shaped, with delicately-traced eyebrows arching over them. Her mouth was small and curved, with a short upper lip. Her hair clustered in curls round her face and fell in ringlets on to her shoulders. Joseph noticed that it was that rare colour—a true brown, with a touch of red in its shadows. Her skin was exceptionally fair, and the effect of its whiteness in conjunction with her dark hair and brilliant blue eyes was most striking. A narrow blue velvet ribbon was threaded through her curls.

Joseph was so enchanted with her appearance that he did not hear what she was saying, and when she paused he had to beg her to repeat herself. Her voice was low and musical, with a soft Scottish intonation.

"Lady Westmoreland will not be able to receive you for some little while. She begs you to excuse her, and told me to endeavour to entertain you until she is ready."

Both Eastlake and Joseph murmured a polite reply to this stilted little speech, though they were more than a little astonished at a young lady, whom neither of them had ever seen before, being sent to entertain two young men entirely by herself.[1] However, she seemed to find nothing unusual in her position, and seating herself on a chair between them, she began the conversation with the greatest composure.

They were too polite to ask what they were longing to know— who she was, and what she was doing here. But Joseph set himself by dint of indirect questions to find out. Had she been long in Rome? Was her visit likely to be a long one? Until two months ago she had never left Scotland, she said. Now she had come to live with her guardian, Lady Westmoreland, and so her movements in the future depended entirely on her.

"They will incline then to be a little uncertain," said Joseph, laughing.

[1] Sharp, *op. cit.*, pp. 150-151.

E

The girl smiled restrainedly and turned the conversation. She was certainly an easy person to talk to, but Joseph, studying her face with quick secret glances, decided that her expression was not a happy one. He tried to put into words the impression he had from her manner. She seemed, although civil and agreeable, to be deliberately withdrawn from them. Her reserve seemed somehow a little strained, as though she were controlling her spontaneous reactions and keeping something in check.

This impression was strengthened by the way in which, when she was just in the middle of a sentence, she stopped abruptly, with a sudden, watchful look in her wide-set eyes. A firm footstep sounded outside the door. Lady Westmoreland swept in and extended a regal hand for Joseph and Eastlake to kiss. She made no reference to their long wait, but burst immediately into a voluble description of Hortense de Beauharnais, whom she had visited at the Villa Paulina earlier in the day. Her compelling personality took command of everyone in the room from the moment she entered. She spoke rapidly, telling them how the ex-Queen of Holland could talk of nothing but herself—the romances she had written, the drawings she had made, the beauties of her villa in Switzerland, and the number of German Princes who had been to see her. Joseph's eyes turned for a moment to the girl at his side. Lady Westmoreland caught his glance. She stopped short in the middle of her typically inconsequential and amusing flow.

"Ah, Miss Montgomerie has been with you. I trust she has not tired you. She had never left Scotland until a few weeks ago. I am endeavouring to educate her." She dismissed her with a nod. "You may go, Elizabeth."

Miss Montgomerie curtsied to the two young men and had just reached the door when Lady Westmoreland called her back.

"And for heaven's sake, child, never let me see you wear that dress again. It makes you look as white as a ghost—quite colourless."

A wave of colour rose into Miss Montgomerie's face and vanished, to leave her skin whiter than before, but she said nothing. Her eyes rested steadily on her guardian before she turned again to the door, which Joseph had opened for her.[1]

This was only the first of many similar humiliations of which Joseph was the unwilling witness. He hated to see Lady Westmoreland, who had always been so kind to him, treating her ward

[1] Sharp, *op. cit.*, pp. 150-151.

with contempt.[1] Miss Montgomerie never answered her back. She did as she was told with an ever-increasing air of unhappiness and desperate self-control which touched Joseph's heart.

Lady Westmoreland sent her on errands, like a servant, unaccompanied, through the streets of Rome. On one occasion, walking from the Vatican, he saw her emerge from a dark little shop. He quickened his step to catch up with her. Pieces of old brocade and embroidery were stretched out on the cobbles at the side of the road, weighted with a stone at either end, and the vendors, seeing a foreign lady, began to importune her to buy. Hands were stretched out clutching every sort of material, with a clamour of praise for colour and texture. Miss Montgomerie did not look at them at first, then she shook her head and Joseph heard her murmur something. Encouraged by this acknowledgment of their presence, the vendors redoubled their efforts. The noise became deafening. Several of them began to follow her along the street, pushing their wares in front of her face, shouting, pleading, whining at her. Miss Montgomerie walked faster and faster.

There were no footpaths in the Roman streets and the cobbles were uneven and covered with refuse. No Roman lady or gentleman would think of walking in their own city. Always they rode in carriages or on horseback. Miss Montgomerie was almost running now. Most of the salesmen had given up, but one, more persistent than the rest, was still keeping pace with her and, giving up hope of a sale, was becoming abusive. Joseph ran forward, and with threatening gestures and a flood of Italian got rid of him. The man retreated to his pitch, whence he shouted a few remarks of an uncomplimentary character, but fortunately his attention was diverted at that moment by the cries of an old woman whose basket of roast chestnuts some children had upset.

"What are you doing here?" asked Joseph severely. "Don't you know that young ladies do not walk about the streets unattended?"

She was wearing a Leghorn bonnet, tied with broad pink ribbons.

"Lady Westmoreland wished me to fetch some silk that she had ordered." She answered the first part of his question.

"But why did she not send you in the carriage? Or, if you must walk, you should have an attendant with you."

Miss Montgomerie only laughed. She had completely recovered her composure.

---

[1] Sharp, *op. cit.*, p. 157.

"I must not keep you, Mr. Severn," she said in her low Scottish voice. "But, believe me, I am very grateful for your kindness."

She turned to walk away, but Joseph followed her.

"I will accompany you home, if you will permit me?"

He smiled at her, and her gentle face relaxed suddenly into an answering, youthful smile. He had the idea that in other surroundings hers would be a happy nature. Always her mouth carried a hint of humour at the corners, only her eyes betrayed her unhappiness.

"I can scarcely refuse such a request from my gallant rescuer," she said, and laughed again. As they walked side by side through the narrow Roman streets, he thought what a pretty voice she had, and what brilliant blue eyes and what a lovely smile.

Miss Montgomerie made him leave her before they reached the gates of the Palazzo. She did not give any reason. As they were parting she turned back, hesitating.

"You won't mention this to—to anyone?"

They both knew whose name had been left unspoken.

The spring of 1827 was a gay one in Rome. The city was full of English visitors, and there were balls and receptions almost every night. Torlonia, the Roman banker, and the French Ambassador, the Prince de Laval, gave frequent parties, and foremost among the English hostesses was the Countess of Westmoreland. She made a great fuss of Joseph at her own parties, and took him as her escort to many of those given by other people, where she introduced him to all the great personages.[1]

Seeing so much of Lady Westmoreland, it was inevitable that he should also see a good deal of her ward. When he called in the evening Miss Montgomerie was often sent down to entertain the visitors until her guardian was ready.[2] But immediately Lady Westmoreland arrived she expected all his attention to be concentrated on herself. When he dined at the Palazzo Rospigliosi she was sometimes there, though at other times Lady Westmoreland made her take her meal in her bedroom. She did not speak much during these evenings, and often she was the butt for her guardian's witty but cruel tongue.

These occasions made Joseph acutely uncomfortable. Not only did he hate to see Miss Montgomerie humiliated, but also he did not relish these glimpses of a darker side to Lady Westmoreland's character. She had been so kind to him always, and he had

[1] Letter, Jan. 14th, 1828. (Keats House.)   [2] Sharp, *op. cit.*, p. 151.

thought her everything that a great lady should be—gifted, witty, and magnificent in appearance and her way of living. At every crisis in his fortunes she had come to his aid. It was she who had written to the President in London when he was hoping for the Royal Academy pension, and it was she again who, on the day the pension ended, had come forward with a commission to paint six historical pictures for her, making it unnecessary for him to return to what he thought of as "the drudgery of portrait." [1] It was she who had introduced him to many of his noble patrons who treated him as a gentleman. He was "the only artist here who is on this footing with the nobility," [2] and he was loth to throw away his advantages by quarrelling with Lady Westmoreland. She had even suggested that she might get him a commission from the King of England that summer.[3]

Until now he had been proud of the regard she felt for him, which she displayed to all the world, but now he felt almost guilty, if Miss Montgomerie were there, to see the contrast in her behaviour towards them both. Fortunately for him, Lady Westmoreland's vanity was such that it never occurred to her that Joseph could feel anything but admiration for her in all her moods. He realized that Miss Montgomerie was very unhappy, but he told himself that there was nothing he could do. If he tried to speak to her ladyship about it, she would be furious with him, and would only be harder on the girl. Her arrogance would permit no criticism of herself.

So he said nothing.

But he made enquiries about Miss Montgomerie, in a discreet way, from some of the English ladies who came to his apartment to play with him on his pianoforte. Entirely disinterested enquiries, he assured himself. Merely to satisfy a reasonable curiosity.

At first he could get only vague hints that she was the natural daughter of a Scottish baronet, who seemed very fond of her. Then, one day, from a lady who lived in Scotland, he heard a more detailed story. She was the illegitimate daughter, he discovered, of Lord Montgomerie, who, if he had lived, would have been the 13th Earl of Eglinton. Her mother, rumour said, was a friend of Lady Montgomerie, a young girl, who had been seduced by Lord Montgomerie just before his marriage. Whether this story was true or not, it was not disputed that Lady Montgomerie had shown the child great kindness.

[1] Letter, Dec. 4th, 1827. (Keats House.)
[2] Letter to Maria, Jan. 14th, 1828. (Keats House.)
[3] Letter to Tom Severn, July 15th, 1827. (Keats House.)

The fact that she brought up her husband's natural daughter
with her own child was thought curious by no one. Many of the
oldest families were in the same position. The Duchess of Devonshire's children had shared their nurseries with their father's
illegitimate brood, and the same was true of many noble house-
holds. Lady Montgomerie's marriage had been planned by her
family since her childhood, and she was only sixteen years old
when the ceremony took place. She was the eventual heiress of
the 11th Earl of Eglinton, and by marrying her cousin, young
Montgomerie, she was reuniting the family estates with the title.
When Montgomerie died of consumption two years after their child,
a son, was born, his widow waited a year and then married again—
a Scottish baronet, Sir Charles Lamb. Elizabeth Montgomerie
went with her half-brother to their new home and lived there
until he was old enough to take up residence in his own house
and control his own estates. Then Elizabeth had gone abroad,
with Lady Westmoreland as her guardian.

Tableaux were the new fashion in Rome that winter. Lady
Westmoreland gave a party, with tableaux representing famous
pictures. She made Joseph arrange them, calling him "her
Commander-in-Chief." [1] All the most beautiful ladies in Rome
were persuaded to take part, in dresses specially made for the
occasion. In the interests of realism Lady Westmoreland went
so far as to bring home the notorious dwarf, Bajocchio, who made
a small fortune begging from the visitors at the Caffè Ruspoli.
She wanted him to represent the dwarf in Van Dyck's picture of
Charles the First. While she was dressing the dwarf for his part
the audience could hear her vehement voice from behind the
scenes,

"Miss Montgomerie, rouge Bajocchio, and then throw away
the rouge-pot!" [2]

Lady Westmoreland had told Joseph that she intended to show
a picture at the end of the evening which he was not to see before-
hand. The curtains in front of the picture-frame parted to reveal
a reproduction of one of his own pictures. Real trees stood in
the background, and Lord Mayhew and two daughters of the
Duchess of Sante were posed as the figures.

Joseph was astonished and delighted at the compliment. When
he murmured his thanks Lady Westmoreland replied, before all
the company, "that she owed him a pleasure." [3]

[1] Letter to Tom, May 26th, 1827.   [2] *Journal of Henry Fox*, p. 312.
[3] Letter, May 26th, 1827. (Keats House.)

The lovely Roman spring matured, and Joseph began to discover in himself feelings towards Miss Montgomerie which he knew were very ill-advised. They met so constantly that a certain intimacy had grown between them, and he would often find himself thinking of those unhappy blue eyes and that attractive voice with its Scottish intonation. Her beauty disturbed him, and he fancied, too, that Miss Montgomerie was not entirely indifferent to him.[1]

He thought it over, sitting in his big studio with its large north window, and decided that he must check this dawning emotion. It would be wiser for him not to see too much of Miss Montgomerie. He felt glad that summer was approaching when all the English visitors would soon be leaving Rome. He was not quite certain of his strength of purpose, if Miss Montgomerie and he continued to meet so often. Perhaps it was as well that she would be leaving.

But she did not leave. In May, Lady Westmoreland suddenly announced that she was going to remain in Rome for ever. She took a fresh lease of the apartments in the Rospigliosi Palace, and began to refurnish most of the rooms with great extravagance but extremely good taste.

Many were the errands that Elizabeth Montgomerie was sent on, and it was surprising how often they seemed to meet, quite by chance, when Joseph had heard the arrangement made the night before. He had been right when he doubted his resolution to keep away from her. "Women in high life are cats," he had once written to his father, but Miss Montgomerie was different from the others. She was so sweet and young and trusting, and she obviously thought of him as her one friend. For, with the departure of so many of her acquaintances, Lady Westmoreland spent more of her time with Elizabeth, and when she was in a bad mood she seemed to take pleasure in insulting and humiliating her.

Joseph's feelings towards Lady Westmoreland began to change that summer. He still admired her as much as ever, but he realized now that she was not the goddess he had once thought her. At the end of July she went to Naples, taking Miss Montgomerie with her, and Joseph joined them for a brief holiday. Lady Westmoreland was as witty as ever; there were many English people staying there; the weather was lovely, and the life was gay. But Joseph did not enjoy his holiday as he had the last one that he had spent in Naples, alone with Lady Westmoreland, two years before.

[1] Letter, July 1827. (Keats House.)

He cut short his stay and returned to Rome, where he painted vehemently every daylight hour, to shut out the picture of a beautiful face, made for laughter, which yet was desperately unhappy.

Several months before, Lady Compton had asked him why he did not marry Miss Montgomerie. This Scottish lady was clever and warm-hearted, besides being very musical. She was one of those who came, when they were in Rome, to play on Joseph's pianoforte. Although her learning and inclination to pedantry had led some people to call her a "blue," she had a woman's love of match-making and intrigue. She extracted a confession from Joseph that he found Miss Montgomerie "the most lovely and amiable girl he ever saw," [1] and if she had not been on the point of leaving Rome for London she would have tried to force him to a decision then. But he had told her that, from a common-sense point of view, he realized that he would be foolish to marry. As a single man he could live in Rome in comfort on £150 a year and still save money. It would cost him £500 a year to live in England in the same style, even without a wife or family. He meant to save while he worked in Rome, so that he could go home a rich man. He could not afford to marry yet.

Autumn came, and the Countess of Westmoreland returned to Rome for the winter. Once more the huge rooms at the Palazzo Rospigliosi were filled with people. "She is a most queenly person and does everything with magnificence," [2] wrote Joseph to his father. Lady Westmoreland had suddenly become engrossed with politics. Her speculations were "wild and fantastic," according to young Mr. Henry Fox, great-nephew of Charles James, but he admitted that her conversation was "always brilliant" although "without method or consistency." [3]

Joseph and Elizabeth Montgomerie met frequently, but he took care not to pay her too much attention when Lady West-moreland was present. For he could not help noticing that whenever he was talking to Miss Montgomerie her ladyship would make some excuse to separate them. She would send her ward to fetch something from another room, or she would call Joseph over to look at some new book of poems or music that had arrived out from England.

The circumspection that was necessary when her ladyship was with them made it seem as though he shared a secret with Miss

---

[1] Letter, July 15th, 1827.   [2] Letter, Dec. 4th, 1827.
[3] *Journal of Henry Fox*, p. 237.

Montgomerie. But he was anxious not to offend Lady West-moreland, and, by her behaviour that winter, she gave him good reason. He had many opportunities of seeing the lengths to which she would go to harm people who had offended her. Her restless spirit of interference was always leading her to meddle with the affairs of her friends. While she was controlling their lives—or thought that she was doing so, for she was a woman of immense vanity—no praise was too high for them, no sacrifice too great. But let them once act in a way of which she did not approve—which meant contrary to her advice—and from that moment nothing they could do or say was right.

Mr. Henry Fox described her as "a dreadful friend." [1] He came several times to Joseph's studio.

"There is nothing she will not say and do to provoke those she likes, if they displease her in the slightest thing," [2] he said. "I never saw a manner so ladylike or a power of conversation so invariably brilliant or agreeable.[3] Her wonderful talents and brilliant conversation make it impossible for me not to have pleasure in her society, notwithstanding the very extraordinary absurdities of her conduct. She is perhaps not mad, but nobody ever approached so near it with so much reason. She has fine and generous impulses, which are almost always either perverted or entirely overwhelmed by the exuberant vanity, violent temper, suspicious distrust, or ungovernable annoyance, that obscure the better feelings of her heart. It is the same with her head. Some-times she has very just views of people's characters and actions, but when they in any way can be made to have the slightest refer-ence to her, or when she is the least blinded by one of her vague suspicions, she instantly forgets all her former observations, and only sees them as her enemies or her friends' enemy, or her enemy's friend: for she divides the world into two classes—her friends and her enemies, which supply in her vocabulary the words good and bad." [4]

Towards Christmas, Lady Westmoreland seemed to lose some-thing of her interest in politics and turned her enthusiasm, instead, to the Roman Catholic religion. Joseph had never lost his strong religious sense, but he remained a robust Protestant. One day at dinner, after Lady Westmoreland had been talking enthusiastically about Catholicism, a Lady Howard leaned across two people and said,

[1] *Journal of Henry Fox*, p. 300.   [2] *Ibid.*, p. 248.   [3] *Ibid.*, p. 261.   [4] *Ibid.*, p. 229.

E*

"So I see the Pope has made a conquest of you."

Lady Westmoreland was furious.

"The vulgar, foolish woman!" she cried, and regarded her as an enemy from that day on.[1]

A few weeks later she embarked on a more bitter and a more public feud. At the end of January, Laval, the French Ambassador, gave an enormous costume-ball. This was the cause of a drama which was to end only with his recall months later.

To his ball he invited Lord and Lady Blessington. They had established themselves in the Villa Negroni some months before— the drunken, fatuous Blessington, his common Irish wife, and her dandyish French lover, Count Alfred d'Orsay, all living in the same house. This much had been accepted by certain portions of society. But even the least squeamish were outraged when Lady Blessington married her lover to her fifteen-year-old step-daughter, Lady Harriet, in order to make it more convenient for him to live in their house.

Many people were surprised to see the Blessingtons at the French Embassy.

"They were dressed gorgeously as Turks," said Henry Fox drily. "But Lady Blessington looked like one of her pro-fession." [2]

Lady Westmoreland was furious with Laval for receiving the notorious Lady Blessington. She immediately tried to persuade the English ladies in Rome to refuse to enter his house. She talked wildly of his inviting Lady Blessington to his parties in order to degrade the English nobility and bring about a revolution in England. Having stirred up as much feeling as she could against Laval, she retired abruptly to Palo for a week, during which time she communed with God, not speaking for seven days and fasting for twenty-four hours.[3]

It happened that the day of her departure from Rome was the first day of the Carnival, and her withdrawal was so suddenly decided upon that Joseph knew nothing about it. He called on her to discuss the details of a picture she had ordered. Miss Montgomerie told him that her ladyship had retired into seclusion for a week. It was only natural that they should discuss the Carnival, and when it transpired that Miss Montgomerie had not yet been to the Corso, Joseph immediately offered to escort her. She would enjoy the battles with sugar-plums and trying to recognize her acquaintances behind mask and domino, even if

---

[1] *Journal of Henry Fox*, p. 260.   [2] *Ibid.*, p. 267.   [3] *Ibid.*, p. 265.

she did not wish to see the little horses race, riderless, down the street, driven on by the sharp spikes which at every bound fell heavily on to their bleeding sides. Miss Montgomerie did not think she would care to see the race, but accepted Joseph's offer to escort her to the Corso most gratefully.

So at noon next day, when the bell from the Capitol rang out its summons to the reign of folly, they were seated together in a carriage in the narrow, crowded street. The windows and balconies on either side were hung with brightly-coloured draperies and filled with gay spectators. The two lines of carriages moved slowly past each other, while the shouting crowds on foot thrust their way between. Almost everyone, like themselves, was masked. Miss Montgomerie wore the dress of an Italian peasant girl, but her fair skin and bright hair attracted much attention. At one moment quite half a dozen masks were hanging together on the back of their carriage, and chattering to them in Italian. Some of their compliments were so outspoken that Joseph hoped she did not understand them.

He had never seen her so happy, so carefree. In her excitement she forgot her troubles, and her laugh rang out again and again as they became involved in furious pitched battles, with sweetmeats for ammunition, against other carriages, until the opposite line moved on and carried their antagonists away from them.

They stayed for nearly an hour, and then Joseph invited her to come and see the sketch he had done for Lady Westmoreland's picture. It was the first time she had been in his studio. She seemed in great spirits. Her gaiety became her and made more fascinating her lovely face. Her delicate, fair skin seemed to gain an extra glow from the happiness in her eyes, and her mouth had surrendered to the humour always lurking at the corners.

She pronounced the sketch quite excellent, but she teased him about the shabbiness of his cap, which was hanging on the easel. She made him put it on and told him it was a terrible colour— and it was so tattered. Why, the embroidery was in shreds. Joseph begged her, if he bought a new cap, to embroider it with something of her own devising, since she thought so poorly of his old one. Miss Montgomerie thought that, from compassion, she could scarcely refuse. Joseph felt he was really seeing her for the first time. She should always look like this.

When they met in company after that they would exchange a secret glance, and when they were separated in a crowded room

each would feel the other's presence.   He bought himself a new
cap and sent it to her with a note.

"Miss Montgomerie—with the Cap.

DR. MISS M.,—Here's the Cap—and I shall expect something
pretty to be done—particularly as you rail at my purple one so—
but pray come and rail again.

Yours,   J. S." [1]

Before the cap was embroidered Lady Westmoreland arrived
back from Palo, wilder and less balanced than ever.

"God must manifest Himself more plainly!" she declared
dramatically.   "I cannot fight His battle any more.   There must
be another Incarnation.   I have said 'God, manifest yourself.'   I
have done all I can do for the cause of virtue; God must complete
the work." [2]

She continued her feud with Laval, and spent much time
composing letters to him.   Towards the end of March she received
a grossly insulting letter from Count d'Orsay.   He was enraged by
her crusade against the Casa Blessington, and retaliated by setting
down in his letter all the unpleasant rumours that had ever been
associated with her name.   He ended by threatening, "if not to
murder, to insult and outrage her." [3]

She was dreadfully distressed by this letter and became so
nervous and irritable that Joseph began to wonder how much
longer Miss Montgomerie would be able to support her life with
her guardian.   Hoping that the French Ambassador would, as a
gentleman, feel compelled to have d'Orsay expelled from the
Papal States, Lady Westmoreland dressed herself in mourning and
handed him the libellous letter in front of many witnesses at an
evening assembly.

"*Cela appartient, monsieur, à la France et pas à moi*," she said with
emotion.

Henry Fox came to see her next morning and reported finding
her "in her dressing-gown, her hair about her neck, and sadly
harassed and broken." [4]   She became every day more restless,
unbalanced, and impossible to live with.

D'Orsay was showing copies of his letter with its scandalous
accusations to anyone whom he could persuade to read it.   Lady

---

[1] This and all the following notes from Joseph to Miss M. in possession of
Margaret Lady Birkenhead.
[2] *Journal of Henry Fox*, p. 274.   [3] *Ibid.*, p. 280.   [4] *Ibid.*, p. 279.

Westmoreland rushed frantically from one acquaintance to another to enlist their support.

Meanwhile Lord Blessington commented to his friends on the extreme chastity of all his family. According to his account, Lady Blessington had a "spine complaint which prevents him from exercising his matrimonial duties. D'Orsay has not and will not consummate his marriage, and he himself does not think *le jeu vaut la chandelle* to make any search among dirty Italian women." [1]

From Henry Fox's Journal, March 24th, 1828.

"In the morning I had a head-ache, and remained in bed. . . . Lady Westmoreland burst for an instant into my room; this dreadful libel has quite unsettled her very unsettled understanding. She was dressed in deep mourning, the expression of her face was haggard and careworn, but wearing the most ghastly mad smile. She did not stay three minutes. All she said was rhapsody about the Divine interference in her behalf, which she says has manifested itself, supported her spirits, and dictated her letters. She then abruptly interrupted herself, and said, 'For eighteen years I have suffered persecution, for eighteen years have I been reviled, ridiculed and libelled. Who am I to thank for this? Lord Westmoreland. Had he a grain of feeling, a spark of honour, or a single Christian thought, what remorse would he now feel to see to what insults he has exposed the woman that bears his name'; and, 'Oh God!' said she, falling on her knees by my bedside and praying earnestly, 'may he feel it, as he should, *bitterly* in this world, but spare him, spare him from remorse and sorrow in the next.' She then suddenly sprang from her knees, and talked on indifferent subjects, with the mock composure of a maniac, for a minute before she rushed back again lest our being together should be spied upon by emissaries from Casa Blessington." [2]

Henry Fox was on her side. He thought she should be protected from the insults of a ruffian, but the majority of the English in Rome did not support her. Many of them had suffered from her passion for interfering in the lives of other people, and they agreed among themselves that she had brought the insult on herself. Lady Westmoreland spent hours at her desk, writing long, long letters about the affair to everyone she knew. Her nerves were raw and she flew into frequent passions of rage, when she would violently abuse Miss Montgomerie. Her only intervals of good

---

[1] *Journal of Henry Fox,* p. 281. [2] *Ibid.,* pp. 281-282.

temper came when she was well pleased with some letter that she had written. Then she would suddenly become charming to her ward, although she could still talk of nothing but the wrongs that had been done her and her own "angelic conduct."

At the end of the first week in April her ladyship was *rayonnante*. She heard reports that the Governor of Rome had requested d'Orsay to leave the city. Casting aside her mourning and her martyrdom, she sallied forth in a blue silk ball-dress and lively spirits. Alas! the rumour was not justified, and the disappointment made her more unreasonable than before. She picked quarrels with everyone who had supported her, even with Henry Fox, who had almost had to fight a duel with d'Orsay over the affair.

That April was one of the hottest in living memory. Lady Westmoreland, worn out by the violence of her emotions, retired to bed for two days' rest before leaving Rome for some cooler air by the sea. Joseph called on her and found her in bed. Miss Montgomerie was summoned to wait on the invalid. When he was taking his leave he managed to press a note into her hand. He had folded the paper into a tiny triangle. Miss Montgomerie's fingers closed round it as she curtsied, with her blue eyes on his. The great heat was making him feel dizzy, but he was shocked at the strained expression of her face. He felt he must help her, speak to her, and find out what he could do.

"They tell me that you are to go to their ball to-night," he had written, "now if you want a Squire I offer you my services. You may tell Lady Westmoreland now, or shall I write.

Yours,   J. S."

He returned to his studio to await an answer. He knew that, with Lady Westmoreland in bed, she would be able to send one of the servants. But, by the time the message came, he was feeling really ill. His head throbbed as he read her little note. She thanked him for his kindness. She would look forward with pleasure to seeing him at the ball, but she had already accepted an offer from another gentleman—she mentioned his name—to escort her there. Although he knew that he was in no condition to go dancing, Joseph felt an unreasonable irritation at her having arranged to go with someone else. He got sulkily into his bed, where, with his head aching, he lay tossing in the hot room, trying vainly to get to sleep.

By the morning his annoyance had vanished. He felt weak

· and ill, but he did not want her to think that he had deserted her. He sent his Italian servant round to the Palazzo Rospigliosi with another note.

"DEAR MISS M.,—I fear you thought me a most unfaithful knight—the truth is I should have gone only on your account, for I was ill and ill-disposed to go—and when I found you had a squire in Mr. D. and feeling myself really ill, I gave up all idea of coming— I had a fever on me all night and I cannot conceive from what cause —this morning I am still ill—so believe me

still yours faithfully,   J. S.

Does Lady W. go to-morrow?"

Lady W. did not "go to-morrow." Rising suddenly from her bed, she abandoned the rôle of invalid and threw everybody's plans into chaos by insisting that she must leave Rome at once.

In the confusion nobody noticed that Miss Montgomerie appeared particularly melancholy this morning. Nor did they notice a sudden change in her demeanour when, as she was on the point of departure, a letter was delivered to her.

"The truth is I should have gone only on your account . . ."

Miss Montgomerie's expression was suddenly cheerful as she climbed into the coach. Perhaps her guardian would make another change in her plans. Perhaps they would not, after all, spend very long in Florence.

They did not return to Rome until mid-June. Scarcely any English people had stayed in Rome for the summer. The heat was terrific, but Joseph painted doggedly all the day. He had eleven pictures on order. He wondered what was happening to Miss Montgomerie and often found himself thinking of her unhappy blue eyes. He received several letters from Lady Westmoreland, each of many sheets. There were pages about her persecution and the Divine support vouchsafed to her, but no mention of her ward. He noticed that she had transferred many of her former champions into the ranks of the agents of darkness.

Immediately he heard of her return to Rome, Joseph went round to the Palazzo Rospigliosi. He managed to exchange a few words with Miss Montgomerie alone. She told him that she had finished the embroidery on his cap, and he begged her to bring it herself to his studio, so that she might see how much work he had done since she went away.

She had just time to murmur that she would come next day,

as Lady Westmoreland swept tempestuously into the room. She did not look very pleased at finding them together, and spoke crossly to Miss Montgomerie before sending her away. Joseph listened to her triumphant tale of how she had had Laval turned out of Rome. He knew that the French Ambassador had been recalled while Lady Westmoreland was away, but he was not certain that it was the result of her appeal to the French Court. However, Lady Westmoreland had no doubt of her own triumph and enjoyed retailing it in detail.

When she had finished she insisted on driving him back to his studio, so that she might see how "The Fountain" was progressing. It was a large picture, similar to "The Vintage," which the Duke of Bedford had bought. A country scene—a fountain in the foreground, a shepherd boy playing on his pipe while his goats were drinking, and barefooted peasant girls fetching water in pitchers; in the distance an Italian village. Joseph had been working on this picture for more than eight months. It was nearly finished, but one or two figures had yet to be painted.

When Miss Montgomerie came to his studio next day he begged her to let him include her portrait as a peasant girl carrying her pitcher to the fountain. She smilingly agreed, but then her expression altered and she said sadly that she doubted if she would be allowed to come.

"Do you mean by Lady Westmoreland?" Joseph asked boldly.

She nodded silently, and then suddenly burst out that she could stand it no longer. Lady Westmoreland was increasingly violent and abusive. She seemed to have some idea that Elizabeth was in league with her enemies. When she had been out of the house, even if she had only been to church, Lady Westmoreland would question her suspiciously about whom she had met and what she had said to them. If they were people with whom she had quarrelled—and that, said Miss Montgomerie bitterly, meant almost everyone she knew—she would fly into a passion and would reproach her bitterly, often in front of other people, for her ingratitude. And when she was not there, Lady Westmoreland would tell people malicious stories about her—all lies, that she had invented to discredit her. She could not stand it much longer.

Her lip was trembling as Joseph took her hand in his and comforted her as best he could. He would have liked to kiss her tear-bright eyes, but instead he talked gently to her, holding her hand, and telling her that she must not do anything impetuously, but that she could rely on him to help her and that she could trust him absolutely if things got any worse at the Palazzo Rospigliosi. Miss Montgomerie quickly regained control of herself and left, afraid to stay any longer in case her absence was noticed.

From that day they were conspirators, with Lady Westmoreland as their avowed enemy. Miss Montgomerie found herself more and more hemmed in with suspicion. Lady Westmoreland seemed to sense that something was not quite right, although Joseph tried to give her no hint of his changed feelings. Her jealous scrutiny made it very difficult for them to meet, except when she sent Miss Montgomerie on some errand on foot, when she would sometimes slip up to Joseph's studio for a moment. Nothing had been said of love. Joseph particularly tried to keep their relationship on a gay, friendly basis, but each time that he looked into her vivid eyes he found it more difficult.

They seldom had more than a minute or two alone together, but little secret notes were folded and refolded, and passed from hand to hand when they met.

"*Wednesday morning July 9th*, 1828.

DEAR MISS M.,

When will you come again,
Or must I ask in vain?
You're just as scarce as rain,
   Now 'per l'amor di Dio'
And every Love profane
   Pray let me see you.

O how I want to trace
Your laughing bonnie face,
My 'Fountain' has a place,
   So pray say 'Yes'
(And 'perche no?') in case
   I say Not Yours   J. S."

She came again at last. While he painted she told him that her mind was made up. She would stay no longer with Lady Westmoreland. She had a little money of her own and she would find some family in Rome who would let her live with them. She was afraid that no English family would help her, she added bitterly, because Lady Westmoreland had set them all against her by the stories she told.

Joseph suggested that he should speak to a friend of his, a

Miss Mackenzie, who would be staying in Rome, at any rate until next spring. It was evident that a young girl could not leave her guardian without there being some ill-natured gossip, and it would be desirable to find some respectable lady of her own nationality to look after her. From his own experience Joseph had no high opinion of the morals of the Italian ladies in Rome.

He saw that she was in earnest about leaving the Palazzo Rospigliosi, and he could not blame her. Her life there had been made wretched by Lady Westmoreland, who had tormented and maligned her. It was dreadful to think of that poor young girl, so innocent and good, suffering such persecution. Lady Westmoreland had, on several occasions, told him stories supposed to illustrate Elizabeth's slyness and ingratitude. He had kept silent, because to arouse her suspicions now would be fatal. She might carry her ward away to Switzerland or France, where he would be unable to help her. Occasionally he could see her alone for a moment, but most of their arrangements were made by stealthy little notes.

"DEAR MISS M.,—I have been thinking that as you are determined not to remain as you are with Lady Westmoreland, and as you have intended to go to an Italian family here in Rome in case of extremity, I am sure my kind friend Miss Leach will receive you—she is now living with her brother (Dr. Leach) at Subiaco (30 miles from Rome) and I will now write her to prepare the way—and I beg you will consider this as a recompense for my missing Miss Mackenzie which after all would only be the same as Miss Leach, who remains in Rome during the Winter.
                    Yours very faithfully,
                                        J. SEVERN."

His efforts to find some suitable lady for her to live with were not very successful. August came and he could see that she was becoming desperate. It was more and more difficult for them to meet undetected. She was frightened to come to his studio even for a moment, since one day she had only just missed meeting Lady Westmoreland as she was leaving. He could not bear to see her so unhappy. He made up his mind to an action which he realized might well ruin his career. He was well established as a fashionable artist in Rome, but he knew Lady Westmoreland's persuasive tongue, and he had witnessed the vindictiveness with which she could use it to avenge herself on those she considered her enemies.

He called at the Palazzo Rospigliosi that evening. He was not left for a moment alone with Miss Montgomerie, but as Lady Westmoreland rose to welcome another guest he was able to pass to Miss Montgomerie a note, asking her to call upon him the next day. It was *most important*.

He received her reply next morning. She dared not come. Lady Westmoreland was watching her all the time and she was afraid of what she would do if she found out that her ward had been to his studio. Joseph was not to be baulked. He had made up his mind, and nothing was going to deter him. He was determined to rescue her from her life of misery, whatever the obstacles. She was too sweet a girl to have her life poisoned in this way. He scribbled another note on a hastily-torn-off scrap of paper, and sent his Italian servant to hang about outside the Palazzo until she found a chance of speaking to Miss Montgomerie.

"I am sorry you cannot take my assurance that there is no harm—and here's an end of it—What I had to say is nothing but from my own head, but I will call at Ave Maria. Pray come to defy her.

Yours,   J. S."

There was no reply. His servant reported that she had de-livered the note to the *bella Inglese*. But she did not come. Once again the servant was sent round to the Palazzo, this time to ring and deliver the letter in the ordinary way. Lady Westmoreland would almost certainly be out in her carriage at this hour.

"DEAR MISS M.,—As it is doubtful my seeing you at Ave Maria—I say to you once more that *I have the power of insuring you 'gainst all you say* if you *yourself* have but the confidence to trust me—take courage and come early to-morrow—do believe me this once,—or I can never presume to show you respect again and fancy myself

Yours,   J. S.

Wednesday, 4 o'clock."

He sat in his library as the shadows lengthened. In the corner of the shelf nearest to him lay the books that Keats had read during his illness—Milton's poems, *Clarissa Harlowe*, *Holy Living and Dying*, several books in Italian, and the little volume of Shakespeare's sonnets which Keats had given him that night when their ship lay becalmed off the Dorset coast. He had not forgotten Keats in his new life, but he was not thinking of him now. He was angry with Miss Montgomerie. After all that he had said and done she did not trust him sufficiently to risk coming to his studio, although he had given her his word that he could protect her from the consequences if she were found out. She had not come to him. Very well, then, he would not go there, as he had promised, at Ave Maria. He sat, frowning, at his bay window, as the bells chimed and night fell softly over Rome.

But he could not sleep that night. The air was sultry and oppressive. He went to bed and then got up again, to march scowling up and down his room. Soon his mood changed. She would be here early in the morning. She must be planning to slip out early, before Lady Westmoreland was awake. He flung himself down on his bed.

He could see her as she would look when she came in—her blue eyes a little doubtful and frightened. And how her face would change when he spoke to her and told her what he planned. . . . He fell asleep.

Early in the morning he awoke. He washed and dressed and sat down to wait for her. Half-past six. Seven o'clock. He went over to the window and watched the street, to see her as she turned the corner. It was a bright, beautiful day. A little donkey came plodding over the cobbles, a great basket of fruit perched on its back, and a black-headed boy trotting at its side. A priest hurried silently by with bowed head. Half-past seven. Eight. She had not come. Joseph left the window and sat down at his writing desk.

"*Thursday morning* 8 o'clock.

Dear Miss M.,—I purposely kept away—your want of confidence annoys me—Yet I will tell you that I have to impart something which secures *your freedom* from Lady W. for ever. Your doubts are unworthy of you, more as I have ever shown myself your true friend, and once more say, I *can* insure you against all, even from Lady W., down to the petty tatlers, but all rests in your faith of my word and power, you have no cause to doubt the one or the other, and my pride is to have them credited—I still hope to see you *here* this morning, and still to call myself

Yours,   J. S.

P.S.—These are the last words *about you*, that I shall *write*, or *say*, or *read*."

She came at last, panting a little from having run up the stone stairs, her blue eyes wide, her white brow puckered in distress.

How *could* he have thought that she did not trust him? He was her only friend. Her faith in him was unbounded. But he must understand that it was very difficult—that she already had enough to bear—that if Lady Westmoreland discovered that she had been to see him, she would redouble her persecution—she would tell more lies about her—she would prevent her from seeing him—

Her faltering words were silenced by Joseph's urgent voice.

"I will take you away from it all—Elizabeth." Her hand was in his. His arm slipped round her. "Will you marry me?"

Miss Montgomerie made him promise that their love should remain a secret until their marriage could be arranged. She was afraid that Lady Westmoreland would find some way to prevent it if she knew. Joseph could not pretend to feel anything but relief at this suggestion. He too was afraid of Lady Westmoreland's violent temperament. He would rather acquaint her with a *fait accompli*.

So, for a little longer, they had to dissemble, while Joseph tried to think how he could best manage the affair, with the minimum of scandal for the gossips. On one point Miss Montgomerie, usually so ready to fall in with his wishes, was adamant. Even if her guardian agreed to the marriage, she would refuse to be married from the Palazzo Rospigliosi, where she had known nothing but unhappiness. But how else could they be married in Rome? And if they went to some other town together to be married, there would undoubtedly be much unpleasant talk, especially as Lady Westmoreland's malice had already put most of the English colony against Miss Montgomerie.

While their plans were still unsettled, things were made more difficult for them by Joseph falling ill with a sharp attack of Roman fever. Fortunately it did not last long. During all this period of worry and excitement they could scarcely ever contrive to be alone together, but little notes were still passed secretly from hand to hand.

"MY PRETTY LASSIE,—I come to-night by invitation early, at Lady W. request—do you mean to say you have said anything to her? I hope not—You were to have written me I do not know what—I am sorry to have you sympathize with me in being ill, for I am miserably ill, and nothing but seeing you will do me good perhaps not even that—however I'd like to try.

Yours,   J. S."

Miss Montgomerie had not said anything to her guardian, but Lady Westmoreland was about to give them the opportunity for which they had been waiting.

On September 24th she removed her household to Florence for a month or two by the sea. In Florence lived Charles Brown, one of Joseph's oldest friends, who, in the old days, had shared his house with Keats. Joseph decided to follow them to Florence. He would stay with Brown, make all arrangements for their marriage, and tell Lady Westmoreland only when it was too late for her to do anything to frustrate them.

"ROME, *Sept.* 30*th*, 1828.

MY DEAR AND BETTER HALF,—These are the last words I shall ever write you and I would that they were the last words I might speak to you in my single life, but we will begin the married one on Sunday with fun and frolic, and now—I sat me down to write you a long, loving letter and somebody has come in, and the post is going, so farewell, and believe me ever and ever

Most sincerely and devotedly yours

J. SEVERN.

On Saturday morning we shall meet, and on Sunday I hope we shall meet again never to part more."

As he was setting off for Florence he received a letter from Charles Brown, urging him to come and stay with him to recuperate after his attack of fever. Brown had added a postscript: "Lady Westmoreland is here: I trust that's no hindrance to your coming." [1] Joseph smiled. He would explain to Brown, when he arrived, exactly why her presence was no hindrance but the reason for his journey.

One more letter he wrote to Miss Montgomerie—when he had arrived in Florence:

"MY DEAR ELIZA,—When I saw my friend Brown I could not conceal it from him, and to my delight he approves it in every respect and rejoices with me. We are going to the Clergyman, and as he thinks of Lady W. as you and I do wishes to arrange it so that she cannot interrupt our marriage. He has offered me his house, but I prefer Siena.

Ever yours,   J. S."

All was arranged. On the Saturday Joseph called on Lady Westmoreland and revealed what he had done. He told her

[1] Sharp, *op. cit.*, p. 157.

directly that Miss Montgomerie and he were to be married at the British Consulate next day. She flew into a passionate rage, abused Miss Montgomerie, threw her benefaction in Joseph's face and rated them both for deceitfulness and ingratitude. Then, with a sudden change from violent rage to a control which was almost more frightening, she said that she would attend the wedding to give her ward away, although she would never, never speak to either of them again after their monstrous behaviour.

With icy demeanour she fulfilled her part in the ceremony, and left them without a word. Ironically enough, they were married in the house of her stepson, Lord Burghersh, who was the British Consul in Florence.

Only once more did Joseph hear from her. He was married on Sunday, October 5th. The next day he received a long, violent letter, full of hints and insinuations which were obviously intended to make him doubt the purity of his wife's conduct before her marriage.[1] If he had known the writer less well, what a cruel stab this would have been. It might have poisoned their marriage from the start.

He read it through to the end and then held the paper to the flame of his candle. It needed no answer. As he watched it curl and shrivel it was as though he were watching the end of his old life. Lady Westmoreland with her turbulent brilliance, her uncurbed passions, her arrogance and wit, had gone for ever. In her place the lovely young Elizabeth with her straight glance, her vivid blue eyes, her honesty and laughter, faced life at his side.

[1] *Journal of Henry Fox*, pp. 347-348.

CHAPTER XI

HIGH NOON

(1828—1837)

THEY were not a very provident couple. When Joseph married he had commissions on hand for eleven pictures. His future seemed rosy. His wife had an allowance from her brother. There seemed no reason why they should not lead a very comfortable life. But Joseph's carefulness was only on the surface, in reality he was quite incapable of managing his financial affairs. He was fond of calculating how much living cost in Rome, but as he could never remember figures, and in any case always chose the ones that suited best his argument of the moment, the results were often surprising.

The first three years of their marriage were overshadowed by a fraudulent lawsuit,[1] which cost him money he could ill afford, but brought him great support from the English colony in Rome and also from the Italians, who were delighted to see someone stand up against the corruption of justice in the Papal States. For six years before he married he had employed an Italian woman, Teresa Bartolomei, to look after his apartment and to cook for him, and he allowed her to live there with her husband and child. The husband was a porter, and Joseph had tried, when he could, to help him by recommending him to his friends. A few months after he was married he found out Teresa in some dishonesty and dismissed her. They had scarcely left the house before he received a legal document from Teresa's husband, demanding five years' wages on the plea of his having been Joseph's servant for that period.

When Joseph enquired into this false claim he found that Giovanni Bartolomei had produced several witnesses, workmen, who swore that while making a new door for the apartment in the Vicolo dei Maroniti they had overheard Joseph promise to pay Giovanni six crowns a week for his services. They even gave the date of this scene—October the first, 1823. Joseph had no idea what he had been doing, or even where he had been, on that day five and a half years ago. He only knew that he had not been engaging Bartolomei as his servant.

Joseph and Elizabeth hunted through all his muddled papers

---

[1] Sharp, *op. cit.*, Appendix I, pp. 289-292.

during a sleepless night, to get a clue as to what he had been doing. Luckily they came across his passport, which showed that in October, 1823, he had been in Venice. He remembered that he had gone there with Charles Brown, and that reminded him that he had not even been living in the Vicolo dei Maroniti at that time but in the Via San Isidoro, more than a mile away. More searching produced the lease of his tenancy of the other house. With these documents in his pocket he felt that even the notorious Papal Courts of Justice could do nothing but dismiss the case at once.

He produced in court the papers which disproved the statements made by Bartolomei's witnesses. The judge, a Signor Manari, then asked Joseph to come into another room and speak to him privately. He received Joseph with great politeness and shook hands with him "in a queer ambiguous manner." Speaking rapidly in Italian, he said that "the whole affair of Bartolomei was nothing less than a conspiracy, and that he should forthwith give the decision in Signor Severn's favour." Joseph was not a little surprised at the judge taking the trouble to see him privately in order to tell him that he knew him innocent, and concluded that he had been grossly prejudiced against Roman justice. Thanking the judge, he left the court, only to find that, the minute he had gone, the judge pronounced the sentence against him.

The truth was that the judge, when shaking hands with him, had expected to receive a bribe. When he found that Joseph did not give him one, he immediately called in the other party and accepted one from them. Then he told them to change their evidence, dating it a year later, so as to correct their error in time and place. The witnesses swore devoutly to this new statement and, without giving Joseph time to prepare a second defence, the judge gave the verdict against him and sentenced him to pay four hundred and twenty-eight crowns (about £100) with costs.

Luckily for Joseph, this happened at a time when he actually had £100 which he could have paid. This gave him the courage to refuse. Through Lord Arundell of Wardour he obtained an interview with the newly-made Cardinal Weld. The English Cardinal listened to his story with evident pain, and undertook to have him granted the right to appeal in a new court. But the new judge confirmed the sentence in the face of Joseph's evidence.

The affair was the talk of Rome. It was discussed in every social gathering and at every café and street corner. The Roman people were delighted that such a thing should have happened to an Englishman. They hoped that the scandal might lead to some reform of the universal corruption among Papal officials. The Englishmen in Rome wanted to use it as a stick with which to beat the Papal Government. They offered to subscribe the whole sum and present it to Joseph if he would give them the facts to publish in the newspapers of the Continent.

He refused, thinking it would be unfair to Cardinal Weld, who was supporting his cause, and also fearing that such an action might put himself and his wife in personal danger. But when Weld obtained for him an interview with the powerful Cardinal Odescalchi, the advice given to him by this Prince of the Church was "to accept the subscription money discreetly, and when they come upon you for permission to publish the case in the European newspapers, to pretend that you had never so understood it."

Joseph ignored this advice, and his friend Chevalier Bunsen, the Prussian Minister, spoke directly to the Pope, pointing out what harm the scandal was doing to the Roman Government. The Pope then offered to repay Joseph all the money he had spent— by now more than £150. This Joseph indignantly refused. He was determined to be vindicated in a court of law. The Secretary of State, Monsignor Tosti, arranged for him to have a new and a fair trial, but at the same time he wrote to M. Kestner, the Hanoverian Minister, expressing his opinion that in the first place Joseph, instead of proving that the man had never been his servant, "should have sworn that he had paid him the money and should have outnumbered the other side's witnesses in swearing to this." Even then the case was not ended. It was tried and re-tried until, with the aid of Cardinal Weld, Joseph won his case and the false witnesses admitted that they "knew quite well that he did not owe the money." It had dragged on for nearly three years, and even when he had won it, he found himself some £95 out of pocket.

He never knew where Bartolomei got the money to sustain his case, for money he had in plenty. The Severns' friends suspected that it came from Lady Westmoreland, and Joseph confessed that he "could not guess who else could have cared to spend so much money upon me, or who had it to spend in such a way." He suspected that Cardinal Weld knew the truth, but he never questioned him.

During the anxieties of these three years Joseph and his young wife were upheld by the kindness of their own countrymen in

Rome. Henry Fox was particularly kind. Twice he lent them his lovely villa at Frascati.[1] There, in the first summer after they were married, a daughter was born to them, whom they named Claudia, and fifteen months later, in Rome, they had a son, Walter. The following summer, 1831, the year that the lawsuit was at last concluded, Joseph fell ill and Henry Fox again lent them his villa. It stood on a thickly-wooded slope with a magnificent view over the Campagna. There were over thirty rooms in the house, all elegantly furnished, and hundreds of English books.

When Elizabeth Severn first saw it, "It is like a dream!" she cried. "Like coming to a fairy palace." [2]

They brought their own pianoforte and Joseph would play on it for hours. He recovered quickly in the healthier air and lovely surroundings, and soon he was hard at work on a large picture, "The Infant of the Apocalypse Caught up to Heaven." Cardinal Weld had ordered it as a present for the Pope, to be placed as an altar-piece in the Cathedral Church of San Paolo fuori le Mura which was just being rebuilt.

Four months they spent at Frascati, and returned to Rome in the autumn. Writing years afterwards, Joseph said: "When we returned to Rome we had the most complete happiness and enjoyment that it is possible for human creatures to know—prosperity, friendship, the best and most entertaining society, no end of brilliant gaieties when we wished them, our love for each other and our children, and above all we had both by this time good health to enjoy all." [3]

He continued his work on the gigantic canvas for Cardinal Weld, who died suddenly before the picture was finished. Joseph grieved for him. It was not only that he knew he would have many anxieties before his picture was safely hung in the restored church, but also that the Cardinal had become a personal friend. He would often appear unannounced in Joseph's studio and stay there a while, watching him at work.

"His Eminence never once enquired what the price would be, or how long the work would take me to do. Once he told me not to hurry it or inconvenience myself, for he could sincerely assure me of the great pleasure it gave him to see me occupied on such a work." [4]

Joseph was often invited to dine with him. "He performed on the French horn with great delicacy and expression, and on

[1] Sharp, *op. cit.*, p. 159.   [2] Letter, July 1st, 1831.

[3] Sharp, *op. cit.*, p. 168.   [4] *Ibid.*, *op. cit.*, p. 293.

every occasion after dinner he requested me to play an accompaniment to him on the piano." Poor Cardinal Weld was not for long allowed to amuse himself thus. "This music after a while was considered to be not quite in accordance with the dignity and gravity of his high position as a Dignitary of the Roman Church, and His Eminence was invited to leave off playing on the French horn." [1]

The years slipped happily by. More children were born. In 1832 came another daughter, Ann Mary, who was to be the most talented child in a talented family. That was the year that two great writers came to Rome. Sir Edward Bulwer Lytton was writing *Rienzi*. He told Joseph with astonishment that "it seemed impossible to buy a Gibbon anywhere in Rome." Joseph confessed that he owned one, but that he could not lend it to him as it was a prohibited book. He had been allowed to buy one through the kindness of Cardinal Weld, and only after giving his word that he would not lend it to anyone. In the end, after vouching for Sir Edward's discretion, he was granted permission to lend him his copy. [2]

Walter Scott arrived in Rome that year, a stricken man, worn out by six years' unceasing labour of creation. His failing mind was filled with sadness for his beloved Lady Compton, who had died in Rome two years before. When Joseph had known her she was fat and middle-aged, but Walter Scott remembered her as a child in Scotland, and still saw her as the singing angel of Raeburn's portrait. She was very musical and used often to come to Joseph's apartment to sing and play on his piano. He had got his brother Tom and Vincent Novello to send new music out for her from London. Scott became very distressed when he thought of her death, and it was some comfort to be able to talk about her to Severn.

Scott's daughter, Anne, told Joseph that his visits did her father good, and by their joint request he would call on them almost every day, bringing some book or picture to interest the invalid. One day he showed him the picture he had painted of Keats reading by the open window. He was saying something about his friend's genius and his tragic death when he saw that Anne Scott had turned away, looking flushed and embarrassed. She and her father probably knew that the attack on Keats in *Blackwood's Magazine* had been written by Lockhart, Scott's son-in-law, and, like so many

---

[1] Sharp, *op. cit.*, p. 294.   [2] *Ibid.*, p. 294.

others who had read *Adonais* or Byron's contemptuous couplet,[1]
they believed that the humiliations heaped on him by reviewers
had contributed to his early death. Joseph stopped short in his
praises of Keats. Scott was visibly distressed. He took Severn's
hand and murmured falteringly, "Yes, yes, the world finds out
these things for itself at last."

A few weeks later Walter Scott died, his body and mind worn
out by the tremendous strain they had been subjected to for six
long years, while he had written and written to clear himself of
debt.[2]

Another year, and another son was born—Henry Augustus.
Joseph began to see Keats's name becoming better known. No
new edition of his poems had been published in England since his
death, but young Englishmen arriving in Rome would sometimes
call on Joseph and introduce themselves as admirers of John Keats.

Although his often-planned visit to England was every year
postponed, he had so many friends and correspondents there that
he was not completely out of touch with his own country. His
sister, Maria, and his mother wrote to him about the family;
Richard Westmacott and Charles Eastlake reported to him on
the successes of the yearly Exhibitions at the Academy; while his
brother Tom, who had become quite a successful composer, told
him the latest musical news and sent him music.

Joseph wrote to Tom in 1837 that he "remembered Mendelssohn
in Rome and was glad to hear of his success in England."[3] He
had stayed some months at a house in the Piazza di Spagna, he
remembered, and Joseph had met him one evening at Bunsen's.
Mendelssohn was then only twenty-one, with a noble head set on
a fragile body. He spoke English well, with a German accent,
talked of Shakespeare and his visit to Scotland the year before.
He was writing a Scottish Symphony. After some singing of
Palestrina's music by Papal singers, Mendelssohn was asked if he
would play. He suggested that the director of the choir should
give him a theme. The director picked out a few notes lightly
with one finger, then Mendelssohn sat down at the piano and
improvised round this theme, playing with it, embroidering and
elaborating it, in the most fascinating manner. Everyone present
had been enchanted by his skill.

[1] " Strange that the mind, that very fiery particle,
        Should let itself be snuffed out by an article."
[2] Joseph Severn, "Vicissitudes of Keats's Fame": published in *The Atlantic Monthly*, 1863.   [3] Letter, April 9th, 1837.

Now he had won fame in England, Tom wrote, and the whole world of music acknowledged his genius. Tom's letter made Joseph long to return home himself, but he was still doing well in Rome. Though he had plenty of pictures ordered he was shrewd enough to guess that he was not so well established that he could carry his fame back with him to England. But he vowed he would be. He felt confident of his powers. Look at what he had accomplished already. It took something like genius to work yourself up to the position he occupied now, when only a few years ago you had arrived in Rome penniless and unknown.

"I long to come and see you all," he wrote to Tom. "It will be seventeen years in October since you and I sailed down the Thames with poor Keats. I can see you now in my mind's eye, and the blue coat you had on, I can never forget you. How pale you looked at the scene we had passed and how I trembled, yet all this was for the best, for I could not expect to have done what I have done here, or certainly made so many friends who are capable of serving my family." [1]

Joseph loyally acknowledged his debt to Keats.
"To poor Keats I owe a great deal of my present good fortune. You would be surprised how often it is mentioned to me—and how I am pointed out as the friend of the poet Keats." [2] "Betwixt you and me I have gained more from poor Keats who is dead and gone than from any other source." [3]

This made him all the more anxious to see a Memoir written of his friend—a book which would bring his unpublished poems before the world, and which would describe his life, his personality and his tragic death. It was now eight years since Charles Brown had undertaken to write such a Memoir, and sixteen years since Keats's death. Sixteen years in which his friends had fought over his memory. Brown asserted that George Keats had taken with him to America money which rightfully belonged to his brother and which he had badly needed. George Keats, supported by Charles Dilke, denied this charge indignantly. Others supported Brown, and each faction had no name bad enough for the other.

Joseph had promised Brown his help, and also an engraving of the miniature that he had painted of Keats for the Academy Exhibition in 1819. But it was not surprising that George Keats was definitely obstructive when he heard of Brown's projected

---

[1] Letter, April 9th, 1837.   [2] Letter to Maria, Oct. 4th, 1824.
[3] Letter to Tom, Nov. 21st, 1825.

Memoir of his brother. Even allowing for this difficulty, Brown did not seem to be working at his task with much energy. He had gone home to England with his son two years ago, so that since then Joseph could only encourage him by letter. He continued to urge him to persevere, even threatening to write a Memoir himself if he did not finish it soon.

"If you will go on I will send you everything I can think of," he wrote. "If you will not, I mean to defy you and try and write his Life myself, which I am sure will make you look about you."

"Here I have heard and heard of Keats's Life which you are doing," he complained. "I have written and written to you about it, and now I hear nothing more, now, when the world is looking for it. Now tell me what you have to say by way of excuse. It cannot be, save that you do not know how high Keats's fame has risen—that if he is not the Poet of the million, he is more, for I would say that, judging of the talents of his admirers, and their rank as scholars, that his fame is a proud one." [1]

So far his protests had been unavailing, and the year 1837 was such a tragic one for him that he had little time to spare for letter-writing until it was almost ended. In the spring their new baby, a little boy of only eight months, whose christening William Wordsworth had attended, was killed. He slipped down through the rail of his cot while he was sleeping and broke his neck. Joseph and his wife were heart-broken, particularly as they felt that it was their fault, that they should have been able to prevent the accident. Mrs. Severn broke down completely, and in the hope of helping her to recover, Joseph insisted on going for an expedition which they had half-arranged before the tragedy. This was a visit to Olevano, a little town in the mountains some forty miles from Rome.

They were here when rumours were heard that cholera had broken out in Rome. There had been outbreaks in other parts of Italy, but the Romans proudly declared that "it would not dare to enter Rome on account of the holiness of the place." Joseph immediately decided to go to Rome and collect what they might need for a long stay. Before leaving he obtained permission to re-enter Olevano so long as the cholera had not been officially declared in Rome. He was only just in time. The few friends he saw were in a state of alarm, and immediately after his return to Olevano he heard that cholera had broken out furiously in Rome.

[1] Letter, March 14th, 1834. Sharp, *op. cit.*, p. 164.

Cordons were thrown at once round each of the towns near the city and no one was allowed to enter, lest they should bring the dread infection with them. Luckily he had his painting materials with him, so he was not idle. But soon his money was exhausted. He could not communicate with his bank in Rome, nor with Chevalier Bunsen, the Prussian Minister, to whom he had just lent some money for his hospital on the Capitol. The Bunsens were equally isolated in Frascati. But the natives of Olevano proved so trusting and hospitable that the Severns suffered little inconvenience.

Their life seemed unreal by contrast with reports from Rome. They lived in the Apennine town in the midst of romantic scenery, while Joseph painted and Elizabeth sketched the children, and both rejoiced to see them thriving in the healthy mountain air. Their only discomfort lay in being confined to the town.

"It is like the plague in Boccaccio's *Decameron*," Joseph said.[1]

In Rome the cholera raged. Occasionally they received a fumigated letter from the city giving terrible accounts of the death of friends and acquaintances of every class. Then they heard of a "state of almost public anarchy. Contagion being the order of the day, all the nobles, and even the Pope himself, had bricked up their palaces, and selfishly left the rest of the city to destruction from plunder and murder. People threw the dead bodies out of windows into the streets to avoid contagion, and it was an appalling thing to see the continued falling of the corpses. The sight after sunset at the Church of San Lorenzo was the most awful that could be imagined. Carts were arriving continually, filled with naked dead bodies, which were at once on their arrival thrown into the fosse. These death-carts came in unbroken procession from sunset until two or three o'clock in the morning. There were innumerable torches to light up the dismal work. During a month, this rude interment was at the rate of three hundred corpses a day."[2]

They did not return to Rome until November. It was a sad home-coming. Within their house every room brought memories of their dead baby; without, every street reminded them of friends claimed by the cholera. Joseph wrote to Brown:

"Our return to Rome seems after an absence of twenty years instead of a few months—the number of deaths, some fifteen

---

[1] Severn's " Reminiscences " ; quoted Sharp, *op. cit.*, p. 180.
[2] *Ibid.*, pp. 180-182.

thousand, the pallid countenances all seemingly sunk in years, the vacant streets and the gloom. . . ."

The whole life of the city was disorganized. He confided in Brown that he had been unlucky with his pictures, "having by me a thousand pounds' worth; this is from the persons who ordered them not being able to pay me. My last commission I am now at work on."[1]

After a moment's pause on this gloomy thought his pen dashed on to a phrase which, in slightly varying forms, was to become the motto of his family for the next twenty years: "The future may turn up some good fortune." Vague and charming, enthusiastic and unmethodical, God-fearing and incurably optimistic, something usually did "turn up" for the Severns.

[1] Letter, Nov. 21st, 1837; quoted Sharp, *op. cit.*, p. 184.

CHAPTER XII

FAMILY LIFE

(1837—1852)

THE children grew up to speak Italian as well as they did English, and they knew the names of Raphael and Michelangelo as soon as they could talk. It was a romantic and colourful world they lived in, peopled by crimson Cardinals and sombre friars. They heard the long-cloaked shepherds sing the old Christmas songs in Papal Rome; they knelt in the streets when the Pope passed; they played their childish games in the Ludovisi Gardens where the violets clustered thickly under the ilex trees. And when they drove outside the city they crossed the desolate Campagna, where the giant ruins of the Claudian aqueduct strode away towards Frascati.

From the first, Mary and Walter showed most talent in drawing and Claudia in music. She was seven years old when the family returned from Olevano, and her father would make her sing the Vintage songs that she had learned in the mountains. He had taught her to play duets with him too. One of their favourites was "Figaro." Mrs. Severn loved to watch them at the piano. Joseph would be carried away by the music, gradually increasing the time from *presto* to *prestissimo*, and bursting into song, while his daughter made desperate efforts with her small childish hands to keep pace with him.[1]

They had not long returned to Rome before an old friend arrived. This was George Richmond, baby of the Academy Class that Joseph had attended while he was still an engraver's apprentice. A portrait that Richmond had painted of William Wilberforce, the great opponent of slavery, had made the artist's name in England. He brought with him his wife, with whom he had eloped to Gretna Green six years before, and their son Thomas, the only surviving child of four babies born to her. She was expecting another shortly.

Joseph was delighted to meet Richmond again and they spent much time together. He took him sight-seeing, and they talked

[1] Letter from Joseph to his daughter Claudia, May 30th, 1873; quoted in *A Victorian Artist*.

of painting and music, and their old friends at the Academy. One day they went into the Church of St. John Lateran, where they saw a crowd prostrating themselves before a picture on the wall. To their astonishment they saw that it was a portrait of King George IV. Greatly scandalized, they hurried away to make representations to the Papal authorities. It was found that the portrait, which Lawrence had painted, had been presented by the King to the Vatican. During some cleaning operations it had been transferred to the church, and had at once been mistaken for a canonized saint and worshipped as such.

The Richmonds had taken a large apartment in an old palazzo, and Mrs. Severn told Mrs. Richmond to send her word if she needed help at any time. Young Mrs. Richmond thanked her new friend gratefully and was reassured to think that there was someone she could turn to in need, as George, though a devoted husband, had a temperament that was more artistic than practical.

One night Richmond was awakened from a deep sleep.

"George!" cried Mrs. Richmond, "you must go at once for Mrs. Severn—my baby is going to be born!"

He decided that his wife's nerves must have been affected by the long journey across Europe. The baby was not expected for several weeks.

"Nonsense, my dear!" he replied firmly. "Compose yourself to sleep," and he followed his own advice.

"George!" called his poor wife some time later. "You really must go for Mrs. Severn! My baby is *here*—in the bed with me!"

"Good gracious!" exclaimed Richmond, really roused at last. "This has made me feel quite faint!"

"Empty some cold water over your head, George," his wife advised, thoughtful to the last.

Many English people arrived in Rome with letters of introduction to Joseph.

"Everywhere Joseph Severn was *persona grata*," wrote Richmond's son long afterwards. "His geniality charmed every member of Roman society, from high officials at the Vatican to the humblest traveller. Severn would do his utmost to render a year's sojourn in the Eternal City pleasant, and having great tact and considerable accomplishments, his house likewise became one of the centres where were to be found the foremost men and women of the day." [1]

[1] *Richmond Papers*, pp 42-44.

Henry Acland, later to be Regius Professor of Medicine at Oxford, was one of those who arrived in Rome with a letter of introduction to Joseph and became a life-long friend of all the Severn family and of the Richmonds too. 1838, the year following the saddest in Joseph's life, opened cheerfully with new friends.

His only enemies were the English Catholics in Rome, who were indignant that a heretic's picture should be hung in San Paolo fuori le Mura. They made frequent efforts to convert him. "On all occasions," he wrote afterwards, "when a convert was *sur le tapis*, the priests of the English College made it their object to call on me and tell me the fact, no doubt in the hope that I might be induced to follow the example set me, for there was a great dearth of respectable converts—indeed they were mostly of such ambiguous character that we were induced to call them 'convicts' instead of 'converts'." [1]

With everyone else he was most popular. He was "always full of anecdote" and told his stories amusingly. His good spirits were invigorating and, although he was no longer so good-looking, for he had put on weight, his charm was undeniable. It was in part due to his enjoyment of life, and partly to his anxiety that everyone should be as happy as he. Though he wrote to Tom that his financial position was not very good and that he had many enemies, he was never depressed for more than a moment by either thought.

Elizabeth Severn, too, had a happy, impulsive temperament, which release from Lady Westmoreland had unfettered. She taught her children that love of God was not incompatible with laughter. She gave them a real religion and surrounded them with gaiety and affection. Their household was run in a rather haphazard way, with more good taste than method. The food would grow cold on the table while the family was at the window admiring a sunset, and Joseph would be late for an important appointment because he was teaching Claudia a new song.

Joseph made two new friends that year, who were to help him in the future. In December, 1838, William Ewart Gladstone arrived in Rome. He was twenty-eight years old, tall, with a pale resolute face, an upright carriage and an expression somewhat severe. He introduced himself to Joseph as an admirer of Keats, and asked him many questions about the poet.[2] He did not approve of the Papal Government. George Richmond went riding with him on one occasion. When they got outside the Papal

---

[1] Sharp, *op. cit.*, p. 294.   [2] *Ibid.*, p. 203.

States Gladstone flung his cap in the air and shouted "Long Live Liberty!" [1]

Gladstone's attention was much occupied by Miss Catherine Glynne, the younger of two beautiful, tall English sisters visiting Rome, whose brothers had been at Oxford with him. Catherine was the exact opposite of William Gladstone. He was logical and austere and had schooled himself to stern habits of self-control. She was impetuous, warm-hearted, unpunctual, unconventional and completely unselfconscious.

Nearly every day they met, and he discovered that she, like himself, was very religious. She was lovely, with her tall, supple figure, her thick, dark, curling hair and her laughing eyes. With the ruined Colosseum towering around them he asked her to marry him. But his suit was unsuccessful and he returned to England. Soon afterwards Lady Glynne followed with her two daughters, and a few months later Joseph heard that William Gladstone and Miss Catherine Glynne were married.

They were to be very good friends to himself and his family.

One last friend remained to be made, and then the first Roman chapter of his life was closed, though there was still to be a Roman epilogue.

In 1840 a delicate young man arrived, travelling with his father and mother. He approached the Severns' apartment with a letter from Henry Acland asking Joseph to be kind to young John Ruskin, who had lately won the Newdigate Prize. At their first meeting they did not exchange a word. Ruskin had climbed laboriously up the stairway, "broad to about the span of an English lane that would allow two carts to pass," of the house in the Via Rasella. "I was within eighteen or twenty steps of Mr. Severn's door, when it opened, and two gentlemen came out, closed it behind them with an expression of excluding the world for ever more from that side of the house, and began to descend the stairs to meet me, holding to my left. One was a rather short, rubicund, serenely beaming person; the other, not much taller, but paler." The first was Joseph, the second George Richmond. "They looked hard at me as they passed, but in my usual shyness . . . I made no sign, and leaving them to descend the reverting stair in peace, climbed at still slackening pace the remaining steps to Mr. Severn's door, and left my card and letter of introduction with the servant." [2]

---

[1] *Richmond Papers*, p. 45.   [2] J. Ruskin, *Praeterita*, vol. 2.

"That man has the face of a poet," said Severn to Richmond as they went on down the staircase.[1] They could not guess the fame that was to come to him, nor could they know that in his old age he was to be tended by a son of Joseph's yet unborn.

"There is nothing in any circle that ever I saw or heard of," wrote Ruskin, "like what Mr. Joseph Severn then was in Rome. He understood everybody, native and foreign, civil and ecclesiastic, in what was nicest in them, and never saw anything else than the nicest; or saw what other people got angry about as only a humorous part of the nature of things. It was the nature of things that the Pope should be at St. Peter's, and the beggars on the Pincian steps. He forgave the Pope his papacy, reverenced the beggar's beard, and felt that alike the steps of the Pincian, and the Aracœli, and the Lateran, and the Capitol, led to heaven, and everybody was going up, somehow; and might be happy where they were in the meantime. Lightly sagacious, lovingly humorous, daintily sentimental, he was in council with the Cardinals to-day, and at picnic in the Campagna with the brightest English belles to-morrow; and caught the hearts of all in the golden net of his good will and good understanding, as if life were but for him the rippling chant of his favourite song: 'Gente, è qui l'uccellatore '."

But Joseph's days in Rome were drawing to a close. Two reasons made him decide to return to England. The first was that his eldest son, Walter, was now nearly eleven years old, and his father wished him to go to an English school. The second was his conviction that Brown would never complete the Memoir of Keats unless he could see him and force him to it. Brown had been living in England now for five years.

So, with a sigh, Severn turned his back on Rome. On the evening of his last day in the city he made a melancholy pilgrimage to the grave of Keats. He had thought, in such a deserted spot, to rest in solitude a while. But, as he approached the grave, he saw, kneeling by it, hand in hand, two lovers, evidently English. He did not disturb them, but from his vantage point made a rapid sketch of the scene. His reaction was the same as that which had prompted him, during his wakeful night by the bedside of his dying friend, to draw his death-like countenance. It was not that his heart was cold, but rather that it overflowed on to the paper. His children were to be the same. At every crisis in their lives the

[1] *Richmond Papers*, p. 46.

Severns reached for paper and a pencil, and by crystallizing their emotion received comfort.

It was in March, 1841, that the Severn family arrived in England. They were soon established in a charming old house in Buckingham Gate. It had wainscot and carvings, panelled walls and a sunny garden behind. There, in the August of the following year, their last children were born to Joseph and Elizabeth—twins whom they named Arthur and Eleanor.

At the time of their birth Joseph's eldest child, Claudia with the beautiful voice, was thirteen. Next came Walter, one year younger, who was sent to Westminster School to be educated, as his father had always planned, as an English boy. Then came Ann Mary, who, at the age of ten, was already showing great artistic talent, and Henry, nine years old, who was entirely practical. He liked to take things to pieces to see how they worked. And now the twins.

Joseph's responsibilities, with so many children to provide for, began to weigh on him. When he first arrived in England there was all the bustle of finding and fitting into a house. Then there was the pleasure of seeing his mother again, very old now but as dear as ever, and his brothers and sisters and their children. There were many old friendships, too, that had been forged in Rome, to take up again in London, and the matter of the Keats Memoir to be investigated.

Joseph's faith in Keats's genius had never wavered during these long years when his friend's name was still comparativly unknown. He felt it his duty to see that a Life of Keats was published, which should put before the public the many poems that had remained unpublished since his death. But when he arrived in London he found that Charles Brown was about to sail for New Zealand. Brown had made an immediate decision on hearing a lecture about the new colony. His son, Carlino, had already gone, and he was full of grandiose schemes for their future. Before he left he handed over all his material for the Life to Mr. Richard Monckton-Milnes, who, seven years before, as an admirer of Keats's poetry, had sought out Joseph in Rome, when he was travelling abroad after having taken his degree at Cambridge. As an undergraduate Milnes, with his friend Arthur Hallam, had been responsible for the reprinting of *Adonais*, but the first reprint of Keats's poems in England was not until 1840, the year after Joseph returned to England, and nearly twenty years after Keats's death.

Once the material was in Monckton-Milnes's hands, Joseph was satisfied that the Memoir would be produced. But he was very distressed when he heard the next year of Charles Brown's death in New Zealand. Brown and Keats and Joseph had been so linked in their old life, and when Keats had died, Brown and Joseph had drawn even closer together through more than ten years when they had both been living in Italy. There was news, too, that year that George Keats had died in Kentucky. Joseph wrote sadly to Charles Eastlake that, with all these friends, "his sense of youth had gone for ever." [1]

Now that his son was at an English school, and the materials for the Life of Keats were in safe hands, Joseph turned again to his painting. But he found it difficult to sell his pictures. He was pleased soon if he had one commissioned picture on hand, and even thought of returning to miniatures, until he found that miniature-painting, too, was out of fashion. His hopes now centred on a new form of work—fresco-painting. There was a great competition to decide who should paint the frescoes at Westminster in the new Houses of Parliament. The subjects were selected from the works of English poets. Joseph submitted his cartoon to the Committee.

His anxiety was very great, so that he was overjoyed to receive a letter from Mr. Gladstone, putting an end to his suspense:

> "13, CARLTON HOUSE TERRACE.
> June 24th, '43. (Night.)
>
> MY DEAR SIR,—Mr. Rogers dined with me this evening, and hearing that the judges had to-day been engaged in passing sentence on the cartoons, I ventured to ask how one, which had for its subject the Princess Eleanor drawing the poison from the wound of Edward in the Holy Land, had been considered to stand. He told me that I had better not tell him whose it was but that I might mention to the artist who drew it, that according to the sentence of all the judges—except Lord Lansdowne, who had not yet seen the cartoons—it was in the number of the successful and selected. It gave me very great pleasure indeed to learn this, and I am anxious, in case it should not have already reached you, to lose no time in making it known.
>
> I remain, my dear Sir, Most faithfully yours,
>
> W. E. GLADSTONE." [2]

Joseph was elated by his success and concentrated all his

---

[1] Sharp, *op. cit.*, p. 201.   [2] *Ibid.*, p. 203.

energies and thoughts on fresco-painting, in spite of a rather
damping letter from John Ruskin in Venice:

". . . I cannot longer defer expressing my sincere gladness at
your well-deserved success, and my sympathy in all the enthusiasm
of your hopes, and I am also glad, for the sake of our national
honour, that you are to be one of its supporters. But with your
hopes for the elevation of English art by means of fresco I cannot
sympathize. I have not the remotest hope of anything of the
kind. . . . I see on our Academy walls nothing but what is ignoble
in small pictures, and would be disgusting in large ones. I never
hear one word of genuine feeling issue from anyone's mouth but
yours, and the two Richmonds', and if it did, I don't believe the
public of the present day would understand it. . . ." [1]

This fresco at Westminster not only gave him work to do but
also brought him another commission when it was ended. The
Countess of Warwick engaged him to decorate a magnificent hall
at the house, Gatton Park, Reigate, which her son had built for
her "in imitation of a fine building in Rome." Here he had
thirteen men working under him, a pianoforte and an organ in
the house, and "a fine library, even of music." He confessed
himself in Paradise. But when the work was finished he had to
look round again. There were not many people in England
who wanted large walls of their houses to be painted with
frescoes.

For the first eight years in England things went fairly well.
Something always "turned up." Mrs. Severn's relations were
very kind to them. Lord Eglinton continued to give his half-
sister an allowance. Joseph went to Scotland to paint "Lady
Eglinton and son, now three years old," [2] and the two eldest
children, Claudia and Walter, went frequently for long visits to
Eglinton Castle and to Rozelle in Ayrshire, where they stayed
with Lord Eglinton's aunt, Lady Jane Hamilton. Claudia was
pretty and sang beautifully when the ladies showed their accomplishments in the evening. All Elizabeth's daughters inherited her air
of distinction and her good taste in dress. As for Walter, he
delighted the ladies by making clever sketches of them skating
or playing croquet, though he preferred to draw stags, and "Stags
in the Snow at Bay" was duly presented to Lord Eglinton as a
birthday present. Lord Eglinton was Walter's hero. "He plays

[1] Sharp, op. cit., p. 205.   [2] Letter, Jan. 21st, 1845.

F*

at racketts (with which game all the gentlemen in Scotland seem to be mad) as at *every other* most perfectly, beats everybody as he seems to do easily in every other game."

Meanwhile the twins, Arthur and Eleanor, lived quietly in the house at Buckingham Gate. Eleanor's earliest memory was of their Roman nurse—her brown neck and her necklace of large coral beads. When she left them to return to Italy, their brother, Henry, used to help his mother to pull the twins along in a little green wooden chaise. There were no perambulators yet. They would go to the Mall and drink milk from the cows that were kept there, and Henry made them little boats and took them to St. James's Park to sail them on the water.

The nursery windows looked over Wellington Barracks, and gazing out of them, at the age of five, Eleanor fell in love with a drummer-boy in the Guards. Through the good offices of her parents' friend, Colonel Palliser, who lived with his family a few doors away, the little boy was brought to the nursery and performed with his drum, while the twins gaped at him in silent hero-worship. The young Pallisers were wild Irish children, and their favourite game was to climb up on the Severns' garden wall and, with a hook and string, pull up sunflowers from Sir Edward Bulwer Lytton's garden. Another favourite game was to dress up Mr. Severn's lay figure as a ghost and then to send Arthur or Eleanor to fetch something from his study.

Henry Severn was the only child to be affected by the change of climate. His health was bad and he lived entirely at home. He was always making engines and machines, and at fourteen developed what his sister called "a talent for electricity." He took exception to the number of cats which wandered into their garden, and put a wire along the top of the wall, together with a saucer of milk. The cats came to drink, received an electric shock and quickly disappeared. One day he gave the old cook a shock. When she was brought round by an anxious Mrs. Severn she could only gasp, "Lor'! What a wonderful boy Master Henry is!"

The following year, 1848, when the twins were six, was the year of the Chartist Riots. Troops were stationed all over London. The Duke of Wellington took charge. Artillery was posted in St. James's Place. The Chartists gathered on Clapham Common. It looked like the beginning of a revolution. Joseph and his son Walter were enrolled as special constables, and for forty-eight hours London was under military rule. The windows of the house in Buckingham Gate were barricaded, but nothing was thrown at them. The twins sat with their mother in the darkened room and heard the heavy stamp of feet passing outside. Arthur had to be restrained from climbing up on to the roof "to pour boiling water on them." Anxiety was great until Walter appeared to tell Mama that the crowds had dispersed and there was no further danger.

The twins often watched the Queen drive out of Buckingham Palace to Drawing-Rooms at St. James's Palace, and more than once they saw the great Duke of Wellington riding down Birdcage Walk. They gazed with awe at the iron shutters of Apsley House, which the Duke had put up after the riots.

Many interesting people came to visit their parents. They heard Mendelssohn play on their father's piano, they listened to Leigh Hunt discoursing on poetry. Young Dante Gabriel Rossetti arrived with a letter of introduction from his father which begged Mrs. Severn to be kind to him as he was very shy.[1] And Mrs. Gladstone came, as lovely and as gay and kind as ever. With her usual carelessness and indifference about what she was wearing, she could not find her hat when she rose to leave. After the room had been turned upside down it was eventually discovered in the coal-scuttle.[2]

Walter was now eighteen years old and, having left Westminster, he was to try for a clerkship in the Privy Council Office. To Mrs. Severn's dismay, he chose, a few days before he was to appear before the Council, to have a fight, which lasted for three-quarters of an hour, with a boy larger than himself. "I remember," wrote Eleanor, "his coming home (he was a day boy) and I ran to the door to open it for him, knowing his knock. I was terribly frightened! There he stood with a black and bruised face quite unrecognizable. He was obliged to remain in bed for a day or two, and when he was better had to go and be seen by 'My Lords' at the P.C. Office. I stood at the bottom of the stairs to see him descend resplendent in his first tail coat. Both his eyes were still black and when he entered the room they remarked on the fact. The President of the Council was old Lord Lansdowne, and he was a great friend of my mother and father. He had been at Westminster himself and, on hearing how Walter had got his black eyes, said, 'A fight—and at Westminster—sit down and tell

[1] Claudia Gale, *A Victorian Artist*.
[2] From the diary of Eleanor Severn.

us all about it!' He was appointed to a clerkship and was in the office for forty years!" [1]

Monckton-Milnes's Life of Keats was published that year and acclaimed by the critics. Joseph painted a portrait of Milnes and another of Mr. Gladstone. Meanwhile his daughter, Mary, was studying with George Richmond.

[1] From the diary of Eleanor Severn.

CHAPTER XIII

MARY

(1852—1857)

THE Richmonds lived at No. 10 York Street, off Portman Square. The two families were great friends, the children treating each other as brothers and sisters. George Richmond was a die-hard Tory, a staunch Churchman and a man of very high ideals. But he was a stern father, and a lapse from grace by any of his ten children was immediately punished by a thrashing. In spite of this he could be "as playful as a child when he unbent." His children loved him and so did the young Severns.

Every Christmas the Richmonds gave a children's party at York Street. It was Joseph who made these parties such a success. His good spirits delighted the children as much as they did an older generation. His jokes and laughter banished shyness and charmed them into complete enjoyment. Little Arthur Severn and Willie Richmond used to be encouraged to wrestle. They were the same age, and at five years old they both wore short white breeches, which were black by the time the match was ended.

"Mr. Joseph Severn was a great acquisition," wrote Willie Richmond later. "He had a time-honoured trick, beloved by the children, of manufacturing a black cat seated on the top of a door with its tail hanging down. The cat was fashioned out of a tea-canister, with gleaming tin eyes; but in order to represent its fur, an old beaver hat was required, of which he cut off the brim. In Mr. Severn's excitement, however, for the success of the trick, he was not always too particular whose hat he got hold of, so that people with good hats found it necessary to hide them, for a beaver hat in those days often cost as much as four pounds!"[1]

Mary Severn was fortunate in her teacher. George Richmond was a drastic critic and would permit no slovenliness of execution. He demanded extreme accuracy and patience. He worked a great deal in crayons and water-colour, and Mary could have had no better teacher in these mediums. He had done portraits of most of the leading men and women of his day. Cardinal Newman, Charlotte Brontë, Mrs. Gaskell and Lord Macaulay were among

[1] *Richmond Papers*, p. 105.

his sitters. He was very fond of Mary, not only because of her charm, which was compounded of great sweetness leavened with lively humour, but also because he saw in her unusual talent, application beyond her years, and a profound belief in God.

Sometimes she would stay at York Street for a week or two, sleeping in Mr. Richmond's dressing-room, which was hung round with his early drawings. When Richmond went out during one of these visits, his wife would give her the key of the studio and leave to bring down any drawings to copy. In return for all this kindness Mary drew portraits of the three youngest children for Mrs. Richmond. She was beginning to show "the greatest power in catching a likeness," and was particularly successful with children.

Mary was nineteen when Claudia married, early in 1852.

With every year, their father had been finding it more difficult to make enough money to support his family. Fortunately Walter was working in the Privy Council Office and Mr. Gladstone had obtained a position for Henry in the Mint. Inspired by his friends Ruskin and Eastlake (now Sir Charles and President of the R.A.), who had both achieved success in writing about art, Joseph tried his hand with the pen. He wrote a novel about Titian in Rome, which was never published, as well as papers and essays on painting and painters. But they had no success. With his vagueness about money he did not realize how serious his financial position was becoming. By thinking about it, he could convert a passing reference in conversation with a friend into a definite order which had only to be confirmed; so that even at his lowest ebb he saw himself as surrounded by promising possibilities which might any of them, at any moment, materialize into a splendid commission.

His wife saw what was coming. She realized that they could not go on living in Buckingham Gate, and found a cheaper house in Belgrave Road. Walter and Claudia were staying at Eglinton Castle for the move, and after some thought, Mama wrote to her eldest son. She had noticed that Mr. Frederick Gale, a young barrister and a well-known amateur cricketer, seemed very impatient for Claudia's return. He was certainly making enough money to marry, and she believed that he wished to marry Claudia, whom he had known for several years. On the other hand, she did not know what Claudia's feelings were towards him, and she was certainly very popular in Scotland, where she had made many friends. So she wrote to Walter. What did he think?

MARY SEVERN
from the self-portrait in the National Portrait Gallery, London.

24th June /49

JOSEPH SEVERN
from a drawing by Mary Severn, 1849

Walter was the most worldly of the Severns, and had a good opinion of himself. His letters home from Eglinton were full of his triumphs. He had been out shooting several times lately and "not very often miss." The governess had taken a tremendous fancy to him and "praises me to everybody in the most absurd way." Even when he had just described how he had been run away with on a horse, he ended complacently, "with a little practice I should soon ride."

He thought over what his mother said, weighing in his mind the apparently eager Mr. Gale in London and the expense of the journey South—oh, but that would be all right, because Lady Eglinton would be certain to give her the money for her ticket, she was always so kind to them all. Claudia was undoubtedly having a great success in Scotland. Everyone seemed to like her and there was at least one gentleman whom Walter suspected of deeper feelings towards her.

"Well, about Claudia returning," he wrote. "Now I think this, that Claudia should go to London (*la Signora pagherà*) for a little time and if Gale is not ready that she should go back and he must then take his chance of future events." [1]

Claudia returned to London and all went as Mrs. Severn had forecast. Frederick Gale proposed and was accepted. They were married in the following February at St. Peter's, Eaton Square.

Mary was beginning to make money. As her father's commissions grew further and further apart, her own were becoming more frequent. She had done several portraits in water-colour or crayon for her friends, and by them she had been recommended to other people. Her twentieth birthday came, and that autumn she went to Ireland, to stay with a brother of Colonel Palliser, to paint his sister and her children. The Colonel came over while she was there and she painted his portrait, too. These pictures were so good that she was invited by several friends of the Pallisers to stay in their houses and to paint their children or the proud Mamas.

"I am in great spirits," she wrote happily, "for I see more and more 'coms,' in perspective. I shall soon make quite a fortune!" She sent money home to her mother, half a ten-pound note in one letter, and the second half in the next. She stayed in several different country houses, the owners being most friendly and helpful to her, and was able to ask ten or fifteen pounds a picture. In one house

---

[1] Letter from Rozelle, Ayr, 1851.

she was introduced to Louisa Marchioness of Waterford, the celebrated beauty and artist. They went on several painting expeditions together.[1] In spite of the pleasure she felt at working well and making enough money to keep herself, she was sometimes irked by the too great comfort and regularity of the life led by her various hosts. She felt homesick for their own haphazard happy household, with its constant interruptions of crisis or excitement.

"Last night we dined with Mrs. Phipps," she wrote. "I sat next to Colonel Phipps who, altho' such an interesting person, full of information, was so absorbed in the discipline of his dishes, his servants, his wines, and his sauces, that I could get little or nothing out of him during such an important time as dinner! I think it is such nonsense people being so particular about the waiting, etc. Surely a little originality is delightful, now and then I long for the Denbigh Terrace irregularities; I think our way of living is after all the most interesting—at all events we have variety!"

Poor Mary was to have rather too much variety when she returned from Ireland.

She was staying at Charleville, in Co. Wicklow, with Lord Monck, when she heard that Claudia had given birth to a daughter in London. She was painting the three little girls and, although the Moncks were very kind to her, she longed to be back with her own family. People's values seemed so different here. They attached importance to things which she had always disregarded or simply accepted as something natural, and in no way remarkable.

"You can have no idea," she wrote to Mama, "how extremely polite Lord and Lady M. are to me. Lord M. took me to the Glens and when he asked me to go he said 'If I would do him the honour to accompany him.' But really you can have no idea to what an extent they carry it. When they were out for a walk Lady M., though tired, insisted on remaining with me and an oldish bachelor and when we were home she said, 'Now you are under *my* charge and I could not think of letting you out of my sight. What would Mrs. Severn say if she heard I let you walk alone with any gentleman?' Lady M. is very proud and does not like people who are not good-looking and well-bred. She seems to think more of me because I am in some way related to the Eglintons. I am sure this is one of the reasons why she likes me. The other day Mr. W. was speaking *very much* against Lady E. I saw Lady M.

---

[1] Claudia Gale, *A Victorian Artist*.

look very uncomfortable, and looking across and not answering him. I took no notice, made a few remarks and thought no more of it. The moment we were out of the room, she came to me in way of apologizing for what Mr. W. had said; 'I am so sorry, so hurt that such a thing was said at my table, but the moment I had an opportunity I told Mr. W. he ought not to have said it before you. But cannot you imagine I was *too* glad to give him the reason.' I see she thinks a good deal of rank, more so than of talent. She is the daughter of the Earl of Rathdowne."

Thank goodness Mary is back, thought Mrs. Severn, as she listened to her daughter talking to little Eleanor while she unpacked. She had not been feeling quite the thing lately, and all this worry had really been wearing her out. She had had days when she could eat nothing, days of dizziness and an aching back. Mary was her great support, she was so sensible and so helpful and considerate. Now here she was to share the family troubles and to help her mother to find some way out. Mrs. Severn gave a sigh of relief.

The other children were not quite the same. Claudia was newly married and could think of nothing but her husband, her house, and her new baby—although it was true that Frederick Gale had been very kind. Walter's reactions to their troubles seemed to be confined so far to indignation at his father's fecklessness. Whenever she spoke to him he flew into a rage about it. Henry's health was still bad. He was an engineer and working at the Mint. Now he was talking about emigrating to Australia at the end of the year. There remained Arthur and Eleanor, the twins, now ten years old. They had been attending a day school. But how shall we educate them now, thought Mrs. Severn despairingly. Well, we must see what turns up. Mary will help with them. They both adore her. But she must be careful not to allow Mary's prospects, which seemed so favourable, to be swept away on the tide of her father's misfortune. She must not be sacrificed for her brothers and sisters— or her father, thought Mama firmly. As for Severn, she thought, he is of little help. He is so unpractical. Even now, I doubt if he realizes how serious the position is.

That evening, when the twins were in bed, Mary and her mother sat up late, adding up the bills, calculating how much could be realized by Papa's pictures and drawings if they were sent to Christie's. They had to face the fact that there was little demand now for his *genre* of painting. Mary, at twenty, was already making as much money as her father. His debts had been accumulating, and although Mama had so far staved off disaster, Mary realized as she went through the papers that at any moment they might be overwhelmed by an avalanche of writs. They talked late into the night and Mama told her all that had happened while she had been away.

Luckily the Severns had many friends. One of the most helpful had been a dour Mr. Lockhart, who had known Mama as a child. He lived on Brixton Hill, at a house called The Elms, with a self-righteous, tight-lipped niece who disapproved of the Severns and their unmethodical, slap-dash ways, though she was as enthusiastic as her uncle about the new craze of table-turning. To Brixton Hill Mama had gone frequently for advice during the last few months. She had got it in plenty, and devastating criticism too. But in the end she usually got the help she sought, although she had several times left the house in tears. Lately, when she had felt one of her attacks coming on, she had gone to rest at Mr. Lockhart's, until she was driven out by Miss Macdonald's nagging, or had to rush away to answer a call from her husband or one of her children.

Eventually Mama said they had talked enough on such a sad subject. Now she must hear all about the pictures Mary had done in Ireland, and then they must arrange one of the rooms as a proper studio for her. Already she had one commission waiting for her—a portrait of that handsome Mrs. Babington—and she must have her own room to work in, where her sitters could come to her. Mary was delighted with the idea. She had been wondering how she could manage. With such an entrancing subject before them they soon forgot their troubles in the excitement of deciding what furniture, carpet and curtains would be most suitable, and how they should be arranged. After various suggestions had been reviewed they went happily up to bed.

Mary Severn's Diary

15th June, 1853. Mama is at Brixton. I do hope she will soon return, for all the bills that are owing come due either to-day or to-morrow, and I wonder what is to be done. Papa has sent "The Pantheon" to Sir T. Medington's in hopes that he may buy the picture. The sketches are to be sold at Christie's on the 17th, and I hope something good will turn up; Mama sends me a pound now and then from Brixton which I lay out as economically as I can for the house. Walter has taken lodgings in Charlwood Street where he has taken *all* his things and some valuable books, not knowing what may happen soon if there is no money!

19th June. Papa's sketches did not sell at all. Friday and Saturday people called for money and it was difficult to send them away. I spent a pleasant evening at the Pallisers' and turned tables, hats, and even Colonel Grant round, tho' I felt very anxious about what we should do to-morrow, for Gardiner's bill for £50 comes due.

Monday, 20th. Mama returned from Brixton, but with no things—not being able to risk them in our house. She and I went out for a long time looking for lodgings as I cannot lose my drawings also, if any Execution takes place. We found a very respectable family in Charlwood Street. Everything was soon arranged. They seemed to like us, and we offered many references. Madame Bunsen and *A.* (*Lord Eglinton*). Said we wished to be here for a week only till our new house was ready. We paid our guinea and said we should send the boxes this evening—We take a hurried tea, pack up. Walter calls a cab, everything is put in and he says he will take me.

"What number is it?" he said. I did not know, but said I knew the house. We went up and down the street, and could not find it; at last we got out of the cab, which followed at a respectful distance, but I could not tell even the street. So we went back to Denbigh Terrace, and Mama came back with us. Walter I saw was angry, but he behaved well and did not "bully." We found the house—the boxes were carried up and locked in the bedroom. I went back with Mama, who was obliged to rush back to Brixton where she was late for dinner, for Mr. Lockhart had a table to turn round and she must go. We tried to persuade Papa not to go there as he had been so often lately, and we wanted him to go at once somewhere in the country for fear of his being arrested, but *no*, he would go to The Elms.

Tuesday. Early in the morning I was woke by Walter standing by my bedside. He told me Papa was gone!

"I am so delighted," I said, tho' I had not the least idea where he was.

Walter—"I walked home with Gale last night, and he says that as there is notice, Papa must go away or he will be arrested. So at two or three this morning, before I went to my lodgings, I came here, knocked up Anne, ran up to Papa, and told him in a few words the state of affairs. And oh how provoking he is! Would you believe it, but as usual he said it was nothing, and began to talk about the tables going round! I really think the man is mad."

"Then he is gone," I said.

"Yes," said Anne, who just came in with my hot water, "he went off at daylight. I never seed him, but I heard him looking for his shoes in the back kitchen!" Poor Papa, I felt sorry for him.

I dressed quickly and joined Walter who waited to see Mama, but she never came, so he went, leaving messages for her. I sat in lone splendour darning Eleanor's stockings, waiting for the many pleasant (?) visitors I expected. Mama soon came. We went off to Fred. Gales to know whether anything could be done. After all the business he told me that Mary Palliser wished me to go at a quarter to five to dine there and hear "Sardanapalus." I was charmed and so afraid if I went home to dress I might not go at all, in the midst of all the business. So we went to Fred. Gale's—and Mama asked him if Jardine's lawyer would be satisfied if Walter and Henry paid £5 each quarter, and in this way pay all the £100, which was for their education.

Walter was sent for from the office, I and Eleanor and Arthur retired in the next room, while all this was settling—but I did not like to hear many altercations. Walter is worried with all the bothers, and gets so soon irritated. He does not agree to the plan. He went away—and Mama and I discussed it quietly with Fred.— Walter and Henry are very good, but this standing security Walter is right would not do; he is already involved in debt without adding to it, and it would do no good—So we decided that the lawyers had better put an execution in the house.

Mama went away leaving me, and Fred kindly took me to Mr. Palliser's. I dined there, saw "Sardanapalus" with which I was delighted, the Nineveh Marbles seem to come to life. But how I longed for my quiet lodgings, and scarcely liked going home. Mama laughed when I said, "Well, some girls wish for a new dress or flowers, but I wish with all my heart I had a lodging!"

Wednesday, 22nd. Mama is well and in great business. I am sent off with Eleanor to my lodgings, where we unpacked, washed and dressed—Mama soon came, told me she had heard from Papa that he had got tin—Mr. Monteith, knowing (for Papa had written) he was in difficulty, gave him a generous present of £20.

The Bunsens had invited us to a party. Mama was most anxious to go—but all her clothes were at Brixton. As she felt afraid of having them at home she gave up all ideas of going, but I was to dress and she would send the cab for me and I was to call at Denbigh Terrace, in case she might go after all. No cab came. I sent for one, and as soon as it came Anne appeared and whispered to me that the broker was in the house, Mama wished to remain there, that I was to make some excuse for her. This was a pleasant thing to hear just as I was stepping in the cab to go to a gay party. Everyone was most kind, the music so fine, Beethoven's, that it almost made one cry. I went to bed thinking of all I had to do next day—I must get up early, and take all my paints to Denbigh Terrace and paint Mrs. B. there—for as something good may turn up we need not tell her all this.

Thursday, 23rd. No sooner was I dressed than Anne arrived, well loaded with things we wished saved: workbox, paint brushes etc. with a few lines from Mama to say that I must paint Mrs. Babington here for there were bothers at our house! Eleanor and I had breakfast, then she arranged the rooms for Mrs. B. When all was arranged I went to Denbigh Terrace that I might the better explain to Mrs. B. the reason of the change. I said we were moving. She was charmed with our house and with Eleanor, who has begun a great friendship with her. I felt extremely anxious about the picture and would not show it to Mrs. Ellis till I had improved it. They said they were delighted with it. While I painted Mama arrived with a clergyman—he came from Mr. Richmond anxious to see some pictures of mine of children, and he said he would like to let me do the picture in the country at his place. I was delighted to think I had another "com" in perspective.

When Mrs. B. went, Eleanor and I dressed ourselves nicely and went to see what had taken place at Denbigh Terrace. How good Mama's description was—she said she had a broker in the dining-room, Miss Macdonald and Fred in one parlour and the Clergyman from Richmond in another room; and had to talk and arrange matters for all these different things!!!

Mama—"Now, Mary, listen to me—I must go off to Papa who is at Islington at his sister's, Mrs. Giles, and consult him about the sketches and tell him also that he must meet Fred. Gale at 9 o'clock to-night.—By the bye, read this letter from Papa."

It ran thus: "I am sure all will go right—Lord Lansdowne has offered to lend me £250, if I can give him proper security for the amount—and I think the Altar piece, but as he does not want pictures, having so many, I have written to Lord Wilton to sell if he can guarantee that the subscriptions will be paid—then Lord L. would give the £250, which will set us all right! I am really quite miserable. It grieved me to leave dear Mary and Eleanor at dawn on Monday without seeing them, and how I trembled under my carpet Bag! Do go to Monteith's Hotel and see if Lord Wilton's answer is there for me."

Mama—"Do let us have a 'spree' and go to Papa's in a hansom cab."

Mary—"No, that's such an expense."

Mama—"Well, I am too done to wander about in and out of those nasty omnibus's, I should never get there—Come let's go."

Arthur would not come but remained flying his kites on the Balcony. Mama, Eleanor and I went. We walked to St. James's Street where Eleanor called a hansom. When we were in it, Mama breathed freely and said:

"Well, however poor I am there are certain things I cannot give up—Hansoms, cold cream and violet powder."

We arrived at Mrs. Giles's little Lodging—found Papa out, but sent a message to him to come directly. Mrs. Giles I had never seen before—a person she seemed who looked as if, if brought up in good society, she would have been a very different person from what she seems now. I was greatly struck watching the difference between Mama and her—Mama quite at her ease sat with one leg over the other, her arms anyhow, and talked etc. while this Mrs. G. seemed constrained and afraid to do anything that we might think *vulgar*. After a pause she asked us if we had got thro' our moving (for Papa as a reason for going off there told her we were changing house and wished him out of the way), she asked this in such a quiet tame way, and Mama and I, who were thinking of anything but a *new* house, burst out laughing, we could not contain ourselves.

Papa arrived. There was a long discussion in Italian about the affairs. Papa said he would not go to Fred. Gale's for these lawyers and duns might pounce upon him—Then we decided that nothing could be done till we knew Lord W.'s answer—and Mama was to call for it that night at the Hotel. Papa talked and talked with Mama. I went downstairs with Eleanor to show them we must go.

Papa walked with us to a cab, for a bus "would not do as we had to go to many places." Mama got out at the Hotel to see if the letter was there. I looked out of the cab window anxiously, but there was none. We drove at once to Fred. Gale's. It was half-past ten, Eleanor was half asleep. She remained outside the room while we talked to Fred. Fred wishes me to go there and stay, but I told him that I could not till Wednesday for I was to

. have my last sitting of Mrs. B. and I could not ask her to come to another house! But he begged me to put away all books of Papa's which I might have about my rooms, and also not to let his creditors know where I was. Mama brought us home in the cab—we were soon in bed.

Friday, 24th. We slept till late. I packed up all the books I could find with " J. Severn" in them. Then we went off to see Mary Palliser and tell her I must give up all idea of Exeter Hall, to-night. Mama came and paid us a hurried visit. She was in a great state of nervousness, for she fancied she had lost some of her tin which she declares quite "sits upon" her, for she is afraid to leave it anywhere, and therefore carries it about with her. She was going off to The Elms, for Lady L. of Lee offered to take her there and back. Then Mama was going to Islington to Papa.

When she had left I had a letter from her, saying: "My dear Mary, I thought you looked pale, and it *vexes* me to think there are so many nice things to talk about, and I had not one minute even to see Mrs. B.'s picture! I am just like a Hare hunted to death—but for your *own* comfort I tell you that by dint of driving here and there and using the *common* sense God has given me, I *firmly* believe that even now at the eleventh hour, I *shall* be able to do something. But if I do succeed it will be only for *this once*, and *no more*, the bills were to have been posted over the house *to-morrow* morning, and the sale to take place on *Tuesday*, but *I think I can prevent it all*"—This was consoling certainly—I pray that all will still be right. All is for some good—we must in some way be "weaned" for this transitory world, and God in his mercy sends each one of us something to bear with. "Through much tribulation" we are to attain Christ's Kingdom—"no Cross, no Crown."

Sunday, 26th. It rained. We did not go to Church till the afternoon—About seven or eight o'clock Arthur ran in with a letter from Mama telling me Mr. Bell and Sir Edwin Landseer had been and seen the pictures. They seemed quite distressed at the state of our affairs, and Mama thinks they will do something. In the letter, she said Henry was with her and that they were watching a mouse, which was obliged to run away from having too much to eat. I could not think this mouse's case was in the least illustrative of us—for as I said to her in my answer, as yet I had nothing but one easel to furnish our empty rooms in the fifty-pound-house Mama always has in her eye.

Monday, 27th. Miss Thornton came with a Gentleman to look

at the picture I am copying. She asked a great deal about my pictures of children. So perhaps I shall have a "com." This is my birthday. I am twenty-one. I never was so pleased with a birthday, for a great deal depends on my being of age. Mr. Richmond and Walter soon came—How kind of Mr. R. Altho' ill, he trailed here and was most kind, and promises me plenty of "coms"—Mama and Henry came carrying a splendid Desk, a present from them! We had great fun, though the circumstances were so melancholy—Mr. R. and Walter sat on the balcony saying they were ruining the ladies' Establishment. Mr. R. looked like an out door Patient, with a handkerchief dipped in Eau de Cologne round his head! We all laughed *very* much—

Tuesday, 28th. Mrs. Babington and her daughter came. It was my last sitting—Mr. Palliser came and greatly amused them with his clever criticisms—the picture quite pleased them—Mrs. B. asked Eleanor and I to go there on Friday and stay for a week.

Eleanor and I were out during the day and met Anne, who said, "Would you like to see your Mama?" And took me into yet another lodging in Charlwood Street where I found Mama surrounded by bundles of clothes, (she had no boxes as all had been used in carrying our own things)—writing letters. I spoke to her for one moment and went to Claudia's. All were well there, C. knowing nothing of all that had happened—the baby looking lovely and all Claudia's hopes, griefs and joys concentrated in this one subject, so even had she known all our annoyances, she had no time for them to disturb her.

Wednesday, 29th. As soon as we could Eleanor and I went to Mama's house. Between the four we have, I often make a confusion! We luncheoned at Walter's office. On our way home we went to Mama's to see if anything had transpired during our absence.

"Mr. Bell has been here, and Sir Edwin Landseer wishes to be introduced to you, and I fixed 4 o'clock to-day—I am so glad you are at home," Mama said.

This was indeed great news. I went home, dressed myself, arranged my pictures. Mama came. We both thought how the sale was going on—at that time our fate was being decided in a great way. Mr. B. and Landseer soon came. They were most kind; Sir E. took my book of sketches with him.

Mr. Vaux came from the sale looking tired and fagged. When he was alone with us, we made him refresh himself with washing, we gave him tea. We laughed over a great many things. He,

poor man, is an antiquary, so he bought in for us all the old rubbish,
which I with all my heart wished at the bottom of the Red Sea!
How good he is—he bought the sofa! Mama and I laughed so
much that we were obliged to give him the reason.

"Did any one see the back of it?" I asked.

"Did any one see the side?" Mama said.

"No," Mr. V. said, "I think not, but why do you ask?"

We gave him the history of the marvellously quick way in
which a cover of 3/9d was "Blown on" by me, when I came from
Ireland and found the sofa in so disgraceful a state, but how right
Mama was not to get a *better one*. It was all beautiful (the cover *I*
made) but one square place which I had not stuff enough to cover,
and great ingenuity was shown by us, in the way in which this
great deficiency was concealed. We placed a portfolio there, which
we took care to keep always empty to insure its being stationary.
About £150 was realized at this Sale—so the Jardine debt and the
part rent no longer "sits upon" us.

Friday, 1st July. Very busy packing and arranging for we go
to Windsor by three o'clock train. Claudia came to see me. She
was rather in my way as I was packing, so I told her to go and
sing downstairs, which was delightful for me. I heard all my
favourite songs thro' the floors.

Saturday, July 9th. Arrived back from Windsor.

Sunday, July 10th. Walter came in, looking so well, and at last
confessed to me he had spent hours at his toilette. We talked
about the hour, the weather and the possibility of our being able
to go to Westminster Abbey. Walter was irritable. I really felt
alarmed—he did not seem to understand the "whys and wherefores"
of any of our plans. When he wanted to know why we did not
all go and live in Scotland, and I said I wished to learn drawing,
he laughed in my face and said I drew better than many artists,
"what the deuce do you want with drawing?" However after a
long time, when we were all too late for Abbey, Church or anything, he became pacified, acknowledged he was wrong and all
was settled. He took up my paint brush and painted some pretty
stags in my sketch book.

Monday, 11th. Mama came and told me she had been break-
fasting with Walter, for she had to tell him all her new ideas, which
she had told no one, about its not being fair to make Walter and
Henry pay Papa's debts. We talked it over. She said she must
go to Brixton and tell Mr. Lockhart at once. "How angry he will
be! I am afraid to see him; still I do not care, I am only doing

my duty as a Mother!" She went—I painted in my new study, worked on Mrs. Synot and the new Mrs. B.

Mama came home looking ill.

"Is Mr. Lockhart civil?" I said.

"O very, but he won't agree." Then she told me what had put her most out was Miss Lockhart asking her whether she was living at Denbigh Terrace? that she might save on the lodgings. This greatly annoyed Mama, and she told Mr. L. she took it quite as an insult asking her now, in all the troubles, why she was not living in an empty house, with nothing but one iron bed, merely because we had paid £10 extra, because we had stayed in it beyond quarter day. All this made Mama very angry. After some time and difficulty Mama told Mr. L. before his niece she wished to speak to him alone. Then she told him the whole of her ideas.

"Now as you do not agree, you are offended as I expected, Mr. L?"

He said, no he was not offended as it was no affair of his—but that his ideas would remain *unchanged*.

When the post came, a letter from Mr. Lockhart. Such a letter! about five sheets of paper—saying he could not account for the sudden change—that Mama was quite wrong—that Mrs. Severn's sons ought to give this moderate sum (£30) for the liquidation of their father's debts, and that however Mama might alter her mind, or however much a noble Lord who she mentioned might be on her side, he would use every endeavour in his power to counteract every influence she used. The letter was rather tremendous, it floored Mama. She put it in her pocket and said she would consult Lord E. about it.

We went to Claudia's. She was upstairs putting the baby to sleep, but Mr. Palliser came up to see us, while Fred and Vaux were smoking in the garden. Mr. Palliser was so kind, saw there was something wrong, and sat by Mama and amused her. Seeing that would not do, he tried to find out the cause of her looking so cast down. She showed him the outside of this letter—then by degrees she told him all in a whisper. From the few words I heard him say, I saw at once *his* view of the case—that Walter and Henry should do no such thing. Mr. Vaux soon came up—we all talked about Music, etc. Mama whispered to me she must go off at once to Lord E. Mama told Mr. Palliser and he kindly said he would take Mama there—half-past eleven p.m.—and Vaux took Eleanor and I home. I sat up for Mama. She said Mr. P. and Lord E. were exactly of her opinion. She described to me so well her waiting in the cab till Lord E. returned from a party. Then as he and Lady E. stepped out of their carriage, Mama met him, leaving Mr. P. in the cab. They were very much surprised to see her. When all the business was arranged and Lord E. had read Mr. Lockhart's note—Lady E. asked Mama if she had come alone.

"No, I have someone in the cab." Then Lady E. again fished, but at last said, "Well, who is it, Mrs. Severn?" Mama said, "Mr. Palliser. You know they are really almost like sons, and I always make use of them to take me anywhere when I can't have Walter." Mama and I sat up till late concocting a letter to Mr. Lockhart.

Tuesday, July 12th. Mama did not send the letter but was writing another. She was up at daylight, went to the Baths, then tried to think well over all the affairs and write to Mr. Lockhart. I wrote to Papa telling him how the affair now stood. I wrote to Sir E. Landseer telling him we would be at his house at ten o'clock next morning. Walter came, changed our ideas as regards Mr. L. by saying he *wished* to pay £20 or £30 for Papa, and that Mama had better, instead of differing from Mr. Lockhart, put all in his hands. Mama then wrote a letter to Mr. L. in answer to his and putting all into his hands.

Wednesday, 13th. I found Mama out: she had gone to Brixton with the letter and walked all the way there!!!! I painted. Mama soon drove up in a cab and asked me whether I was ready for Landseer's, but we were late already. I soon dressed. We left Eleanor at home. Sir E. did not appear for some time—he was having breakfast. How kind, gentlemanlike and polite he is! He asked me all about my drawing—told me my book was at the Queen's, but that he had been ordered not to go there as Measles were at the Palace—so he could tell me nothing. He was most encouraging and said in a funny way, that I had got the A B C of the Art. He asked me if I knew Swinton's things, and said, smiling, that if I gave him a few lessons it would do him good. He asked me to copy some of Brocking's heads—and kindly wrote two notes for me, one to Colnaghi, recommending me, and begging him to lend me one or two drawings to copy—and a note to S. Rogers, whom I am going to see out of curiosity. McDowell, the sculptor, came in, to whom Landseer introduced us. Mr. M. offered to show us his studio—so as it was near we said goodbye and thanked this kind Sir E. L. and went with McDowell to his house. We saw beautiful things—he lives in Margaret Street, where we saw houses to let, and altho' Mama was dead tired, she went in to see one.

I drew—and quite finished Mrs. B. and was making arrangements for going out when Tom and Mary Richmond arrived to
carry me off there to tea! "Duty before Pleasure," I said to them—
So they went with me. Colnaghi was most polite and lent me the
picture. I then asked him as a great favour to allow me to have
the envelope of Landseer's letter; he read the letter over, then
said—

"This is a letter that ought to be in your possession more than
mine—"

'Dear Sir—Could you lend Miss S. one or two of Brocking's
drawings—a young beauty and old man with a fine beard—It
would be doing her a great kindness—she is worthy of it, has
great feeling for the Art, (besides poor Severn is in great
difficulties).'

Colnaghi then asked me to lend him some drawings of mine
to see—I said Goodbye to Tom and Mary—by the bye he gave
me a book *Talford's Tragedies* as a B.D. present. I went to Claudia's
—that I might talk to Gale—and also to get a muslin dress of
Claudia's like mine, which Gale won't let her wear as he thinks it
ugly, to mend mine.

Thursday, 14th. Mama told me that she had decided that all
was to be as Mr. Lockhart and Mr. Gale wished, that Walter was
to pay £30 a year and Henry £20. She really has been so worried
with all parties, for if they detect one little mistake (which is very
seldom if ever) these men and Miss Lockhart pounce upon her.
Why surely without her nothing could have been done, and how
mean it is of them to try and find the spots.

Friday, 15th. Mama up since 5 a.m. arranging all the bills of
the different creditors to take to F. Gale to-day. This house is
mine, I am of age, and all in it is my own property. Fred. Gale
tells me perhaps I shall have to swear to this—that no one may
touch my things thinking they are Papa's.

Tuesday, 19th. A letter from Gale, telling me to go off there
at once to give my affidavit. I went with Eleanor. He said since
he had written to me, he had heard from the lawyers at the County
Court who said that they would withdraw the summons, having
heard from Gale that Papa had no property and no house, and that
he was calling the Creditors together and telling them what Walter
and Henry were going to do. So Fred said I need not trouble
myself about this any longer as there was nothing else pending,
and that the lodgings etc. and things were all mine and no one
could touch them.

At last, with the aid of their friends, the family ship was righted. Joseph had already fled to Jersey to evade his creditors and was lucky enough to get commissions for two pictures there. Henry carried his point, obtained a position in the Australian Mint and departed, leaving the twins in tears, and carrying with him a testimony of his skill from the engineer, Fairbairn, in Manchester. Walter remained at the Privy Council Office, though his spare time was devoted to painting and etching. Mama proclaimed that it was an ideal opportunity for Mary to study in Paris and for the twins to learn French. In any case, the change would do them all good after what they had been through.

Filled with enthusiasm she swept them off to France. Mary went to work under Ary Scheffer, who was particularly pleased with one pencil drawing she made of Eleanor sitting with folded hands and eyes downcast. He held it up for his French pupils to see, telling them to look at a drawing by a young English girl that was better than anything they could do.[1] It is a proof of Mary's great charm that, even after this, she remained popular with her fellow-pupils.

When Joseph got back to London he lived in Mary's little house in Coleshill Street, off Eaton Square. Mama brought Arthur back with her, arranged for him to live with Papa and go to a day school. Then she returned to Paris, where she had established Eleanor in a little school of French girls. Joseph lived quietly in London, painting, seeing his friends—Richmond, Leigh Hunt, his brothers and sisters. The poet Frederick Locker-Lampson, who was taken by Joseph to meet Leigh Hunt, wrote of him:

"Mr. Joseph Severn was a jaunty, fresh-natured, irresponsible sort of being, leading a jocile, slip-shod, dressing-gowny artistic existence in Pimlico. Like his friend Hunt, he was not rich, but never seemed to be in actual want of anything, unless perhaps it might be a brush or a comb. . . . Mr. Severn was the most buoyant of Britons, a man of cheerful yesterdays and confident to-morrows. He had a prosperous laugh and coruscated with cheerfulness. . . . Severn was especially amusing when he indulged in the melancholy looking-back vein. 'Ah! Mr. Locker, our youth! That was the time when Hope and Fruition went hand in hand—*altri tempi, altri tempi*. What is left to us? Vain anxieties, delusive hopes, unexpected issues!'"[2]

---

[1] *The Times*, Jan. 23rd, 1866.
[2] Frederick Locker-Lampson, *My Confidences*, p. 342.

One delightfully unexpected issue was to come from Mary's stay in Paris.

Eleanor continued at her French school while Mama attended to her English education by taking her young daughter to the Bois in the summer, where they sat together on the grass and read Shakespeare's plays. Although her methods of education were not conventional, Mama certainly succeeded in making her children appreciative of beauty. Mary had written to her from Ireland, "Whenever I meet with a beautiful thought in poetry I always think how it would please you," and even the little twins' letters to each other, when they were only ten or eleven years old, were full of descriptions of pictures they had seen and books they had read.

Their return to London was again and again postponed. First Mary must finish the copies of two Van Dycks at the Louvre. Then she had a commission to do a chalk head of Lady Elgin and, after that, of Lady Elgin's sister, Lady Augusta Bruce. Finally, at the end of a letter from Mama describing a visit they all had made to Winterhalter's studio, where they had seen a *beautiful* picture of the Empress in a red velvet dress with her little baby— at the very end of this letter, in a scrawled postscript, Joseph read that Mary was "drawing the Prince Imperial."

So hurried and so much an afterthought was the postscript that he did not believe it. He wrote to Eleanor, "The mater says that Mary is drawing the Prince Imperial. It must be a mistake in her hurried letter."

But it was no mistake. Mary returned, in the spring of 1857, with her mother and sister, having completed her first Royal commission.

Mama and Eleanor settled down in the little house in Coleshill Street, but Mary began a round of visits where business and pleasure were to be combined. First she went to Bath, to stay with the sister of her grandfather, Lord Montgomerie, Lady Jane Hamilton. Lady Jane had been ill and was taking the waters at Bath, where she had Lord Eglinton's daughter, Egidia, staying with her. As the twins were the same age as Egidia, Mary took Arthur to be a companion for her. She stayed there for several weeks and painted a portrait of Lady Jane and two of Egidia. Then, after a few days in London, she was off again.

This time she went to Eton to stay with a housemaster, the Rev. Wharton Marriott, who wished her to do portraits of several boys who were leaving his house. She took Eleanor with her, who was now fifteen years old. While Mary was busy with her painting, Eleanor wrote long letters to Mama to keep her informed of their doings, and played with the little Marriott children.

Mama, living in the small London house with Papa and Arthur, looked forward to those long, lively letters from her youngest daughter, whose spelling since her stay in Paris showed a strong French influence. First she heard about Mary's sitters—two sons of Sir Charles Wood. "Wood Majeure" often went up to Windsor to ride with the Prince of Wales. He was so handsome and gentlemanlike that Eleanor found it "quite a pleasure to talk to him." There were descriptions of their life at Eton and prayers with the boys morning and evening. "Sixty-six eyes upon one. Rather nervous work."

Then she heard that young Dugdale Astley, son of Mama's friend, Sir Thomas Astley, had been to see them several times. He was an officer in the Guards, had fought in the Crimea, and now was stationed at Windsor. He had invited Mary and Eleanor to the Castle for a theatrical performance. Mama's optimistic heart rose at the news. She knew that Dugdale was fond of her daughter, although Mary had seemed determined not to notice it.

I am glad that she is doing so well with her painting, thought Mama, but I *should* like to see her married to a nice young man. I should feel so much safer about her—and about Eleanor too. Severn has made so little money lately and if anything were to happen to me, or to Archie (this is what Mrs. Severn called Lord Eglinton), I do not know what they would do. Mary is so pretty and so gay and good and clever, but she never seems to think of marriage—though she has a romantic nature, or she would not love poetry so much. (Mary's copies of Tennyson and Keats, with passages marked and underlined, were a family joke, and drew many acid comments from Walter, who preferred facts, science and Darwin.) Now if she would marry Dugdale—or Tom Richmond—I know he is very fond of her . . . But she treats him like a brother, which I am quite sure is not what he wants, thought Mrs. Severn.

While Mama was musing over her daughter's future, startling news came from Eleanor. Mary was painting the Queen's mother, the Duchess of Kent, at Frogmore. Scarcely had the excitement of this announcement subsided in the family, when an even greater event was foreshadowed.

"Mary is very busy," wrote Eleanor, "so I am going to write

you an eloquent letter. Mary received a command from a cabman, in the shape of Lady Augusta Bruce, which will take her to Court to-day at 3.30 to see the QUEEN. Fancy!!! This morning we had risen from our morning slumbers and Mary was taking her bath when lo and behold, a tap on the door and Mary the Maid brought THE summons. It ran thus:

> H.R.H. would like you to come at 3 p.m. and the Queen will be here at 3.30 p.m. to look at H.R.H.'s portrait and H.R.H. would like you to be present when Her Majesty is here.

Thus ran the elegant and acceptable epistle of Lady Augusta, and my dear sister Mary Hann is to go to Frogmore to-day to be present at the looking of the Queen at her August Mother's portrait. Next piece of business I have to make known is that we can't come home on Saturday because Mrs. Marriott is actually going to give a party on purpose for us. By the bye, I think you will be pleased to hear that *Dugdale* came here yesterday or the day before, I forget which." [1]

The Queen came to Frogmore, and another Royal commission was given. Mary was to do a sketch of the Prince of Wales, a fair-haired boy of sixteen, with large blue eyes, whom she had already met at Frogmore. She wrote to her mother two weeks later:

"I had such a pleasant visit from Papa to-day. He was really pleased with my Duchess. I want you to see the drawing, as it is one of my best. Mr. Hilliard came with Papa and told me the copy Papa has done for him is lovely.

I must tell you about the Prince's picture. You must know that I've been sadly hurried, for he went away, and just when you know all the important touches come at the last sitting I had to hurry so over it that I almost felt inclined to give it up! And then feeling this was *the* picture of all others I wanted to do well made me quite nervous, but he was so kind and gave me an hour's sitting on Saturday and Monday, but had to sit with his watch in his hand because he had to go to a Funeral at eleven. He saw my fuss, and like an Angel, offered to sit next Monday week in Coleshill Street on his way to Portsmouth. But when he saw my delight at this prospect he advised me not to reckon too much on it, in case he could not manage it. But how I shall like you to see him—only I think you will agree with me that my picture

[1] Letter, Oct. 26th, 1857.

does him so little justice and has not got his good honest look, but still, considering all, I hope it will come like. I shall ask to show it to the Queen, and if I see she likes it, I'll make a real point about his sitting in London, but how I wish I could draw him again. I can't tell you how low about it I felt on Friday, and how I hid the drawing under the bed in my room that no one might see it, who might call while I was out. But now I feel happy about it, and Papa thinks it is so *well* coloured and drawn, and it does look very gentlemanlike, so I hope it will all go smooth.

Mr. Coleridge thinks my prices so much too low. He told me just now that I ought to say twenty guineas decidedly for H.R.H., but ten guineas for the Prince as it is only a sketch. The Prince and I had a long conversation about Prices. He said that that awful sketch Ross did of him cost *Seventy Guineas*. 'I wish I had half the money,' he said, 'that they (the Royal Family) spend a year in portraits.' He says it's their Mania." [1]

The Queen was very pleased with the sketch of the Prince and, hearing from Lady Augusta that Mary had done a charming little picture of the baby Prince Imperial, she requested her to paint the little Princess Beatrice, who was just eight months old.

The Marriotts were going to their house in the Lake District for the Christmas holidays, and invited Eleanor to go with them. Mama gave her assent, after a few threats that she *must* go to a school of some sort directly she came home. Either she must go to an English school—here Eleanor protested violently—or to one abroad—well, that would be better, she had been very happy at her school in Paris, but *of course* Mama must come too. The question was left to be decided after the Christmas holidays, and off went Eleanor to the Lakes, to send back lyrical descriptions of the scenery and the sunsets—"if only Mary or Arthur were here— such splendid views—we would go out and draw all day long!"

Mary moved to the White Hart Hotel at Windsor, conveniently near to the Castle, and took Arthur with her as a companion. From here she wrote:

"MY DEAR MAMA,—I have just returned from the Castle. I went at 9 a.m. this morning and finished my lovely Princess, but as I did it on that 'crust of bread' paper, I could not make it as like as I should like, and told the Queen (for I saw her again for

[1] Letter, Sunday, Nov. 15th, 1857.

so long) that I could make a drawing of the Princess *her image*, so the Queen said I might do what I liked, and leave that one as it was, for she liked it so much, and do another on white paper. I could have jumped, I was so pleased at this for I must do *one* good, just to let them see what I can do. For I feel I have many rivals, at least I see and hear of others painting this Baby, but that *no* one is like Sir W. Ross, so as I know I can do mine better than anyone, if I'd only a chance, I said I was going to stay at Windsor, and if the Queen would let me go and draw in the nursery—which was at once granted! I believe it was such a thing my asking to go up *there*, as *no* stranger, not even the ladies in waiting, ever go there—it is such a sanctum—so don't tell anyone. But fancy, there I sat, and the little Princes were *quite charmed*. I drew pictures for them and they only want me to go again. They are so handsome and so gentlemanlike. I can't tell you how I like everyone at the Castle. As for the Princesses they are the nicest girls I ever saw. They took me to their room and made me sit down and look at pictures, and when the Princess Royal regretted I could not see one at Osborne, the Princess Alice said, 'O but some day she *will* see it.' And they always put their arms round me and they asked why I had a Scotch accent so I told them about you, and I think they were all the nicer." [1]

She wrote again the next day:

". . . I couldn't go to my little Royal Baby till half-past two and when I went I found the Queen had sent to see my sketch, and said she would so much have liked a different view, for I'd done the same view as the *first* one, and that she wished so much for a front face, so I at once did it over again. But the Baby had not slept and was cross, so I could only do so little and I am afraid it won't be able to sit to-morrow (New Year's Day) and if so I can't finish till Saturday, but whatever I do, don't you think I am right to do all to please the Queen, and also to do a *good* portrait of this Baby? and Lady Augusta said it would lead to my doing the other children. She was so *delighted* when she heard I had it to do. I will if I see Miss Hillyard show Arthur's drawings. The Queen looked at Walter's but said nothing.

Little Prince Leopold, five years old—said, 'I wish you would draw a lady drawing you.' And fancy the Queen sent me word, when I was in the Princesses' room, whether it would be the same to me whether I would go to the Audience Room (next her own

[1] Letter, Dec. 30th, 1857.

room and where I draw) a little earlier as she would want the
room at half-past three. But it was all so politely put—I can't
even say it—her manners and all she says and does is so kind and
nice—most people would only have said the room was wanted
and I must come at another time.

Fancy, I drew Monday and Tuesday in the Audience Room,
a little room next the Queen's own, where the Queen sees all her
Ministers and everyone I think. And the Queen sent a maid to
say that if I wanted anything I was to go in *there*. This Audience
room is hung with heads of the Royal family by Gainsborough.
I never saw such painting, it was so luminous. . . ." [1]

One last note came from Mary before she returned home:

"We are sorry we were not at your Dinner—but tho' my little
sketch was most successful yet I want to make it quite right. I
am to be at the Castle to-morrow at 9 a.m.

I saw the nice Queen again. She really is pretty, for her
manners, the way she bows, the way she moves is so graceful that
this afternoon I thought her quite handsome, and if she would
only sit in warm rooms she really would be better looking, but
to me it seems as if she were frozen, quite *trembling* and no fires!
Her hands were blue and shaking so she could hardly point to
the pictures. I agree with you about beauty and warmth, and on
the strength of it I bought some *brown* stockings.

I must stay to do Lady Augusta, for she goes immediately to
Paris, poor Lady Elgin is so ill. She comes to sit *here*.

Arthur wants a very well-starched shirt which is in the top of
his trunk. He took a drive with his friend Lady Fanny, all over
Windsor Park. He looked so nice in the Royal Carriage sitting
by her. We are reading Southey's *Life of Nelson*!" [2]

---

[1] Letter, Dec, 31st, 1857.   [2] Letter, Jan. 1858.

CHAPTER XIV

MR. NEWTON

(1858—1861)

THEY were sitting in the parlour at 83A Eccleston Square. Mama had settled the family in the new house before she went off to Hanover, where she had taken Eleanor to learn German. They were still away and Papa was in the country copying a Gainsborough —one of his rare commissions.

Walter, Arthur and Mary, with her friend Mary Palliser, had been laughing too much and drawing caricatures all the evening. Now they were "quite done up."

Mary lay with her feet up on a sofa, her wide skirt spreading over on to the floor, a periodical in her hand. Her dark, waving hair was drawn back from her smooth forehead into a net. Arthur lounged in an armchair by the fire, his legs, which were too long for his trousers, thrust out in front of him. Walter, now aged twenty-eight, stood by the table, an erect, slender young man, very correctly dressed, with a fashionable short dark beard. He was showing some of his etchings to Mary Palliser. Scraps of paper, covered with drawings, lay scattered about the floor.

Mr. Vaux, sitting on the other side of the fire, looked at them all with affection. He was the antiquary who had bought in the furniture for them at their Sale. He worked at the British Museum. He was middle-aged, short, fat, and rather bald. He had known the Severns and the Pallisers for a long time now, and was fond of both families—the handsome Irish Pallisers and the talented, impetuous Severns. Walter is the only one with any real, practical sense, he thought, and Henry, of course, in Australia. But what charm they have got.

Mary looked up from her paper. "Have you seen any of these things that have been discovered at Halicarnassus, Mr. Vaux?" she asked, holding up the paper to show him what she was reading.

The discovery of the Tomb of Mausolus, one of the Seven Wonders of the Ancient World, by an Englishman, Charles Newton, had created a sensation. Now he had arrived back in England, bringing his discoveries with him for the British Museum. The Press was full of it.

"I was talking to the discoverer only this afternoon," said
Mr. Vaux. "About restorations." He hesitated. "He is trying
to find someone to make drawings of the marbles. To be truthful,
I had half-wondered if I should suggest your name. But I didn't
know if you would like such work . . ."

"Oh, I would, very much," said Mary eagerly, sitting up on
the sofa. She had felt she was getting a little stale in her work
lately. Since finishing her portraits of the older Princesses she
had exhibited several pictures at the Academy and had plenty
of commissions, but somehow she felt dissatisfied and restless.
"It would be something quite new," she said enthusiastically,
"and *so* good for me. I should learn a great deal about Greek
Art."

"There is only one objection," said Mr. Vaux hesitantly.

"What is that?" asked Walter, looking up from his etchings.

"Well, he's rather a difficult fellow in some ways—Newton.
And I don't know if he'd—er—if he'd choose—well, I mean, if
he'd *trust* a lady to draw his marbles."

"Mary would draw them as well as any man," said Mary
Palliser loyally, and Walter nodded his agreement.

"I could show him some of my drawings," said Mary. "Oh,
do let me try, Mr. Vaux. At any rate, let me *see* the marbles, even
if you don't think Mr. Newton would like me to draw them.
I've been so interested reading about them. How exciting it
must be to find beautiful statues that no one has seen or touched
for two thousand years!"

Her large, deep-set, grey-blue eyes were shining. She had a
most expressive face, and when she became excited she used her
hands with more gestures than most Englishwomen. Perhaps it
was her childhood spent among Italians that had taught her this,
or perhaps it was the knowledge that it was with her hands that
she could ultimately best express herself.

Mary Palliser begged to be allowed to come too. Mr. Vaux
at length agreed and appointed a time. As he let himself in to
his little house near the British Museum he wondered whether
Newton would bite his head off if he suggested Miss Severn's
name—he had such a sarcastic tongue.

Mary stood back from her easel and examined her work. Yes,
she quite thought she had got the effect she wanted at last. It
had not been easy. She looked across at Mary Palliser, who was
drawing at her easel on the farther side of the big, cold room.

With a frown of concentration she was trying on an enormous paper to reproduce one of the stone lions from Halicarnassus, which crouched, stood, and lay before her, most of them with at least one limb missing. The Artemis that Mary herself had been working on for so many hours was without a nose.

She smiled as she thought of the shock they had both had when the intimidating Mr. Newton had led them into this room. She had been so elated that he was going to give her a chance to show what she could do, but her heart had sunk as she looked around her. Lions' heads without bodies, lions' bodies without legs, gods without heads, goddesses with shattered arms, a headless horse with only the legs of a rider still gripping its body. For a moment it seemed a nightmare. But then, as they moved slowly round the room, she looked more into the detail of the work and was astonished by its perfection. Mary Palliser, less knowledgeable, seemed bewildered.

Mr. Newton had not spoken much as he led them round. Sometimes he stopped to point out some particular statue, or to conjecture the rightful place of some almost unrecognizable fragment. Mary glanced sideways at him. He still looked as forbidding as when Mr. Vaux had first introduced them to him. Such a noble face. He was quite like a Greek god himself—the stern profile, the firm mouth, even his hair and beard seemed to grow in sculptural form. She would like to draw him. Suddenly she found his penetrating dark eyes turned on her and looked away in confusion. Her glance lighted on a female statue, and she made one of her graceful gestures, asking whom it represented. His face lit up and he leaned over to stroke the marble cheek with his long-fingered hand—like a Van Dyck's, thought Mary.

"The public don't deserve to see my Artemis," he said in his deep voice. "They don't appreciate her beauty."

Mary had just restrained herself from replying that it wasn't surprising as the poor creature had no nose or mouth—only a chin, but that stern face did not encourage flippancy. She had been thankful that she had not spoken, since she had heard his caustic tongue at work on other people.

The door opened and he came in. He was tall and held himself well. He was forty years old and his body was spare and strong. With his stern face and unconscious air of distinction the whole impression given was one of austerity, until you noticed

the rather grim lines of humour round the mouth and piercing
eyes. He came straight over to Mary, who drew back in silence
to let him see her drawing. He stood for several minutes in front
of it, his elbows out, his long hands clasped in front of him. His
back was turned to her so that she could not see his face. She
felt her heart beating as she waited for his judgment. She would
so like to do the other drawings. She *knew* that she could do
them well. He turned.

"I congratulate you, Miss Severn," he said, in a harsh voice
that sounded anything but congratulatory.

Mary smiled at him in relief and pleasure. When she smiled
her big eyes shone, and her expression of sweetness and friendliness
was almost irresistible. Mr. Newton's eyes searched her face.

"I should like you to begin work here at the same time to-
morrow morning," he said gruffly. "Is that convenient?"

"Oh, *quite* convenient, thank you, Mr. Newton."

"Good. And your friend will accompany you?" He made a
gesture towards Mary Palliser, who was still concentrating on her
drawing, trying desperately to improve it before this frightening
man should see it.

"Oh, yes, she would be very pleased."

He strode over to the other easel. Again there was a silence
while he gazed at Mary Palliser's lions.

"Humph. One would think these were drawings for *Punch*,"
he grunted sardonically, and, with a brief "Good-day" to poor
Miss Palliser, he left the room.

He was not always so abrupt. He did not make friends easily,
he mistrusted the other sex. But there was something peculiarly
winning about Mary's manner and her enthusiasm for learning—
he found that she had read widely—mingled with a certain naïveté
and piquancy of expression. He came to inspect their work every
day, and sometimes he would stay to talk.

Mary loved to listen to him. He was so learned. He knew so
much. She sat as a disciple at his feet while he talked about
Greek Art, about the Athenian Empire in the days of Pericles, and
the immortal work of Phidias. She was fascinated by his
description of the statue of Athene Parthenos, which stood in
the Parthenon, for whose adornment the Athenian people had given
gold to the value of £115,000. As their friendship matured he
talked of more personal subjects. She learned that, after he had
graduated at Christ Church, he had taken the post of Assistant to the

Antiquities Department at the British Museum, "where they had classical, Oriental and Medieval objects all jumbled together in one department, and no single classical archaeologist among the officers." He broke off to scowl over this unsatisfactory state of affairs, which was still no better. They would have to alter it soon.

After twelve years in London, he had become Vice-Consul at Mitylene, so that he could explore the islands and coasts of Asia Minor. He had discovered inscriptions on the island of Calymnos and then he had declined the Regius Professorship of Greek at Oxford, so that he might continue his search for fragments of a past civilization. The next year, 1856, he had discovered the Mausoleum at Halicarnassus. It had taken nearly two years to disinter the whole colossal tomb.

Mary came to look forward eagerly to these long talks. Usually he stood by her easel, or paced up and down as he talked. Sometimes Mary Palliser came over from the other side of the big, draughty room, picking her way between horses' heads, marble hands and arms, all the unidentified fragments that lay about the floor waiting for restoration. Sometimes they would help Mr. Newton in his well-nigh impossible task of fitting them together. Mary, pointing to a fragment, would cry helpfully, "Don't you think it looks like a horse's tail?" "No," would come the uncompromising reply. "I am thinking it is undoubtedly a lion's neck!"

Another day he suddenly decided that drawing from the antique should be done from touch. Both girls had to climb on ladders, which they propped against the bigger statues, in order to feel the features with their hands.

They stood on tiptoe, looking strangely out of place beside those grey stones shaped two thousand years ago, with their wide skirts and tiny waists, and their smooth hair drawn back into little knots at the nape of their necks. Below them Mr. Newton stood, as always fastidiously dressed, his beard jutting, his dark eyes alight, his long Van Dyck hands gesturing to show them what he wanted.

Another day Mary brought some clay to the Museum and thought she would try her hand at modelling one of the friezes. She looked up to find the saturnine Mr. Newton standing by her side.

"Do look, Mr. Newton," she cried. "Haven't I got on well?"

"A very tolerable mud pie," replied Mr. Newton dampingly.

She was not hurt by his cutting remarks. She was used to criticism from her own brothers. She knew that he did not mean them to hurt and that they were due to his naturally sardonic turn of humour; she even wondered sometimes if they might not cover an unexpectedly sensitive nature.

Then he called one evening at Eccleston Square. He had come to talk over some work with Mary, he said. There did not seem to be anything very important in what he had to say to her, but he was soon on good terms with her family. He seemed charmed by Papa's easy geniality. He discussed Darwin with Walter, and smiled when he heard of the argument, lasting into the small hours, between Walter and Mary, which had been started by Mary incautiously asserting that Beauty was Truth. As they talked, Mary felt conscious for the first time of the idiosyncrasies of her family. She had never given them a thought before, had just accepted them as part of her happy world, but now that Mr. Newton's piercing eyes were scrutinizing them, she felt afraid of what sardonic judgment might be forming in his mind.

However, he couldn't have disliked them, because he accepted Papa's invitation to dine with them one night with becoming gratitude. He came to dinner and they were all on their best behaviour. Mary wore her new muslin dress and a gold net on her dark hair. To her relief, Mr. Newton never once made one of his biting comments.

One morning, not long afterwards, she was drawing at the British Museum. She was pleased with the last few drawings she had done. They were bold and masterly, and she had got her effects with the smallest possible amount of detail. For once she was alone. Mary Palliser, who usually worked with her (partly because she loved drawing and partly to make Mary's position more *convenable*), was away from London. Sometimes Gertrude Jekyll, "a good creature and so willing," would accompany her, or on rarer occasions John Ruskin. To-day it was Arthur who had come with her to the Museum, but he had suddenly abandoned his drawing because he wanted to see Mr. Vaux. He went off to look for him, and scarcely had he gone when Mr. Newton entered. She smiled at him, but he only muttered a gruff "Good morning" as he came over and took up his stand beside her, watching her at work. He was looking very gloomy. She hoped he had no bad news.

After standing for a few minutes in silence, he said abruptly that he had to leave England almost immediately. He must go back to Greece. Mary was taken by surprise. She raised her startled face to his, and tears that surprised even herself brightened her grey eyes. The rather harsh lines round his mouth softened.

G*

His face blurred above her and drew suddenly nearer as he stooped and kissed her.

She smoothed her crisp dark hair and smiled up at him. He frowned back.

"When will you marry me?" he asked abruptly.

All her happiness suddenly dropped away from her. How could she marry? Papa made so little money, and although Walter had a good position in the Privy Council Office he was not very highly paid. She was the bread-winner of the family. It was the money she made from her work that enabled them to live in Eccleston Square, and to send Arthur to school, while Mama, with her allowance from Lord Eglinton, stayed in Hanover with Eleanor. She could not desert them, especially dear Mama, who relied on her so completely. She tried to explain all this to him. She was afraid he would be impatient, but he took her hands gently in his and said,

"If I believed in God I should think you were an angel."

She did not quite realize the second half of what he said until later.

"Oh, but don't you?" she asked, distressed. "Believe in God, I mean?"

"I believe only what I can prove to be true."

"But don't you *feel* Him—in the beauty of your statues—you must feel Him there?"

"No, I feel only the greatness and the skill of man."

Mary sighed. She did not want to spoil this moment that she would always remember by arguing with him. All their ideas seemed to be at variance with each other. He despised her beloved Keats and Tennyson. She hated the idea of a life bounded by facts. She said she must go home. He did not try to stop her, but he raised her hand to his lips as they parted, and as she looked down at the thick curling hair on the head that was bowed over her hand, she knew that it didn't signify if his beliefs were different from hers on every subject under the sun, she would still love him, and only him, until she died.

He wrote to her often from Greece. Letters and poems, too. Mary kept them carefully hidden away in her bedroom and would spend her evenings there, taking them all out to read. His letters were beautifully expressed. They were learned, affectionate, lover-like. Mary, sitting on the bedroom floor—her dress a dark pool round her—would glow with happiness as she read. How lovely she had looked with that gold net on her dark hair, how beautiful she was, how slender, how graceful. It was really extraordinary that he should remember the colour of her dresses, and she loved to hear in which he had most admired her.

She wrote him back long, racy letters illustrated by little drawings. She described her life, and the work she was doing, the people she met and talked with, hitting off their characters by a few words of dialogue inserted, bringing the whole atmosphere in which she lived before him, and assuring him in simple, glowing words of her love for him.

Their devotion to each other seemed to intensify rather than diminish with separation, although their letters made clear how different were their conceptions of life and art. It was a clash between the Romantic Spirit and the Classical. But whereas she did not want her Philosopher, as she called him, to change in any way, he was determined that she should learn more of the true principles of ancient Greek art, and was convinced that then she would cast aside her inferior gods. He told her frequently that it was her personality that had attracted him, and not her art. He disapproved of George Richmond's influence. He wanted her to cease portrait-painting in water-colours, and to do more work in oils.

Eager though she was to please him, this last was at the moment more than she could promise. It was by her portraits in water-colour and crayon that she was well known. She had painted the Queen's children in these mediums. She had exhibited at the Academy in three different years (on the last occasion *The Times* had even proclaimed with avuncular jocularity that Miss Severn deserved to be made an R.A. herself).[1] She could get as many commissions now as she wanted, while Papa had almost none. But this criticism from one she loved so much was very disturbing.

Mama noticed it at once when she returned from Hanover with Eleanor, who could now speak fluent German. Mary did not concentrate on her painting as she used to, although she still worked very hard. She would leave her easel suddenly, to come and sit on the floor at her mother's feet. Mama would go on with her sewing while Mary, with her palette forgotten in her hand, would talk about Greek Art and Mausolus, until they were interrupted by Eleanor dashing in to say she would be late for her music-lesson, or Claudia come to beg Mary's help with the children that afternoon.

[1] Obituary, the *Gentleman's Magazine*, March, 1866.

Mr. Newton had been back to England once—for a short visit when he had just been appointed British Consul in Rome. That was a few weeks before Mama's return. Although he was necessarily very busy, he had spent a good deal of time at Eccleston Square. There had been many happy evenings. By this time all the Severn family were taking a proprietorial interest in everything to do with Halicarnassus, and they attended in a body the lecture Newton gave on the Mausoleum, which was illustrated by Mary's drawings.

There were other, less formal evenings. One picture Mary remembered of him, in the drawing-room at Eccleston Square, seated by the fire, elegant and unmoved, while the Severns disputed who could draw the best caricature of him. A competition followed. Arthur's picture was entitled "The Lecture, 14th Nov. 1859. The lecture comes off at last! Great exhibition of diagrams! Astonishment of the British Public!" and showed Mr. Newton lecturing from a platform to a crowded auditorium, with a long stick ready to point to Mary's drawings, which were hung round the room. While the others were talking he drew a second picture: "The Fog, 14th Nov. 1859. The party from 83A experience a sudden and disagreeable change from the atmosphere of Halicarnassus (to which they had been transported by Mr. Newton's eloquence) and Greek Art to a dense London fog,—no cabs, only a link to guide them."

Papa drew him in almost the same attitude as his posthumous portrait of Shelley at the Baths of Caracalla. Mr. Newton was shown gazing over Rome, an unrolled scroll in one hand. Papa wrote across the top: "'Othello's occupation gone.' Mr. Newton at Rome, cogitates how he can change the Castle of St. Angelo into the Mausoleum of Halicarnassus." Mary drew him in a chariot drawn by lions, behind him a signpost "From London to Rome."

Mr. Newton remained unperturbed in the midst of their excitement. Occasionally he made some ironical comment, but for the most part he preferred to gaze into the fire, his long legs crossed, his shapely hands folded across his chest, his head bowed, until the drawings were shown to him, when he could give full vent to his talent for sarcastic criticism.

In spite of these moments, the visit had not been a very happy one. Whenever he and Mary were left alone he would urge her to marry him at once. Did she not love him? It had been agony for her to rouse his anger. But she could not desert her family, when they needed her so much. In a few days his visit had ended, and to her relief, Charles Newton's letters from Rome showed that in his heart he realized the difficulties of her position. He told her how he had wandered about the haunts of her childhood, and had been to see the house where she had once lived in Rome.

Then Mama and Eleanor came home.

Eleanor was sitting to Mary. It was June, 1860. Outside the sun blazed down on the dusty London streets.

"Oh, Mary, cannot we go out for a little? The room is so stuffy, and it would be lovely by the water in St. James's Park."

"I must just finish this hand," said her sister absently, her eyes on her canvas.

There was a knock at the door. They both turned as the maid looked in.

"Mr. Newton from Rome in the drawing-room," she said and shut the door.

Mary's palette fell to the ground with a clatter. The brush followed it, as she threw open the door and sped down the stairs, her skirt flying out behind. Eleanor followed more slowly. From the top of the stair, she saw Mary pause for a moment at the mirror outside the drawing-room, to smooth her hair with nervous fingers, before she darted through the open door into the drawing-room.

Eleanor went slowly down the stairs. She wanted to see this Mr. Newton. Mary had known him while she and Mama were away, and she said he was "a very nice person." When she came into the drawing-room they were standing together by the window, not speaking, but gazing at each other. Mr. Newton was tall and *very* distinguished-looking, thought Eleanor, as her sister introduced them to each other. Then Mama came in and was introduced too, and soon afterwards Eleanor had to leave, because she had promised to spend the day with Claudia and her children.

When she returned that evening, Mama told her that Mary was going next day to Bredwardine in Herefordshire, to stay with Mrs. Newton, her friend's mother. Mr. Charles Newton would be there too. Mama did not add that she had told her daughter and Mr. Newton that she saw no reason why they should not be engaged, and though the position *was* a little difficult at the moment, something would be sure to "turn up." Then Mr. Newton had explained his plan. They were reorganizing the Antiquities Department at the British Museum and dividing it into several different branches. He would try to get the position of Keeper of the Greek and Roman section. He would then do his utmost to get Mr. Severn appointed British Consul in Rome in his place.

Mama was all enthusiasm for this scheme. Severn spoke Italian just as well as English, and he knew so *many* people in Rome. It would surely help in these difficult times if the new Consul were already acquainted with most of the Italians. What a *good* idea! How *kind* of Mr. Newton to suggest it! One look at Mary's radiant face had been enough to assure her mother of her happiness.

Next morning Mary left for Bredwardine, and the morning after came a note for Papa, asking his permission for Mr. Charles Newton to marry his daughter, Mary. They were engaged at last.

Oh, those long walks in Herefordshire in summer! The hills and the orchards and the blue sky! Heaven must be like this, thought Mary blissfully.

Two of the Severn family were missing from the usual big Christmas party at the Richmonds'. Young Thomas Richmond looked in vain for Mary, who was spending Christmas with old Mrs. Newton in Herefordshire. Claudia was not there either, because her little boy had died a few days before. She was left with three little girls, and was already expecting another baby in the spring. Mr. Newton arrived back in London soon after the New Year. The first part of his plan had been achieved. He had been appointed Keeper of the Greek and Roman section of the Antiquities Department in the British Museum. Now he was determined to do everything possible to ensure that Mr. Severn should be his successor in Rome.

Severn, too, left no influential friend unapproached. He was "a candidate for the Consulship at Rome," he wrote, "about to be vacated by Mr. Charles 'Mausoleum' Newton (who is about to become my son-in-law), he preferring the British Museum." [1] Mr. Gladstone spoke in his favour. Mary had an encouraging answer from the Queen. Ruskin wrote about his suitability for the post:

"What testimonial can I offer to you, that will not be a thousandfold out-testified by the consent of all who know you, and who knew, in those old times of happy dwelling in the ruinous Immortality of Rome: where English and Italians alike used always to think of Mr. Severn as a gleam of living sunshine which set at one, and melted into golden fellowship, all comfortless shadows and separations of society or of heart. . . . As I cannot fancy any-

[1] Letter to Monckton-Milnes, Oct. 22nd, 1860.

thing pleasanter for English people at Rome than to have you for Consul, so I can fancy nothing more profitable for English people at home than that your zeal and judgment should be on the watch for straying treasures as in these changeable times may be obtainable of otherwise unhoped for Italian art.

I would say much more, but in the hearing of your many dear friends I feel all that I can say would be but impertinence, and so pray you only to believe in my most earnest wishes for your success, on all conceivable grounds: and to believe me here and at Rome and everywhere,

Affectionately yours,

J. RUSKIN." [1]

Baron Bunsen, that faithful friend of Roman days, wrote from his death-bed to Lord John Russell, the Prime Minister:

"MY DEAR LORD JOHN,—I have no hesitation in recommending to your kind notice Mr. Joseph Severn, who I understand is anxious to obtain the British Consulship, now vacant, at Rome. I believe Mr. Gladstone has already given him a warm testimonial, but having known Mr. Severn for many years at Rome I can testify to his peculiar fitness as Consul there, for during the years he spent at Rome he made himself universally useful and popular among the English residents. . . . From his intimate knowledge of Italian affairs and his social relations with Romans of all classes, I should also consider him as very likely to be useful to your diplomatic agents. I will conclude by saying that I never knew an artist possessing so much *practical* knowledge and ability as Mr. Severn." [2]

On January 30th, Mama was reading to Eleanor when Papa walked in.

"You will be glad to hear that I'm appointed Consul at Rome!"

He was full of joy. A great longing had come over him to be back in Rome. His children had been educated. The *Life of Keats* had appeared, with the hitherto unpublished poems. "I think I shall be among the English poets after my death," Keats had written, a few days before his twenty-third birthday.[3] Now, nearly forty years after his death, his friend had lived to see his name among the greatest of English poets.

Joseph's four eldest children were all well settled in secure positions. Only the twins would be living at home when Mary

[1] Sharp, *op. cit.*, p. 218.   [2] *Ibid.*, p. 216.   [3] *Letters of John Keats*, p. 232.

had married. He longed to return to Rome, the city of his prosperity
and his youth, with Elizabeth by his side, and to resume life *da capo*
in Italy. The Consul's salary was certainly not large, but at least
it was assured, and he had faced the fact that, although he loved
his "darling painting" as much as ever, fashion had outstripped
him and left him far behind.

Although no one would have guessed it from his youthful
appearance, he was now sixty-seven years old. He was active and
upright, his face was youthful, his hair unflecked with grey, but
this matter of his age was very worrying. There was a rule at the
Foreign Office that no Consul, on his first appointment, should
be more than fifty years of age. As Joseph airily remarked, he
was "just on the wrong side of it," [1] but fortunately his extra-
ordinarily youthful appearance had prevented the authorities from
suspecting it.

Fearful lest any delay should allow them to discover his secret,
Severn had a few days' instruction in his duties from Mr. Newton,
and set out in less than a fortnight for Rome. Mama accompanied
him as far as Folkestone. They stayed there together for two
days, and then Joseph crossed the Channel, pleased as a boy to
be carrying despatches and a diplomatic passport. Mama must
stay behind until Mary was married, and their affairs in London
settled. In any case, her health had been bad lately, and it would
be better for her to follow by easy stages. She could bring the
twins and a few of their best pieces of furniture with her. Papa
would travel light.

[1] Sharp, *op. cit.*, p. 215.

CHAPTER XV

BRITISH CONSUL

(1861—1872)

How happy he was to be back in Rome, to pick up old friendships (John Gibson was still there, as he had been on Joseph's first arrival in Rome, and Overbeck, the German painter, and many more old friends), to find himself again a figure of importance, to hear the Italian rolling off his tongue as easily as though he had never been away. The clear air and the brilliant sunshine refreshed his spirit after the murkiness of London. The air in February was crisp and the Tramontana blew. The flower-stalls were banked high in the Piazza di Spagna, as they had been that evening when he and John Keats had driven into Rome in their little carriage forty years before. The sound of chanting voices drifted down from the church above, and he rejoiced to hear again the splash of fountains, as he wandered through the streets.

One of his first thoughts was to visit Keats's grave. He was no longer a solitary mourner, but only one of hundreds who came to stand reverently by that honoured plot. The *custode* complained that the flowers planted on Keats's grave were constantly picked by the visitors. Joseph felt only a quiet exultation as he stood in the old Protestant burial-ground, but even now he could not pass the house in the Piazza di Spagna, where Keats had died in his arms, without "a throb at his heart." [1]

A man of less buoyant temperament would have been appalled at the difficulties of his position in Rome. During the time of Joseph's stay in England, the provinces of Central Italy had been united under Victor Emmanuel. Only five months before Joseph arrived as British Consul in Rome, Garibaldi had seized the Kingdom of Naples, and the whole of Southern Italy and Sicily had been annexed to the new Kingdom of Italy. At the same time Italian troops had invaded the Papal States. Umbria and the Roman Marches had been occupied, and only a small strip of land round Rome was left to the Pope. Had it not been for the French garrison that Napoleon III maintained in Rome, the capital would have fallen too.

[1] Sharp, *op. cit.*, p. 249.

The very air reeked of intrigue, of plot and counter-plot. The Inquisition was at work, and a man could be sent for five years to the galleys for failing to remove his hat in church.[1] Sinister, dark-faced Cardinal Antonelli was Pope in all but name. Timid Pius found his interests in evolving new religious dogma, while the unscrupulous Cardinal encouraged corruption, from which he profited himself, and refused to make even the mildest of social reforms, or to compromise in any way with the liberals or the Italian Government.

The natural capital of Italy was Rome, but the French garrison stood ready to defend the city against Italian troops. Napoleon III himself sympathized with Italian aspirations, but he needed support at home from the French Catholics, and perhaps he was influenced by the Empress, who was very devout. Unwillingly he stood guardian of the Pope.

The national feeling of frustration was increased by the behaviour of the Papal Government. Not only was its rule tyrannical and corrupt, but it gave sanctuary within its domain to all the enemies of Italy. From across the border the dispossessed Italian Dukes and the ex-King of Naples schemed and plotted against Italy. They organized brigand bands under the protection of the Pope, and sent them to spread crime and confusion in the South of Italy. Such a state of affairs could not last long, and in the city itself the urge of patriotism and the longing for freedom were no less strong for being ruthlessly suppressed.

To the Papal Government everything modern was anathema. Railways, telegraphs, vaccination, modern literature, all belonged to the nineteenth century and therefore were abhorred as working against the authority of the Church. Feeling in Rome ran high. Liberal conspirators took their lives in their hands when they plotted a rising in the city. In the secret strife between them and the unyielding Church party, the few voices raised for compromise went unheeded. It was in vain that they argued that the Pope's spiritual authority would not be lessened, but reinforced, if he were to relinquish voluntarily his temporal power.

The official policy of England was non-intervention. At such a troubled time Joseph was the ideal man for his position. He accepted the reactionary Papal Government for what it was, fully appreciating its lack of justice (had he not suffered from it himself?) and its conception that laws made by priests were God-given, and therefore superior to those forged by man. Equally he accepted

---

[1] Bolton King, *History of Italian Unity*, vol. ii. p. 10.

the fact that there were men whose ideal of freedom would never allow them to remain passive under tyranny. He did not align himself with either side, but even in his first days as Consul he found that his rôle could be a useful one. His great facility in the Italian tongue, his knowledge of Rome, and especially his ability to joke in their own language, helped him to soften their rancour, and often to reach some sort of agreement in small matters between the two parties.

In March, when Joseph had been a month in Rome, Charles Newton was sent there to acquire the Castellani Collection of sculptures for the British Museum. He brought young Arthur with him, as his father had taken an apartment "large enough for *all* the Severns." Arthur would keep his father company, and it would make Mrs. Severn's journey easier if she had only Eleanor to bring with her. As soon as he got back to London Mr. Newton was besieged with enquiries about Papa. To Mary, who was finishing a commission in the country, he wrote, with their wedding only a few weeks distant:

"He gives a most flourishing account of himself. He seems to have taken to the Consular service as kindly as he did to the uniform.

Arnold has sent me his three lectures on Homer which I will bring with me. Darling, do not let them keep you over Sunday.

I send you many kisses. Ever your affectionate

C. T. NEWTON." [1]

"I am now well 'in my saddle,'" wrote Joseph to his brother, "and the great variety of things are more pleasing than not, for I am equal to any amount of business. I have just had four rooms with divers persons in them, all with individual affairs going on, so I went from room to room, while my secretary and my son Arthur were helping. . . .

My appointment has caused great envy, for there is no end of people here who were candidates. Here all is uncertainty, no one can even guess what is to transpire. The city is full of French soldiers, every monastery is now a barracks and you see monks and soldiers shouldering each other. What a marvellous state of things, what an important moment, what a crisis, almost bursting with the future.

As yet I have not sought an audience with the Pope, but now it must come off and I am preparing. Cardinal Antonelli received

[1] Letter from Travellers' Club, March 7th, 1861.

me most graciously and assured me how acceptable my appointment was to the whole Government. Indeed I see that everything
here turns on old, old associations. So in this I stand really
well. . . .

My sole care is my dear, dear wife's health. For she has too
much upon her hands now I am absent, and I regret that I did not
oblige her to come with me. But the approaching marriage of
my daughter made it impossible." [1]

After all, Mama was not able to be at Mary's wedding, on the
third of May. She had been to Folkestone to recuperate after one
of her attacks, and became ill again only a few days before the
wedding, so that she could not come to London. Claudia was not
there either, because a baby boy had been born to her ten days
before the wedding, and she had been very ill. Only two of
Mary's own family were in the church. Eleanor was a bridesmaid,
with Claudia's three little girls, and Walter gave the bride away.
Mr. Vaux, who had introduced Mary to Charles at the British
Museum, was the best man.

Eleanor wrote to Papa that Charles looked "really very handsome indeed—I never saw him look so well." They were married
at St. Michael's in Chester Square, and there was a wedding
breakfast afterwards at Eccleston Square, where toasts were drunk
to Papa and Mama and old Mrs. Newton. When the happy couple
had driven away, Eleanor, with ten of the younger guests, went
"down to the Crystal Palace by the new railway."

It now only remained for Mama to wind up the family affairs
in London, and then she and Eleanor would be ready to leave
England, to travel by easy stages to Marseilles, and then by
boat to Civita Vecchia and on to Rome. Mama, as always, was
pleasurably excited by the thought of change. By the end of June
she pronounced herself quite recovered, and returned to London.
Two months were needed to arrange everything. Then Mama
and Eleanor said goodbye to Walter, to Claudia, who was still
convalescent, and to Mary, who had just moved into her new house
in Gower Street. She was painting the dining-room walls with a
frieze from the Elgin Marbles, which were now under Charles's
supervision.

It was a terrible wrench for her to part with Mama and Eleanor,
but they consoled themselves with plans for meetings in Rome. A
few days later she received the letter that Eleanor had promised to

[1] Letter to Tom, April 6th, 1861.

write. They had crossed the Channel, stayed a few nights at Calais and were now at Dunkirk. Mary laughed as she read of Mama's characteristic behaviour.

"When we arrived at Dunkerque we got the omnibus of the 'Hôtel du Chapeau Rouge' and when we were in it Mama saw on another omnibus 'Hôtel des Bains de Mer.' This attracted Mama very much, and she wished very much to get out and go to that Hotel, but I persuaded her not, so we came here. Next day we went *to see* the 'Hôtel des Bains de Mer' for Mama could not *rest* until we had gone, for she was sure it would be very nice. It was a very long drive, quite twenty minutes, and when we arrived we did thank our stars we had not gone. Such smells! Oh dear!

Mama thought she'd like to see a doctor so we called upon the Consul, Major Pringle. He was so civil and we all became friends at once. He is a Scotchman and knew the E.s. So he was very civil and went with us to the doctor's. How lucky we got the doctor. Next day Mama was laid up with a bad bilious attack and lumbago and she is still in bed."

They were still in Dunkirk when news came that Lord Eglinton had died. Mama was terribly distressed. Not only was she very fond of him, but he had always been there for her to turn to when she was in trouble, and also she could not think how she could manage without the money he allowed her. Within a few days, however, her fears on that account were temporarily allayed, when an instalment of her allowance, which was due, was paid into her account in the usual way.

Meanwhile Papa and Arthur were living in Rome. Papa had taken an apartment of five noble rooms in the enormous Palazzo Poli, looking down on the Fountain of Trevi. Below them the water rushed over the rocks where Neptune sat in stony state, and splashed down into the great marble basin. It was like living on the edge of a waterfall. The rush of the water was with them day and night. It was astonishingly pure—the same highly-prized Aqua Virgine that flowed into Rome in the days of Augustus—and Arthur loved to watch the girls come to fill their pitchers in the mornings, balancing them on their heads as they walked gracefully away, while the water foamed between the rocks, and swirled and sparkled in the sunlight.

Unfortunately Joseph's purse did not permit him to furnish the large rooms of the palazzo. "As yet only two rooms are habitable," he wrote to his sister in November, "my office and my sitting-room. But the grandeur of the rooms carries the day and does not permit anything really modern, for the Palace is in the old style, so I pick up old carved things at sales. How you'd be amused to see me at dinner with Arthur, in a large saloon thirty-two feet square and twenty-eight feet high, with nothing in it but ourselves and the dinner! The first night I awoke in the night and coughed, and was frightened at the deep echo through the empty rooms, for I had left the door open!" [1]

On December 13th Mama and Eleanor arrived at Marseilles, where Mama was taken ill again. Severn was longing for his wife to join him. "I am at a loss without her, for in the difficult things I have to do her clever Scotch head would greatly help me." [2]

Walter came out to Rome at the end of December, spending a few days with Eleanor and Mama on the way. It was the Season in Rome, and Walter and Arthur, who was determined, in spite of his father's opposition, to become a professional artist, enjoyed what gaieties there were to the full. Joseph did not think much of them, compared to the brilliance of the Roman Season when he was a young man, but he enjoyed wearing his full-dress uniform to the Ball at the French Embassy.

"My two boys have danced most of the flesh off their bones," he reported, "but by day they have drawn admirably." [3]

Ill as she was, Mama was still full of plans for the benefit of her family. How fortunate it would be if Walter were to marry Miss Arbuthnot, an heiress whom Mary had known in Ireland, and who was luckily spending the winter in Rome. Arthur sent her all the news.

"We have been to one rather splendid Ball at the house of an American banker, and he had all the best of the Italian society and Walter immediately got introduced to half a dozen Contessas and Marchesas all covered with jewels. Walter speaks Italian so very well and everybody likes him so much.

People in shops are delighted when he (stroking his beard) tells them, '*Io sono romano, sono nato qui a Roma.*' I will keep Walter up to Miss Arbuthnot, and if not to Miss Leigh Smyth who is such a nice person and a most splendid rider. She rides every day over the Campagna."

But, alas, Walter left Rome at the end of his holiday, without being engaged either to the heiress or the Amazon.

[1] Letter to Maria, Nov. 19th, 1861.   [2] *Ibid.*
[3] Letter to Tom, Tuesday, March 18th, 1862.

In spite of enemies among the English converts, several of whom had had pretensions to the Consulship themselves, Joseph was finding that by the exercise of tact and patience he could do much good. He was able to rescue his secretary's brother from prison in Rome by clever handling of the Papal authorities, and got him a position on the Naples railways through his influence with the Government of Italy. By the autumn he could point with pride to nearly forty similar cases.

Unruffled, he went to and fro between the two parties, siding with neither, always serene, affable, ready with a joke, mediating between bitter opponents, pleading for moderation if not under-standing. His leisure moments he spent at his easel. He had begun a picture of Keats's grave. But he was grateful that he had not returned to Rome only for his painting, "for all the fine arts are for the moment at a standstill in this disturbed state of things, and the artists are complaining bitterly of 'no coms.'" [1]

Anxiously he waited to hear that his wife had recovered and was continuing her journey. But the news from Marseilles was not encouraging. Elizabeth wrote to her husband in March that she was still too weak to be able to turn over in bed. But she said cheerfully that she had heard of some wonderful baths near Geneva which might completely cure her. What worried her most was the expense of her illness. Their financial outlook had seemed so much more promising, if they could have lived quietly with the twins in Rome. Now her illness was costing a guinea a day and they were not even together. How ever would they find the money? Joseph could not tell her. He could only hope that "something may turn up."

To add to their unhappiness he dared not leave Rome to go to her. He was popular with papalists and liberals alike, but he knew that he had enemies among the English Catholics in Rome; that was why he had repeatedly warned his brother Tom not to mention his true age to anyone. He knew that these people were jealous of his influence with the leaders of their own party. "While I am active at my post, they are afraid of me," he wrote, "and I can afford to pass them over, strong as I am in the affections of the Roman people. They are jealous that I am so in favour with the Governor of Rome that some fifty prisoners have been liberated through me." [2] But he knew that, if he left Rome, they would intrigue against him, and, with this unforeseen expense of his wife's illness, he must at all costs keep his position as Consul.

[1] Letter to Maria, April 30th, 1861.   [2] Letter to Tom, Tuesday, March 18th, 1862.

Mama wrote anxiously that the apartment in the Palazzo Poli sounded rather too large for them. Arthur replied :

"All you say about a *small* house is of course quite right. I laughed so much at that part of your letter when you say that a *cottage* is better than a large dirty house. I could hear you say *dirty house* quite plain, as if you had been speaking to me in your Scotch accent. Papa has got people looking for a small house for us at this moment." [1]

Then, suddenly, the telegram came. Joseph was wakened at midnight to receive it. It was from Eleanor. Mama was dying. Would Papa come at once. He threw a few things into a little trunk. His poor dear Eliza, so far from him. He should never have left her behind. Surely the doctors must be mistaken. There must be something they could do. He must move her to Rome directly—she had always been well there. He would find her somewhere to live in the hills, at Frascati or Albano, where the air was cooler than in Rome. Then she would get well. She *must* get well. He needed her so much.

He was ready to start by dawn. He took his passport to the police, for it must be signed by them or he would be turned back at Civita Vecchia. The inefficiency of the Roman administration was brought home to him then in the most painful way. For twenty-four hours he stormed, cajoled, pleaded to be allowed his passport. Nothing would hurry them. At last, almost distraught, he got it back. It had taken them a day and a half to have one signature affixed to it. He rushed to Civita Vecchia and boarded the first boat to Marseilles. [2]

In the Hôtel des Bains des Catalans at Marseilles Mama lay dying. Eleanor sat at her bedside, her young face pale and haggard. She was nineteen years old. If only Papa would come. She was alone. The doctor, the English clergyman, and the wife of the British Consul were her only friends in Marseilles. Mary and Charles had been there for several days only a fortnight before, but no one had realized then how serious Mama's illness was. Now it was only a question of how long, the doctor said. If only Papa would come in time.

She wrote to Claudia, who had not yet recovered from the birth of her little son a year ago. Only a year ago—Claudia's baby born, Mary about to be married, Mama at Folkestone, Arthur

---

[1] Letter from Arthur in Rome to Mama in Marseilles, undated.
[2] Letter to Tom, May 2nd, 1862.

just left to join Papa in Rome. It seemed like twenty years, not one.

She had been so vexed that morning. The nun who nursed Mama had shown in the Mother Superior.

"She talked very kindly to Mama for a little while," wrote Eleanor. "Then, 'Would you not like to see someone who speaks English?' she asked. So poor Mama, not knowing what was coming, said 'Yes.' Then the Mother Superior said, 'Our bishop speaks English and I am sure you would rather see one of our priests than your minister.' I bent down and told dear good Mama what she said, and she whispered, 'Don't offend her but tell her No.' It made me cry, a thing I try as much as possible to prevent when I am with her. I said to the Mother—'Madame is a confirmed Protestant and, God willing, will die in the religion that she has been brought up in.' She *actually* had the impudence to tell me not to talk to Mama about religion, not to influence her in any way! I could not help saying, 'I shall do *my duty* and shall speak to her as I think proper.' Oh, it made me feel so unhappy, but it is over now, and that woman shall not see Mama again, and if she dared to send a priest I should send him away quickly. Oh how I do pray that Papa may be in time. . . ." [1]

The nights were so long. Eleanor dared not leave her mother for long. She was so afraid that she would die alone. When Mama could speak she asked if Papa were there, and Eleanor could only shake her head, with tears in her eyes, and say that he was coming very soon. The tired white eyelids dropped again over the blue eyes.

Soon she was too weak to speak. Eleanor sat by her side for hour after hour, running to the window whenever she heard the wheels of a carriage, scanning the sea for the boat from Italy. At her lowest moment, she took her pencil and a scrap of paper and painfully sketched her mother's profile—her thin, sharp face under the white cap. She sat there through the night and drew her dying mother, just as, forty-one years before, her father had sat by Keats's bedside, in the house in Rome, and drawn him, with the damp hair clinging to his brow.

Joseph arrived too late. His wife had died the day before. If the passport had not delayed him he would have been in time—in time to speak to her, to hold her hand, to comfort her. How cruel, thought Joseph, overcome by misery. If I had known

[1] Letter to Claudia, Monday, April 14th, 1862.

there was no hope I could have brought her on to Rome, to a house of her own—and to me. But the doctors deceived us all with false hopes. They told us that the journey to Rome might impede her recovery. Thank God that Eleanor was with her. To die, alone, in a hotel in a foreign land—that would have been too dreadful. And she was in agony at the expense that she knew was falling on me. If only I had insisted on her coming out to Rome with me at the beginning. Then I would not have been cut off from the last precious days of our thirty-four years of anxious life.[1]

All his energies had been concentrated on getting to Marseilles in time to see her, to speak words of affection and comfort. Now he had arrived too late. She was already buried. He had not even seen her face again. He felt limp and empty. The one purpose that had filled his whole mind, since the moment he had received that telegram in Rome, had gone. He roused himself when Frederick Gale, who had arrived the day before him, came to talk to him about Eleanor. Claudia wanted him to take her back to England to live with them, at any rate for a time, until she had got over the shock of her mother's death. She would be with her two sisters. Her mother had whispered, before she died, that this was what she wished.

Joseph agreed miserably that it would be best. Then they discussed money. He had sent his wife £60 in January, but the hotel and doctor's bills amounted to £240 and by French law there was a further fine of 1000 francs (about £40) because poor Mama had died in a hotel. Joseph nodded dumb agreement to all his son-in-law's proposals about ways to pay this debt. Then Gale said briskly that there was no point in waiting about in Marseilles. He would arrange to leave with Eleanor next day.

It was Easter Sunday. She had been dead for three days now. The whole journey had been a nightmare. He couldn't believe that it was true. All that Easter Sunday he spent on the boat which was carrying him back to Rome. The tranquil Mediterranean lapped placidly round him under an April sky, as he sat on deck and wrote about her. He wrote down all his memories of her. Her beauty, her elegant impulsive distinction, her humour and her ready kindliness. What a wonderful mother she had been, untiring in her care, and what a loyal, courageous wife. He wrote about her as a beautiful girl, as a young mother playing with her children among the scarlet anemones in the gardens of the Pamphili Doria, as a brave resourceful wife in times of trouble.

[1] Letters, May 2nd, 1862, and June 12th, 1862.

So he sat and wrote about her, while the tears ran down his cheeks and the blue sea slipped past in a slow stream, silent as Time itself.[1]

Fortunately when he got back to Rome there was a great deal of work for him to do. It comforted him to fill every minute of the day, and his energy, for a man of sixty-eight, was astonishing. No one in Rome had any idea that he was so old. He was generally supposed to be about fifty, and in appearance and in vigour he was certainly no more. It gave him a childish pleasure when people asked him, as they often did, about "his father and Keats." [2]

He warned his brother, Tom, "Let me still be your younger brother and I will sell you my birth-right for a mess of potage, to keep me out of the mess my age might place me in." [3]

A letter came to him at the beginning of May, which did much to cheer him. It was from General Durando, the Foreign Minister of the King of Italy.

> "DEPARTMENT OF FOREIGN AFFAIRS,
> TURIN,
> *May 1st, 186½.*

SIR,—Since the month of September, 1860, the protection obligingly given by the French Embassy to His Majesty's subjects in the Pontifical State having been withdrawn, the British Government consented that similar protection should be afforded by its Agent in Rome, and you, most excellent Sir, as British Consul there, have on every occasion that has occurred performed this kind office with a courtesy, goodwill and readiness, corresponding fully with the intentions of your own Government as well as with the wishes of His Majesty, our King, and have thus acquired a just title to our particular gratitude.

Having been lately called to the direction of this Department it is now my very agreeable duty to express to you, Sir, these my sincere sentiments of satisfaction and acknowledgment, whilst I feel confident that you will continue as hitherto to adopt the same good offices with the Roman Authorities as regards the safety of the persons and interests of His Majesty's subjects, thus rendering yourself evermore well deserving of our Government which has already so much to praise for your indulgent assistance bestowed upon the above persons.

[1] Letter to Tom, May 2nd, 1862.   [2] Letter to Tom, May 19th, 1863.
[3] Letter to Tom, April 8th, 1863.

Meanwhile I avail myself of the present opportunity to assure you of my highest consideration.

GIACOMO DURANDO."

Joseph sent the original of this letter to Lord John Russell, together with an English translation, "to show that the Italian Cabinet approves my efforts and that I have done even more than was expected of me." [1]

He sent another copy to his brother, explaining, "The Foreign Minister was thanking me for my services in liberating upwards of fifty-five of His Majesty's subjects from the Roman prisons, which you must understand I have not done officially, but solely by good-natured intercessions with the Roman Ministers and trying to 'fascinate them off their feet!'" [2]

This was Joseph's way. He knew just how to handle the Roman officials. He was on the best of terms with them all, and through his personal relationship with them, he was able to get concessions which they would never have granted to him as an official.

In the autumn he was able to exercise his influence when the Prince of Wales and the Princess Royal came to Rome.

"Whilst the Prince was here," he wrote to Tom, "the Pope ordered the English ladies who had been to visit Garibaldi to be expelled from Rome. I visited Cardinal Antonelli and was so fortunate as to get this hard sentence reversed. I assured him that our ladies always have a fashionable hobby and that now it happens to be this hero of Romance. And so I have saved eight ladies now here. This affair got me great credit at the Royal table." [3] He had dined with them and both had "gratified him with the warmest compliments on his dear daughter Mary."

So that he might pay the debt, nearly £300, incurred by his wife's illness, he had reduced his living expenses by almost half, let part of his apartment, and now lived in the most frugal way. On Walter's advice Arthur was sent home, still determined to be a professional painter. By Easter of the next year, 1863, the debt was paid off completely.

He had long letters from his children, which kept him in touch with their lives. Claudia's health was no better. She had yet another baby and was almost an invalid. Walter had received praise from *The Times* for his etchings and designs for *The Golden*

[1] June 21st, 1862.   [2] Letter, June 21st, 1862.   [3] Letter, Nov. 29th, 1862.

Calendar, which had just been published. Arthur was working hard at water-colours. Mary seemed very happy with Charles Newton. She led a full and interesting life, but she was worried that, so far, there was no sign of a child. She, who loved children and painted them so well, was not destined to be a mother herself.

She lived among clever people. Her father heard from her when she and Charles were staying at Oxford with Dean Liddell of Christ Church, who was delighted with the portrait she painted of his lovely wife. They would stay in Oxford, too, with Dr. Acland, now Regius Professor of Medicine. He was a friend of her husband's whom Mary had already met at her father's house, and with George Richmond. Dr. Acland was fond of the sea. As he lived so far away from it he consoled himself by the creation of what he called "The Acland Eight." Mrs. Acland would steer the boat, her husband was stroke, and the sons would take the other oars in order of seniority. During the summer this crew would make its stately way up and down the river.

Mary wrote happily about these visits to Oxford, and once they stayed with Dean Liddell in the holiday home he had built for his family on the seashore, near Llandudno. George Richmond's twenty-two-year-old son was there too, painting his picture of the three Liddell sisters, of whom the youngest was to be immortalized by Lewis Carroll. Charles drove over to visit Mr. Gladstone who lived near by, while Mary amused herself by decorating the doors of various rooms with charmingly designed flower-pictures.[1]

But in London Charles made her work as hard as he did himself. She had to make all the drawings to illustrate his lectures. He was fond of company, and when they got home from the Museum, where they had been working all day, he liked to dine out with friends. Mary charmed everyone with her easy, clever conversation and her sweetness and grace. But she often wished that they could have stayed quietly at home, though she never said so to Charles. He was a spare, strong, nerveless man. He drove her as he drove himself, but she was more delicately made.

Joseph heard that Mary and Charles were going to Rhodes and Constantinople on Museum business, taking their friend, Gertrude Jekyll, with them. They would be away for some months—perhaps even a year or more. As Claudia was now almost an invalid, the family decided that Eleanor should go to Rome and live there with Papa, whose financial troubles were, for the moment, ended.

[1] *Richmond Papers*, p. 139.

Walter travelled out with her. He was surprised at his father's youthful appearance. Joseph told him, chuckling, that the Governor of Rome had had to guess his age for a document. "He actually put me at forty-five! What fun! I didn't contradict, for I never cry 'stinking fish' and my well-being turns on my age. My enemies would dash me to the ground if they knew of it." [1]

Eleanor proved a great asset to her father. She spoke German and French fluently—Mama had seen to that—and she soon picked up Italian, too. She went everywhere with her father. She became quite a figure in Roman Society and was known as the "Consulina," the little Consul.[2] She accompanied him to balls and receptions at the different Embassies. She translated letters for him. She sat sketching in the Vatican while her father talked with Antonelli in another room. The Papal Chancellor would accompany her father when he returned, and compliment her on her drawing. She would reply politely to his suave compliments, but she was repelled by his fine, wicked face, with its hard black eyes and brutal mouth.

At the beginning of his third year as Consul, Joseph was appointed, with the consent of Lord John Russell and Antonelli, Consul acting for the Kingdom of Italy in Rome. This added to his responsibilities, also to his salary and his importance. When feelings were strained to the utmost, he was the only mediator between Rome and Turin. In the absence of an Ambassador, he was the representative of Britain. He had made for himself a unique position. "'Tis at the same time the most felicitous position," he said. "For while I have all the power of an Ambassador yet I have no etiquette to keep up, and go about my painting in the true artistic style." [3] He was on such good terms with the Papal Government that they would grant requests if made by him which they would otherwise have rejected indignantly.

Many were the acts of kindness that he was able to perform. Many were the prisoners, unjustly detained, who owed their life and liberty to him. Englishmen or Italians in Rome came to him for aid in trouble; with secret police everywhere, it was easy enough to be reported for an indiscreet remark. But he never sided with either party, and both factions showed appreciation of his fairness. "The Governor of Rome lends me his gendarmes on every occasion," he wrote, "and the other day Cardinal

---

[1] Letter, Nov. 22nd, 1864. [2] Letter, Nov. 12th, 1864.
[3] Letter, July 29th, 1865.

Antonelli assured me that I had gained more power than anyone in Rome. For I had got the affection of the Roman people and also the Government." [1] On the other side, King Victor Emmanuel offered him his Royal villa at Frascati for the summer of 1864, and again the following year.[2] Orders were given that he was to be received with "all the honours of a Cardinal." [3]

In big matters and in small he tried to use his influence for good. When the English colony were forbidden to act a play in Lent, it was Joseph who got the decision revoked. When a young Scotsman won a steeplechase in the Doria colours, green jacket and red waistcoat, and, by adding the customary white belt worn by a gentleman riding against professional jockeys, combined the wicked colours of Italy, it was Joseph who persuaded the Pope to overlook the joyful demonstration of the crowd and to countermand the order for his expulsion from Rome.[4] When the Papal party, who "did not like meetings," forbade the Archaeological Society to meet, the order was revoked as soon as it was known that it was to take place in Signor Severn's house. "I am trusted in everything," [5] he said proudly.

Eleanor and he lived happily together. "She begins to be a *bel pezzo di donna*," he would boast. He loved to hear her talking in German or French, and he beamed with pride when people talked admiringly of "the Consulina." Sometimes he complained of the late hours he had to keep, taking her to balls and parties, and watching her dance until the early hours of the morning. Sometimes she felt a restless depression, a sense of missing something, and she wished that her father were not so old. But on the whole they got on very well.

Then came dreadful news. Mary was dead.

She died in London. She had been thin and pale before her trip to Rhodes. When she got back to England her family thought the holiday had done her no good. She was sleeping badly. She told Claudia that she would start awake in the night, not refreshed by her sleep, but with a sensation that she had been drawing, drawing all the night. Her brain would not rest, and she worked all the harder to keep the miserable thought from her that she might never have a child. Then she caught measles from a little boy whose portrait she was painting. She became very ill. While

[1] Letter, Nov. 24th, 1863.
[2] Letters, Sept. 14th, 1864, and Nov. 12th, 1864.
[3] Letter to Walter, Sept. 2nd, 1864.
[4] Letter, April 25th, 1865. [5] Letter, Feb. 8th, 1866.

she lay in bed, with a high fever, in her house in Gower Street, she saw a maidservant fall from the top window of the opposite house. She was terribly affected by the girl's scream as she fell. That evening the doctor told Newton that she was suffering from brain-fever—the next day no hope—the third day she was dead.

Charles Newton was stricken, but he hid his hurt behind an icy control. Arthur, who was with him, reported that he had behaved that evening just as usual. He had eaten his dinner and opened his paper afterwards without a word about his wife. The only time that his control had broken was when someone had asked about Mary's room—her studio, where her unfinished canvases leaned against the walls, her pallets and brushes lay neatly in their places, her easel stood lonely, in the middle of the room,—where Mary's personality filled the air and everything spoke of her and waited, waited for her return. When the maid asked, after the funeral, if she should tidy up the studio, he turned on her in a fury and ordered that nothing in the room was to be changed—that if she so much as touched a single thing she should leave the house that day.

He went round to Claudia's house and was comforted a little by talking to her about Mary. Claudia, with the family cleverness of hand, made a cross of flowers to rest on the coffin, from them all. For Eleanor she made a chaplet of sweet-scented leaves and violets. Charles kept his eyes fixed on them as they were lowered into the ground. Afterwards he wrote a note to Claudia—"Dearest Mary was so fond of flowers."

To Joseph and Eleanor in Rome the shock was terrible. It was nearly four years now since Mama had died in Eleanor's arms in the little hotel bedroom at Marseilles, with the black-robed nun standing silently beside them. Now Mary was dead too. Mary the loving, Mary the clever, the good, the gifted. To Eleanor she had been the dearest of them all since Mama's death, dearer even than Arthur, her twin. To Joseph she had been the favourite child. "Mary was my greatest pride," he said sadly. "I can scarcely believe that I have lost her for ever." [1] He referred to her always as "my gifted daughter." The complimentary notices in The Times and other papers he read with pride, and was comforted by news of the Queen's sympathy—a note sent by Lady Augusta, "so kind and full of feeling." [2]

His distress made him ill, and he became crippled with rheumatism. For two months he was in great pain and could only creep

[1] Letter, Feb. 8th, 1866.   [2] Letter, Jan. 23rd, 1866.

about, his spirits quenched, his laughter stilled.   There was talk of an
attack on Rome—a rising in Venice—the French were going to
withdraw—Garibaldi would attack—the Pope would treat with
the King—rumours were flying all over the city.   Joseph sat sadly
in the Palazzo Poli, where the Trevi fountain filled the high-ceilinged
rooms with the rush and splash of water.

At the end of the year he was left alone.   Eleanor went home
to be a bridesmaid at Walter's wedding.   He was to marry Mary
Dalrymple-Ferguson of Newhailes, near Musselburgh, the sister
of a Scottish baronet.   Joseph remarked the coincidence that his
eldest son would have a bride from Scotland, and at the same age
as he, himself, had married Walter's mother.

Time seemed to stand still for a while when Eleanor had left.
The struggles and fevers of the Papal power in its death-throes
made no impression on Joseph Severn.   He did his best to help
those who appealed to him, but he could not share their excitement, their hopes and their fears.   Under the terms of their Convention with the Italian Government, the French evacuated Rome
in December.   But the powerful Catholic party in France compelled the Emperor to keep a force of 20,000 troops at Toulon,
ready to sail for Italy if Rome were attacked.[1]

Meanwhile the British Government had been defeated on the
Reform Bill, and four Liberal Ministers came out to Rome for a
holiday with their families—Mr. Gladstone and the Duke of
Argyll among them.   Naturally their presence in Rome made a
stir, not only in the Vatican, but at Turin.   Both sides hoped for
support from Mr. Gladstone, the great Liberal Churchman.   Joseph
saw a great deal of him during his visit.   Mrs. Gladstone was as
charming as ever, and their apartments in the Piazza di Spagna
were the rendezvous of the best of Roman society.   Joseph was
much cheered by their company, and flattered by their attention.
He became less melancholy and, when young Willie Richmond
appeared in Rome, he reported that Joseph had introduced him
to Gladstone "in his bright tactful way."[2]

Another friend who helped to console him during the spring
of 1867 was the Abbé Liszt.   This strange brilliant man, with his
alternating moods of dazzling vivacity and sombre melancholy
would climb the steep stairs to Joseph's apartment and play to him
by the hour.   When Eleanor had been living with her father, and
they were leaving the apartment for any considerable time, she

[1] Bolton King, *History of Italian Unity*, p. 259.   [2] *Richmond Papers*, p. 219.

would carefully lock the pianoforte, which was a very fine instrument, and remove the key. This was to prevent the Abbé playing on it, because, if it was left to him, they would invariably find a couple of broken strings when they returned.

In the summer Joseph went to Tolfa, where he could take baths for his rheumatism. There was no longer any semblance of law in the country outside Rome. The villagers were terrorized by bands of brigands—many of them the same men whom the Pope had allowed to gather on his territory before descending on Southern Italy to burn and plunder. At Tolfa Joseph found all the local landowners being blackmailed by these bands. He evaded them by passing himself off as a simple *pittore*. They did not bother with such small fry.[1] The baths relieved him a little. He was able to move more freely and with less pain. His loyal secretary, a Roman named Frantz, had helped him to conceal how serious his illness had become. When he had first gone to Tolfa his feet were so swollen that he could not wear shoes. Frantz told him that he had not been so successful in obtaining concessions from the Papal Government while Joseph had been away, and that he thought much depended on his personal influence with the Ministers.[2] A storm seemed to be brewing in Rome.

"Just think, on my arrival here," Severn wrote to Tom when he got back to the Palazzo Poli, "I received a despatch and memorial from the Italian Prime Minister, requesting me to constrain Cardinal Antonelli to do away with the arrests of Italians in Rome. The memorial was very violent and threatening and so I felt obliged to request the Minister to send me a more moderate one, as I should never be able to get an answer to the violent one, but the Papal Ministers permitted me to reason with them in a friendly way. The Italian Minister thanked me and granted me full leave to do it all in my own way, and this I have done with great success."[3]

Alas for Joseph's efforts for peace and conciliation. The Italian Government could not control its own hot-heads. On October 23rd the long-looked-for rising broke out in Rome, and Garibaldi crossed the frontier at the head of seven thousand volunteers. Eight hundred rebels in the city, armed with a few revolvers and bombs, captured one of the gates and advanced on the Capitol. For three days there was fierce fighting in the city, but by the end of the third day the last struggle was overcome in the slums of Trastevere district and order was restored. Joseph

[1] Letter, July 30th, 1867.   [2] Letter, Oct. 14th, 1867.
[3] Letter, Oct. 14th, 1867.

took the opportunity to get a good three days' work on his new picture, which was destined for the Ashburton collection.

The Papal Government was triumphant, but it was also panic-stricken. It knew that its troops could put up no effective resistance to Garibaldi, who had already captured Monte Rotondo and was advancing towards Rome. The Pope was appealing to France, but no one knew whether his call would be answered. The Irish and English monks rushed to claim Mr. Severn's protection, and, in case the city was taken, he engaged to give sanctuary to a Cardinal and twenty-two nuns in his own house.

But the Catholics in France had forced the Emperor to act. The French troops sailed from Toulon. They landed at Civita Vecchia, marched inland, and met and defeated Garibaldi's volunteers at Mentana. It was clear that Rome would never be taken while the French were ready to protect the Pope. The uneasy stalemate continued. The French troops withdrew, but only to Civita Vecchia. Everyone knew that it was only the strength of France that prevented the fall of the Temporal Power.

Joseph's position was a difficult one. Everything savouring of Liberalism was anathema in Rome. English residents became increasingly uneasy, and when an English priest was attacked in the street many of them fled. Rome was boiling in the crucible of transition. Within the city there was universal uneasiness, and a feeling of approaching, unprecedented change was in the air. It led to an increasing amount of disorder and crime. Joseph remained unaffected by the pervading fears. He loved Rome. It was his true home. His only fear was lest it should be plundered by a victorious army. Apart from that he felt no apprehension.

When the Romans were rioting in the streets outside his window, when shouts of "*Viva il Re!*" mingled with jeers and cat-calls at the Papal troops, Joseph sat, unperturbed, at his easel, puzzling over his "Marriage at Cana" and how he should give the effect of water changing into wine. While Papalists looked with dread towards the day when France should again withdraw her troops, and while Liberals plotted, with the fear of the Inquisition chilling their blood, Joseph went serenely about his consular work, and painted, and entertained his friends. There were still old friends with whom he could talk about *tempi passati*, and there were even new friends too.

There was Madame de Llanos, whom he met during his early months as Consul. To his delight he found that she was Fanny Keats, John Keats's little sister. He had met her as a little girl,

'H *

and now she had appeared in Rome with her daughter and her son-in-law, who was an engineer. Fanny Keats de Llanos was now an elderly woman, but the memory of her favourite brother was a link that bridged the years since their last meeting. Clara Novello, of the beautiful voice, and daughter of that Vincent Novello whose musical parties Joseph and Keats had attended in London, was in Rome too. Then there were visitors who came to his studio to see his pictures. But they were not so carelessly munificent as those noble patrons who had thronged to Rome when Joseph was a young man. Since his return to Italy he had only sold two pictures. Yet with each visitor his hopes rose anew. Something always seemed to turn up, and meanwhile he would only spend what was absolutely necessary, so that he would be able to save some money for Eleanor, and to send five or ten pounds at intervals to his sister Maria, who had never married.

His consular duties kept him very busy. After the fiasco at Mentana, the Italian Government sent him 3000 francs for the wounded Garibaldi prisoners. "Each man on leaving the hospital receives from me 40 francs." [1] The victory of the Papal forces (for the Pope's troops spread the story that they had already defeated Garibaldi's men before the French soldiers had arrived on the scene) had given a triumphant impetus to the reactionaries among the Papalists.

"I am fighting with the Inquisition," he wrote, "which from day to day is taking away the many privileges I have gained from the Papal Ministers. But Mr. Odo Russell says that he is sure I have an extraordinary influence over the said Ministers, and that they have at times been induced to grant me more than was convenient or in order, so that now the Inquisition has stepped in to correct this mistake." [2]

Although the sulphur baths at Tolfa the summer before had relieved the pain of his rheumatism, and reduced the swellings on his hands and feet, the trouble kept recurring, and then he found it difficult to sign so many letters, and painful even to move. If his secretary had not been so efficient and devoted, he might have been ousted from the Consulate as unfit for his duties. But Frantz had never forgotten Joseph's kindness in negotiating his brother's release from a Roman prison. Now this brother joined him, and together, when Joseph was ill, they stood between him and the outside world, and by stratagem and subterfuge protected him from prying eyes.

[1] Letter, Dec. 26th, 1867.   [2] Letter, March 25th, 1868.

"I fear I shall never get rid of this rheumatism," he said rue-fully. "It sticks to one like a creditor."

But he still looked amazingly young, and no one could have guessed that he was seventy-five years old. His twins, Arthur and Eleanor, came out to stay with him, and cheered him with their laughter and good looks. Arthur had now made a name for himself as a painter in water-colours. His success had been sudden. Six months after Mary's death, his picture of "A Breaking Wave" was exhibited at the Dudley Gallery. Two sketches by Mary, painted at Scutari and Rhodes, had been favourably noticed, but Arthur's picture was praised by all the critics, and pronounced one of the outstanding works at the Exhibition. It was bought by the Duchess of Argyll, and Arthur found himself, if not famous, well known overnight.

They left the old man in the spring of 1869. His evenings seemed lonely after they had gone, for he did not go out much after dark. The disorders in the Holy City were becoming worse. Anarchy was spreading right up to the city walls. A suburban train was attacked and pillaged by brigands, and seventeen murders were committed or attempted in Rome within three months. The Pope chose this moment to canonize twenty-one new saints. "If His Holiness had given orders for the construction of twenty-one more trains, or for the execution of twenty-one notorious assassins, or for the release of twenty-one unjustly imprisoned citizens," said Joseph, "or even for the banishment of twenty-one mischief-pandering Princes of the Church, his action would have been more to the point and infinitely more appreciated." [1]

Then came 1870. In May Eleanor was married in England to Henry Furneaux, a Fellow of Corpus Christi. War was looming over Europe. On July 20th the long-threatened conflict broke out between France and Prussia. The French troops were recalled from Italy to defend the motherland. The French Empire tottered to its fall.

News of the collapse at Sedan reached Rome on September 3rd. Two days later a French Republic was proclaimed in Paris. On September 11th the Italian troops crossed the frontier, with the avowed intention of occupying Rome and making her the capital of United Italy.

[1] Sharp, *op. cit.*, p. 277.

CHAPTER XVI

ROMAN TWILIGHT

(1874—1879)

You left the Trevi Fountain, with its rocky Neptune wet with spray, where the tourists threw their pennies into the clear water, and laughed or sighed at the superstition which foretold their sure return to Rome. You entered the huge Palazzo Poli and climbed the steps of the Scala Dante. You turned along a dim carpetless gallery, and pulled the bell which hung by an unpretentious door. It sounded, sweet and faint, like a muted echo from another century.

Then the old servant, Betta, opened the door for you, and you asked for Mr. Severn. She begged you to wait *un momento*, while she asked if her master could see you. When she was gone you looked about you at the little lobby, half hall, half sitting-room, whose walls were hung with a few engravings. Then, after some delay, you were shown into the studio, and Mr. Severn greeted you. He was eighty years old, but there was scarcely a wrinkle on his face, which was round and pink, and his hair was, even now, not grey.

It was two years since his Consulate had come to an end. Soon after "the Capital had come to Rome" he had received a despatch from the Foreign Office. As the Legation was removing to Rome, Lord Granville did not feel justified in continuing the office of Consul, but intended to name Mr. Severn for a pension "adequate to the services he has rendered."

The Times commented in London: "It seems a pity the abolition of the Consulate could not have been deferred during Mr. Severn's lifetime. His services have been sufficiently important to merit great consideration. The office he has filled during a time of considerable difficulty has been one requiring great tact and discretion, for notwithstanding that we have had an unaccredited Minister in the person of Mr. Odo Russell, duties have necessarily devolved on Mr. Severn beyond those usually attached to the consular office, which duties he has performed to the satisfaction of both his own and the Papal Government. In how much estimation he was held by the Ministers of His Holiness is shown by his having been able to obtain the release of a number of political prisoners, so great that on the entry of the Italians he received a complete ovation from them." [1]

His Consulate had officially ended in 1872, the same year in which his son, Arthur, had married Ruskin's ward, Joan Agnew. Arthur had proposed to her and had been accepted in the room in Mr. Richmond's house in York Street where the famous Christmas parties had been held. Now Arthur was well known as a painter in water-colours, and he and his wife lived with John Ruskin at Brantwood. They were to nurse him there through all his long, painful illness.

Joseph had received honourable recognition of his work from King Victor Emmanuel, who made him Officer of the Order of the Crown of Italy.

His official pension of £80 had been supplemented by a further £60 from the Civil List. It was not much to live on, but in Rome he had managed fairly well. He shared his apartment with a Dr. Valeriani and his wife. The Signora kept house, the doctor defended him against his enemy, the rheumatism which lurked, watching for a traitorous draught, or a damp day, to cripple him. Then there was his faithful Betta, his servant since he returned to Rome. She tended him devotedly. How fortunate that he had that gift of rousing friendship, and from such different people— Keats, Leigh Hunt, Bunsen, Trelawny, Kirkup, Landor, Richmond, Ruskin, Acland, Gladstone. His charm still worked for him. His servant, his doctor, the doctor's wife, and Frantz, once his secretary and now British Vice-Consul—no trouble was too great for any of them, if it would give him pleasure.

Something of this serene, happy confidence beamed at you out of those still-young eyes. He reacted buoyantly to the presence of a visitor, though he would probably be a little tired when you were gone. He told you proudly how he spent his days.

"I am up at six, breakfast at seven, read my newspapers at nine, paint till one, dine at two, have forty winks till three. At four I cab it to San Pietro in Montorio where I remain walking till six, then cab it again three miles home."

He talked to you about his pictures. "Painting is no fatigue to me, whereas doing nothing is. My new picture is from Keats's poem of 'Isabella or the Pot of Basil.'" [2]

[1] *The Times*, Nov. 8th, 1871.   [2] Letter, Sept. 24th, 1874.

An American lady had just bought his picture of Keats's grave. You tell him that you are a great admirer of Keats's poetry, and you lead him on to talk about his friend. It is not difficult. His days of youth are now more real to him than the mists of middle age. His thoughts turn often to his father and life at Mason's Court, to the days when John Keats had just renounced the calling of a surgeon, when the hopes of his friends ran high, and Joseph was admitted to the friendship of three devoted brothers.

So he talked and you listened, and occasionally prompted him with a question. Perhaps, if you had made a good impression, he would show you the book of Shakespeare's Sonnets that had belonged to Keats, with the poem "Bright Star" that he had written in it. You would hear how, on that far-off night when the *Maria Crowther* slept becalmed, Keats had pressed the book into this old man's hand. Perhaps, if you were very lucky, he would tear a corner from some old letter and give it to you. Then you would own a precious scrap of paper on which the words had been traced, more than fifty years before, by the hand of Keats.

The shutters exiled the sun from the lofty room. It was untidy and dark. Letters were scattered about on the marble floor, and paints and brushes. In the half-dark the old voice talked of dead men and forgotten days, until you began to feel that in this strange, untidy room, Time had no power.

He grew silent. You felt that perhaps you had overtired him. You hastened to rise and take your leave, thanking him for his kindness in seeing you and for the fragment of Keats's letter. He beamed at your obvious pleasure and turned serenely back to his letter that you had interrupted, while you closed the big door softly behind you.

In the dusky room, with its tall windows darkened to thwart the searching sun, he sat at the table and wrote to his sister Maria, and to his brother Tom. In the still air the words and thoughts of so many letters in the past, and of letters not yet written, rose and mingled in the timeless shadows.

"Walter writes me that the great preacher—Stopford Brooke— preached a sermon on the subject of my friendship for Keats in the church in York Street, St. James's Square, and I hope to get a copy of it, for I am gratified (not so much personally) as it shows that friendship still holds society together, and that mine is noticed after half a century!" [1]

"'Tis now 80° F. and whilst I sit painting, without coat or waistcoat, I'm as it were in a bath." [2]

"I am calling up all my recollections of Keats in notes to the beautiful poem of *Adonais* by Shelley, in which he mentions me. All this I had done when someone stole all my papers and left me to do it all over again. 'Tis true I receive many admirers of Keats, both American and English, and someone with an overflowing love carried off all my papers. . . .

"The picture I am preparing is of Keats, Shelley and myself, when I drew Keats's picture and Shelley read his essay on poetry. . . .

"I am consoled that all my works are in the collection of noblemen and sovereigns, and I have never had to supplicate picture-dealers like the present race of artists." [3]

"After this attack of rheumatism my hands are sadly out of drawing. Even now my music gets a little thrown out and I can't play true, but I can do enough to amuse me in the long winter evenings.

"My friends, the Doctor and his ladies, are good company but don't care about painting or music. This is a drawback." [4]

"I would not allow my good friends, the Doctor and his ladies, to keep my 81st birthday, for 'tis sad that all my old friends are dead and gone and I cannot bear to rejoice without 'em. Yet as good luck would have it, just then arrived young Willie Richmond and his wife—he is like my son, for his Father and I have been like brothers—and so the dinner was got up and was very pleasant. With two young Italian ladies we were eight in all, and Dr. Valeriani was very joyous and I was pronounced to be a fine specimen of Roman Antiquities. But 'tis enough that I am 'bobbish' and am painting to my heart's delight. I dread the cold winter and the long drear evenings, when I can do nothing but keep the fire warm, for I am a very chilly body." [5]

"I hear such a good account of my dear children. Arthur has sold his picture of Venice and Walter also has sold his drawing." [6]

"A sad incident has befallen us. The sister of Dr. Valeriani died lately. As she was a fine, strong woman of sixty-three it was a painful surprise." [7]

[1] Letter, July 1st, 1873.
[2] Letter, July 8th, 1873.
[3] Letter, Aug. 10th, 1873.
[4] Letter, Sept. 24th, 1874.
[5] Letter, Dec. 7th, 1874.
[6] Letter, Feb. 14th, 1875.
[7] Letter, March 21st, 1875.

"I was asked to give a Lecture on Keats, but I declined as my nerves would not stand it. His tomb has been well repaired by Sir Vincent Eyre.

"I am sorry to say my painting languishes, as I can't shake off a certain apathy or idleness (call it what you will). My pictures unfinished stand round me like starving children and reproach me with cruelty, but I hope to pick up as the Spring advances." [1]

"I begin to feel the loneliness of having lived too long." [2]

"You will be surprised and amused when I tell you that Walter has sold the letter of Keats's to Sir Charles Dilke for £5. As for the two letters of the brothers, I don't think they are of any value. I have four letters of Keats and many MSS. of which I give a scrap sometimes to his admirers as a great favour." [3]

"I have discovered that Keats's letter sold to Sir Charles Dilke for £5 was worth more than double, as a letter sold lately for £13, 5s. od." [4]

"You will be glad to hear that I have done a life-size portrait of Keats, and it seems to me very like the dear fellow." [5]

One day in March, 1878, his son, Walter, sat in the same place and wrote in his turn to *his* sister Eleanor. Walter suspected that his father's sudden collapse had been partly brought on by reading Keats's letters to Fanny Brawne. Thirty-seven letters had just been published, in a volume dedicated to Mr. Joseph Severn. Joseph had been waiting to read them with happy impatience. He expressed his "joy at these thirty-seven letters, which I am told are of a beauty beyond his poems. Buxton Forman tells me there has never been anything like it." [6] But when he opened the book, such a searing agony of soul had risen from the pages, such a vivid resurrection of his tortured friend, that the shock had shattered him.

At one moment the doctor had held out no hope, but his robust body refused to give way, and now he seemed better. Walter sat at his father's writing-table and looked down on the Fountain of Trevi. It, at least, had not changed since their childhood in Rome. But it seemed strange to see the flag of Italy flying over the Castle of St. Angelo, and Italian soldiers strolling about the streets.

"MY DEAREST ELEANOR" (he wrote),—"Your charming letter

---

[1] Letter, March 21st, 1875. [2] Letter, May 18th, 1876.
[3] Letter, April 23rd, 1875. [4] Letter, May 18th, 1876.
[5] Letter, Oct. 5th, 1877.   [6] Letter to Maria, Dec. 9th, 1877.

came after mine to you had gone, so I must write again. As Papa
was not so well yesterday I did not think he could attend to it,
so instead of reading it I constantly referred to your letter. In this
way I got him to think about it so much that this morning (he is
always more lively in the morning) he *asked me* to read it, and I
thoroughly enjoyed doing so, sitting on the end of his bed, while
he sat up on the side of the bed with his feet on the ground, and
propped up behind with lots of cushions. We had our breakfast
together as usual, and he repeated several times that he was better
to-day. His perpetual cough is not so irritating—you would be
surprised how well he looks this morning—quite himself, and he
stopped me several times while reading your letter to tell me about
the carpet you had made for his room when you were here, and
various other kind and clever things you had done.

He does not seem to approve much of your destroying all the
official despatches, but I *strongly approve* of all you did. I daresay
you know the kind of look the dear old Pater puts on when he
does not want to express approval of a thing, which he really knows
quite well was done for his good! Everyone is most kind and he is
well attended to and looked after. Betta even sleeps on a mattress
in the room. When he had to be taken up to have his bed made
right a man came to help lift him, but now he is much better and
he has even taken two or three small walks outside the screen.

Papa made his Will and took the Comⁿ. a few days before I
arrived. Frantz and the doctor are the Trustees. Papa has left
all the Keats MSS. to the doctor and all the money remaining from
the Italian Consulship, about £150, to Betta. He leaves certain
pictures and medals to each of his children and *all else to me*. I
only hope this means that I shall not have to *pay a good deal* instead
of *receiving anything*. I could not help feeling a little sorry about the
Keats MSS. but the thing is *done* and so I have not even hinted
that I was displeased, but on the contrary have already talked to
the doctor about the disposal of them to Sir Charles Dilke and what
he ought to get. Papa thinks about £50, but the doctor evidently
reckons on much more.

The Will is done and so I think it must remain. I can't help
having a feeling of having been singularly unfortunate. Everything I care for has gone to others. Even the pictures curiously
enough. The only ones I like are left to Frantz and others, and
precisely those that I do not care for are left to me! with conditions
which I fear could never be carried out, such as getting his large
Magdalen accepted by the National Gallery."

Joseph's heart, which had faltered, made a gallant rally. For more than a year he lived on, still tended devotedly by his little band of friends. Twelve months after Walter's letter he was telling Maria that he had not been out for a month on account of the damp, but nevertheless he was feeling "bobbish." "Keats's MSS. begin to sell high, to my great surprise," he added. "What I thought worth £10 goes for £100. I have given them all to the Doctor, as I could not give him money." [1]

So, to the last moment of his eighty-six years of life, his devotion to John Keats continued to repay him a thousand-fold. In the days of Joseph's prosperity Keats's name was scarcely known. But in all the crises of his long life, Keats, though dead, was yet most powerful. It was as Keats's friend that he had been sought out by Englishmen of rank and influence, though it was his own happy charm that had warmed their feelings into friendship. It was their influence that had won him the Consulship in Rome, and the addition to the pension when he retired.

Even then his benefits were not ended. Though his painting was out of fashion, he could always sell a portrait of Keats; and though there was no market for his novels, his article on "The Vicissitudes of Keats's Fame" was published in *The Atlantic Monthly* and quoted in book after book. The MSS. and letters among his papers went to pay his doctor. His last picture was of Keats. He died peacefully on August 3rd, 1879.

For some time before his death Severn had not been able to see visitors or to leave the house. By the busy Roman world, humming with the energy of a young, proud country, he was forgotten. His last links with that modern world had been broken the year before, when in one short winter had died a King and a Pope: Victor Emmanuel, first King of United Italy, and Pius IX, whose weak nature had been dominated by the sinister Antonelli.

After these deaths that seemed to end an era, few people remarked the little funeral procession of a mere British ex-Consul. None raised a voice to protest against his burial on the fringe of the new Protestant cemetery. But soon the news reached England. There was a leading article in *The Times* about his death. [2] Then letters were written asking why the British Ambassador had not attended the funeral, saying that it was shameful that England had not done more honour to him, and through him to one of the greatest of her poets.

---

[1] Letter, March 15th, 1879.   [2] August 1879.

Two years after his death they moved his body from the new, unfriendly cemetery and buried him beside John Keats. Tennyson, Rossetti, Monckton-Milnes, all suggested inscriptions for his tomb. In the end the words proposed by Milnes, now Lord Houghton, were cut into the stone.

"To the memory of Joseph Severn, Devoted Friend and Deathbed Companion of John Keats, whom he lived to see numbered among the Immortal Poets of England. An Artist eminent for his Representations of Italian Life and Nature. British Consul at Rome from 1861 to 1872: And Officer of the Crown of Italy. In recognition of his services to Freedom and Humanity."

He lies, among his friends, in the sunny field where violets riot over the graves, and the shadow of the Pyramid chases the hours silently across the grass.

BIBLIOGRAPHY

The Life and Letters of Joseph Severn, William Sharp, 1892.
Life, Letters and Literary Remains of John Keats, Monckton-Milnes, 1848.
John Keats, Sidney Colvin, 1918.
Adonaïs, Dorothy Hewlett, 1937.
Letters of John Keats, edited by Maurice Buxton Forman, 1935.
John Keats Memorial Volume, 1921.
Keats, Betty Askwith, 1941.
Recollections of Writers, Charles and Mary Cowden Clarke, 1892.
My Long Life, Mary Cowden Clarke, 1896.
Leigh Hunt, Edmund Blunden, 1930.
Autobiography and Memoirs of B. R. Haydon, edited by T. Taylor, 1926.
The Biography of John Gibson, R.A., edited by T. Matthews, 1911.
The Richmond Papers, edited A. M. W. Stirling, 1926.
Life of John Keats, Charles Armitage Brown, 1937.
Eaton's Rome in the 19th Century, 1920.
The Diary of an Invalid, Henry Matthews, 1822.
The Journal of the Hon. Henry Edward Fox, edited by the Earl of Ilchester, 1923.
Trelawny, Margaret Armstrong, 1941.
"Keats and Joseph Severn," Article by B. Ifor Evans, *London Mercury*, August, 1934.
Catherine Gladstone, Mary Drew, 1919.
My Confidences, Frederick Locker-Lampson.
History of Italian Unity, Bolton King, 1899.

Large collection at the Keats Museum in Hampstead of unpublished letters from Joseph Severn to his parents and brothers and sisters, covering whole period from arrival in Italy 1820 to his death in 1879. The majority of these letters belong to Mrs. Stanley Unwin, granddaughter of Thomas Severn. Extracts from them were quoted by Professor B. Ifor Evans in his article "Keats and Joseph Severn," *London Mercury*, August, 1934.

Notes folded to pass from hand to hand, written by Joseph Severn to Miss Montgomerie, afterwards his wife. Also letters from Claudia, Walter, Mary, Arthur and Eleanor Severn to their mother, and Diaries of Mary and Eleanor Severn. All in possession of Margaret Countess of Birkenhead.

Albums of Sketches and illustrated letters by Mary Severn, in possession of Colonel Claude Furneaux and Margaret Countess of Birkenhead.

Unpublished paper about Mary Severn, "A Victorian Artist," by Miss Claudia Gale, eldest daughter of Claudia Severn.

INDEX